MY BROTHER'S NAME IS
KENNY

THE GREATEST TRUE HIP-HOP STORY EVER TOLD

KENNY PARKER
& ROSE DANIELS

"My Brother's Name Is Kenny"
Written by Kenny Parker
Co-written by Rose Daniels
Jersey City, NJ 2020
Copyright @ 2019 Kenny Parker
ISBN: 978-1-7362756-3-4

List Of Contributors:
Back cover photo courtesy of Mr. Mass
Page 283 photo courtesy of Ernie Paniccioli

To my brother Kris: Thank you for allowing me to tell the whole story. This book would not have been possible without your blessing.

Thank you, Rose Daniels, for helping me put my life into words. Your contributions to this book are immeasurable.

Thank you, Darrell Bailey, for permitting me to tell your family's story in mine.

Thank you, Kim Armstead, for suggesting I write a book so the world could hear my tale.

Thank you, Cydney, for patiently listening to all my stories for all those years.

Thank you, Vy Tran, for the funny facial expression that gave me direction for my book. Ha!

Everyone who helped along the way, thank you.

Finally, I'd like to dedicate this book to Daryl "Dee-Ski" Gardner, the greatest man I've ever known. R.I.P.

CONTENTS

Chapter 1 - One Giant Leap | 7

Chapter 2 - Big Wheels | 22

Chapter 3 - The Devil Is In The Details | 45

Chapter 4 - This Is Not A Test | 67

Chapter 5 - Milk Carton | 89

Chapter 6 - Dog Days Of Summer | 111

Chapter 7 - Rice & Butter | 118

Chapter 8 - Baseline | 139

Chapter 9 - Meal Ticket | 144

Chapter 10 - Hoe Stroll | 164

Chapter 11 - Sho Nuff | 188

Chapter 12 - Little Green Radio | 202

Chapter 13 - Parker Brother | 237

Chapter 14 - Peaches & Herb | 254

Chapter 15 - The Voice | 277

CHAPTER 1
ONE GIANT LEAP

"*Sometimes the dreams that come true are the dreams you never even knew you had*" - Alice Sebold, The Lovely Bones

I was a teenager...wandering the streets of Brooklyn in the dead of winter with nowhere to go. I was trying to make sense of what happened. I needed to make a quick decision, so it was the subway train for the night since there was nowhere else to sleep. The seats were small, hard, and surrounded by random trash. The stench of various homeless individuals filled the air. If you've only slept in a bed, like I had, trying to sleep on a bench-style seat was difficult. I didn't dare lean on the passengers seated next to me, so there was very little sleep to be had that night. I woke up cold and starving but had to do it all over again the following night. I smelled horrible, my scalp itched, and the hairs would stick together when I scratched my head. How did my life get to this point? Where was it heading?

First, allow me to pose a few questions. Have you ever experienced a series of events so profound that they caused you to reflect on your entire life? Have you ever revisited all your early hopes and aspirations to see how they turned out? If so, have you ever examined the decision-making process at critical moments in your life? How do these decisions alter your entire timeline? In reality, we make decisions every day. Some of them have dramatic implications for future events in our lives we may never know. No one has the infinite wisdom to predict how things could or should turn out. I still find myself thinking about past decisions quite often. Not only the decisions I made but the arrangements made for me. Who or what influenced those decisions? Do we have a choice at all? Is decision-making an illusion to mask the reality of destiny? It's the age-old question with the simplest of answers, who knows?

While we ponder this philosophical mystery, I'd like to tell you an unbelievable but true story of how destiny or decision-making shaped the lives of two African-American boys from New York City. I happened to be one of those two young boys. Allow me to start at the very beginning, with my earliest memory. It was July 20th, 1969. I was three years old, and I recall watching a man step foot on the moon for the first time. The reason this memory is so vivid in my mind is because of the coverage. The Apollo landing was the only program airing on television. My mother searched for something for me to watch on tv, but every time she changed the channel, the same feed would show on each station. Despite being three years old, I was very aware that this moon landing was unusual. That historical event was my lone memory of three years old. My next coherent memory was of my fourth birthday.

I had just gotten a new pair of sneakers, and I wanted to race all of my friends. I was under the impression that new sneakers made you run faster. My family, "The Parkers," lived in a Harlem apartment complex called Lenox Terrace. It was a high-rise building on 135th street and 5th avenue, across from Harlem Hospital. Lenox Terrace housed several African-American celebrities and politicians. Even the legendary Harlem gangster "Bumpy" Johnson once called Lenox Terrace home. Our address was 10 West Lenox Terrace. We were a middle-class family, which in Harlem, in the early 1970s, would rank us as pretty well off.

The Parker family consisted of four members. I was the youngest, born on July 9th, 1966. I was named Kenneth after the boyfriend of my mother's friend, who abruptly left her. This woman was so distraught over her man leaving her that she asked my mother, who was pregnant at the time, if she had a boy, would she please consider calling him Kenneth. My mother liked the name and agreed to her friend's request. Then, there was my older brother Lawrence. My mother named him after a motion picture she viewed while pregnant with him. The Academy Award-winning 'Lawrence Of Arabia.' Larry is less than a year older than I am. He was born on August 20th, 1965, making us only ten months apart. Some people call this "Irish Twins."

Next was my mother, a light-complexioned African-American woman born in Brooklyn on January 10th, 1946. Her mother died when she was only a year old. A foster family, who she said treated her poorly, adopted her. At the age of seventeen, my mother left the foster home, found a job, and moved into an apartment. For some reason, she rarely spoke much about her childhood. By 1970, my mother worked as a receptionist in the same apartment complex in which we lived. The

Larry & Kenny very young

family's final member was my father, John, who worked security at The United Nations. He was born in Monroe, Louisiana, in 1926, which made him 20 years older than my mother. John was a dark-skinned, burly man with a short haircut and a deep voice.

The Parker family owned two cars in the Lenox Terrace reserved parking lot. John drove a black sedan given to him by The United Nations, which he used for work. Most of the time, we rode around in a blue family station wagon. Lenox Terrace had a uniformed doorman stationed in the lobby who would open the door when you entered or exited the building. Larry once got yelled at for standing at the entrance and waiting for the doorman to open the door for him instead of pulling the handle himself. The doorman thought it was funny, "He thinks he's a little man." My mother found no humor in Larry's stunt. She shouted, "You have some nerve; you don't pay no bills around here!"

Every other summer, we would take a family trip. Since John was from Louisiana, we would fly down to visit his family during alternating summers. When the weather permitted, we took several family picnic outings to Heckscher State Park in Long Island or Riis Beach in Far Rockaway, Queens. Still, our apartment was the highlight. Along the wall in the living room was a sizable fish tank featuring all sorts of exotic fish. On the opposite wall, John built a raised, fully stocked bar. Next to the bar was an entertainment system with a color television, stereo record player, and a reel-to-reel tape recorder. Most families in our neighborhood didn't own a color television, but we had cable television installed in our apartment in 1971. Lenox Terrace was one of the first buildings in all of Harlem, NY, wired for cable service. In 1971, cable was rare in most parts of the country but, Larry and I had a separate cable box hooked up in our bedroom. A couch, loveseat, rocking chair, and a rug were present in the living room, but our parents forbid us, children, from entering that entire section alone.

Along with working, my mother cooked dinner every night, and we sat at the dining room table as a family and ate. She prepared various meals, including chicken, steak, seafood, and liver (yuck). On occasion, we would eat lunch prepared in a fondue pot. Our parents bought Larry and me all the latest clothes, from bell-bottomed pants to plaid shirts to colorful pajamas with animals on them. There would be a large tree in the living room that John would personally bring home from upstate New York during Christmas time. Of course, Santa Claus would bring us kids a treasure trove full of gifts. We possessed more toys than we could play with at one time. When my parent's friends would visit, they would marvel at our apartment.

As luxurious as Lenox Terrace appeared to be, the surrounding area was a different story. Across the street from our complex were several pre-war tenement buildings. Dozens of low-income families featuring some pretty rough kids lived there. I felt a sense of pride as a child because most of the kids I'd met had absentee fathers. With both married parents living at home, I felt unique and privileged. Harlem, in general, was an impoverished and segregated neighborhood. On any given day, you would find heaps of garbage piled up along the sidewalk. There was trash scattered everywhere. Broken bottles, glass, soda cans, and paper wrappers littered the streets. Dog feces were everywhere. It was like walking through a poop minefield. Acts of violence were commonplace. Drug addicts and alcoholics roamed the streets day and night. There were many graffiti-covered abandoned buildings, the length of an entire city block. It appeared like Harlem once had a booming economy but was now an old, dried-up shell of its former self. My immediate environment was nothing like this, though. My building was clean and well kept. The bushes stayed trimmed, and there was no graffiti anywhere. I can remember our building switching from its old incinerator system to a new trash compacter. Our 16th-floor apartment held a balcony with a view of the entire neighborhood. I could look down on Harlem in both a literal and figurative sense. To be blunt, Lenox Terrace was like this fancy oasis in the middle of a shit hole.

My mother, an avid reader, was earnest about education. She began reading to us at an early age and bought us a large assortment of children's books. I also loved to read. It didn't take me long to finish off all our books. My mother began purchasing children's books written in cursive. Soon I could read and write cursive as well as tell time before entering the first grade. I can remember being quite frustrated when Larry headed off to school, but I was still too young to attend. When my turn came, I breezed through Kindergarten. By the time I entered the first grade, it was apparent that I was different from the other kids in my class. When the teacher would assign writing assignments, I would always finish first. I would sit there and watch the other students struggle. A few of them couldn't write a single letter. I began to wonder if they ever read a book or seen a complete sentence before. After a while, it became clear that I was far advanced compared to the other students. The teacher began separating me from the other kids altogether. Soon, I started hearing the term "Teacher's Pet" used to describe me. I had to ask my mother what does that mean? My teacher realized my case required a different academic approach. The first-grade books weren't challenging me, so she assigned a different book to read. It was a Huckleberry Finn or Tom Sawyer type of book. She told me to take it home and begin reading it. When I arrived home with the book, there was an immediate problem. You see, my mother was a very proud and militant Black woman. She grew up during the Jim Crow era.

Whites and Blacks drank from separate water fountains. Blacks sat on the back of the bus, and segregation was the law. My mother was very active during the Civil Rights Movement. She held a deep distrust of White People and their agenda. She contemplated enrolling us in an organization called 'The Junior Black Panthers.' My mother would speak of an impending revolution if the racial situation didn't improve in America. I had no experience with or understood racism at age six. Still, I recognized some cultural differences between Black People and mainstream White America. However, my mother never allowed us to speak "broken English." If she asked me what I was doing and I said "Nuttin'," she would yell, "Nuttin'?

What kind of word is that?" I would have to say, "Nothing." She would say, "You can't talk like that in the White Man's world; you'll never get ahead." She never let any slang words slide, ever. When my mother saw the novel the teacher assigned in class, she said, "Who gave you this?" I told her my teacher gave it to me, and she said, "Oh no, you're not reading this book." She called the school and berated my teacher, "Why are you giving my child this White People stuff to read?" If you want to give him something to read, provide some African or Black history books to read." The teacher was very apologetic. She said, "I meant no harm. I wanted to give him something to challenge him. Our current curriculum isn't pushing him." My mother's response was adamant, "I don't care, I do not want my child reading this stuff!" Period. Later, there was a discussion between my parents and teacher about moving me up a grade early. My mother rejected the proposal. She felt I wasn't mature enough for such a drastic move.

Meanwhile, my brother Larry was a different story. He was struggling to meet the school's academic requirements. There was already a separation forming on how we were both perceived. Kenny is a bright student who's excelling in school, but Larry is, uh, different. Larry began exhibiting early behavioral problems in school. By the time he was in second grade, I overheard a phone conversation my mother was having with one of her friends. She was expressing how the school wanted to put Larry on some type of medication. He was too hyperactive in class. My mother sounded frustrated with him but was against the idea. She felt like these drugs could have some sort of long-term effect on his mental capacity. She refused the medication. My parents had other ways of dealing with Larry's behavior.

Kenny, Larry and Mom

"Music gives a soul to the universe, wings to the mind, flight to the imagination and life to everything"
- Plato

One of the significant components of my early childhood was the constant presence of music in our home. The radio was always playing in the background, like a movie score. Our station of choice was 107.5 WBLS FM, a Black-owned, R&B station. They played all the Motown hits and the latest funk songs. When we ate dinner in the evening as a family, music was always playing in the background. My favorite group was The Jackson 5 because of the incredible young phenom named Michael Jackson. I related to him because he was a little kid just like I was. My favorite Jackson 5's song was called, 'ABC.' That was right up my alley. One time, I remember watching a massive building fire from our window that was several blocks away. A feeling of sadness came over me because I knew whoever lived in that building lost everything. The song playing in the background was Marvin Gaye's 'What's Going On.' That song time-stamped the tragic event in my mind forever. Although we had an excellent stereo system, children were not allowed to touch it. My parents were strict disciplinarians who required complete obedience at all times. Still, I always felt like they loved us children, and we loved them as well. Our parents appeared to have a healthy, loving relationship. Things were pretty amazing, or so it seemed.

Our Parents began allowing us to play unsupervised around the apartment complex. I was around five years old, and Larry was six. The rules were simple: Do not leave the complex area! That was fine with us. Lenox Terrace was an excellent place for kids to have as much fun as their little hearts desired. Unfortunately, the kids from the tenements across the street felt the same way. They would invade the area in small mobs. Some of them wanted to play with us, but others weren't so friendly. Soon they began picking fights with us for no reason at all. We had no idea how to deal with their aggression. We did the only thing we knew how to do, run! Those little hooligans chased us into our building. We fled upstairs, happy to have escaped their clutches. Our father saw us sitting there in the living room and asked, "Why are you upstairs so soon?" I confessed that these kids from across the street chased us back into the building. He said, "Come on, we're going back downstairs." When we arrived downstairs, he told us to walk up in front of him a little bit. He said, "I'm gonna watch from here." It didn't take but 30 seconds for those kids to come running back over to us with more threats. Out of nowhere, our father appeared and threatened the kids. He warned them of dire consequences if they bothered us again. The terrified kids ran away. I can recall being ecstatic my father scared those kids away. Yes! In reality, a terrible thing happened that day. What my father should have done was made his five-year-old son stand up to those bullies right then and there. Instead, he taught me how to run home, hide, and wait for my father to save me. He made a colossal mistake that would cost me for years to come.

With those tenement goons defeated, we were once again confident to resume playing outside. Our parents gave both Larry and me more freedom. That meant more contact with other unsupervised kids, which meant more bullying. Being harassed became a regular occurrence wherever I went. When I was six, my mother enrolled me in an after school program at The YMCA. Older kids attended as well. When your six years old, an eight or nine-year-old can be a terror. They would hit me with wet towels from the pool and do other annoying things. I put up almost zero resistance. After a while, I got used to it.

Unfortunately, the source of our bullying wasn't only limited to the kids from across the street. My mother hired an afternoon babysitter to watch Larry and me, who had a seven-year-old son. Unbeknownst to my mother, this woman would leave the house to run errands. She would leave us under the supervision of her seven-year-old son. One day while "watching" us, he came up with a beautiful idea. He approached us, holding a small plastic bag. He explained that it was a bag full of candy, and he was going to share it with us. It was a nice gesture. As it turned out, what he offered us was a bag of mothballs! Now I don't know if we were either afraid of the consequences or wanted his approval but…We both ate a mothball. I had more than one. I can't imagine how awful mothballs must have tasted, but we sure ate some. We were both sworn to secrecy by the devious seven-year-old. The next morning my mother woke Larry up for school, and he was feeling sick. I couldn't get out of bed. My mother became confused. How could we both become sick like this overnight? After putting Larry under some extensive interrogation, he finally broke. Larry confessed, "We ate mothballs." My mother freaked out as one might expect. She rushed us to Harlem Hospital, which was right across the street. They pumped our stomachs and keep us under observation for days. Of course, my mother found a new sitter. This incident was my first brush with potential death.

On my childhood stress level scale, bullying was about a level eight out of ten—the only thing that ranked higher than bullying was occurring at home, the beatings. A beating is different than a "spanking." One could argue the effectiveness of taking a belt and striking a child over a dozen times all over his body as he screams in agony. Indeed the need to discipline a child is necessary for obvious reasons, but when does it become excessive? My father's beatings were different than my mother's. Her spankings didn't last long. She would hit you a few times with a belt, and that was it. Now, my father was brutal. He owned an assortment of thick leather belts. Sometimes he used the belt right off of his waist. He once beat my brother Larry so severely that it left red welt marks all over his body. Afterward, they needed to soak him in the bathtub. I don't remember what caused most of my beatings. Most likely, they had something to do with "not listening." Phrases like, "Don't make me tell you again!" and "You got one more time!" were thrown around quite often. Although I don't recall the origins of my beatings, I do remember the frequency. Despite my best efforts, I somehow managed to get beat every other day. I don't know how I accomplished that feat since the mere mention of the belt would strike terror in my heart. My only consolation was, at least, I wasn't Larry. He found a way to get a beating every single day! I could not understand why he refused to listen to my parents. I felt like I was obeying their rules, but somehow I got into trouble too, so who knows? Invoking the wrath of my parents seemed to be Larry's favorite pastime. Sometimes, he got beat twice in one day. This type of discipline would seem excessive by modern standards. The 'Baby Boomer' generation did not "spare the rod" at all. The belt was the remedy for any childhood problems that would arise.

    I once received a beating right out of my sleep. I was relaxing on the couch, reading a book, and dozed off. Apparently, before my nap, I forgot to complete some assigned task. As I laid there fast asleep, I felt a painful sensation. My dormant body began to react. What is this? Pow! The second hit jolted from my sleep as the third hit strikes, Pow!!! Now I realized I was under attack, Ahhh!!!! The transition from fast asleep to being beaten by a belt is traumatic. To open your eyes just in time to see an incoming belt would be difficult for anyone to deal with, much less a five-year-old child. Add the fact that I'm also trying to understand the ramblings of my screaming mother as I regain consciousness. What could a five-year-old have done to deserve this type of drastic measure? Who knows, but it stuck with me for life.

    Along with his daily misdeeds, Larry also developed a bedwetting problem. Bedwetting was a sure-fire reason to receive a beating. Why wouldn't Larry get up at night to use the bathroom? It was a big mystery. The answer may have lied in the way he slept...like a rock. Larry and I had bunk beds in our room. I slept on the bottom, Larry, on the top. The guard rail for the top bunk was either broken or lost. Periodically, Larry would roll over and fall from the top bunk onto the floor during his sleep. Believe it or not, it wouldn't even phase him. I would wake up in the morning and find Larry lying right next to me on the floor. Either he fell from the bunk, and the impact failed to wake him up, or the fall woke him up, and he was too lazy to climb back up into his bunk. Either explanation is crazy. A loud thud once woke me up. It turned out to be Larry hitting the floor. He just laid there and slept. Hilarious.

As time went on, my parents became more creative with their punishments. One day they devised a devious plot to discipline their youngest child, me. We possessed a large fish tank in our living room with an array of fish. I used to love to feed the fish and would go with my father to the pet store to buy food. One day, he returned home after a business trip with a brand new species of fish, a Piranha! At the time, it was illegal for anyone to own a piranha in The State of New York. I have no idea how my father came to possess this dangerous fish, but there it was. This particular species was so ferocious that we kept it isolated in a separate tank. To feed the piranha, we had to buy extra goldfish to use as food. You would take the goldfish and drop him into the piranha tank. The goldfish would begin frantically swimming back and forth, knowing the piranha was nearby. Without warning, the piranha would rush the goldfish and rip it to shreds. I used to sit there and watch the entire process from beginning to end.

One day my mother says, "You know Kenny, we're tired of your behavior. You refuse to obey our rules, so we've decided to stick your foot in the piranha tank." WHAT?? I began screaming, "Noooo!!" I saw firsthand what the piranha was capable of doing. I was in a sheer state of panic as my mother said, "Hurry up and pick which foot we're gonna stick in the piranha tank!" Oh, my God! At six years old, I had to decide which of my feet was more important to me. I can remember thinking to myself, "How can my mother and father stick their own son's foot in a piranha tank?" I was crying as I chose my left foot. They were like, "Ok, now we're gonna blindfold you."

After blindfolding me, my father held me tight and stuck my foot in the water. I could feel the piranha biting at the bottom of my foot. I was beyond myself with fear. I began to scream and convulse, so they took my foot out of the water. My mother said, "Boy, you are lucky; the piranha must not have been hungry." She then said, "Ok, we're gonna bandage up your foot." She wrapped my foot in a gauze bandage. When they took off the blindfold, I saw the blood-soaked bandage on my foot. I was distraught. My mother ordered, "Now go to your room!" I began limping off to my room. My mother yelled, "Stand up, straight boy!" I cried out, "I can't; the piranha bit my foot!" I was in pain. My mother barked, "Walk straight! There's nothing wrong with you, boy!" How could she say that after what happened to my foot? I struggled to reach my room, convinced I had the cruelest parents on earth.

Larry was standing right there and saw the whole thing. It would be a few weeks before he finally told me what happened. I didn't know that my father stuck my foot, not in the piranha tank, but a basin of water hidden nearby. The biting I felt on my foot was my mother pinching my foot in the water. I couldn't see anything because of the blindfold. They wrapped my foot and poured the now banned 'Mercurochrome' on the bandage. It stained the bandage red and gave the appearance of blood. Their charade was so convincing that when I finally saw the dressing and the "blood," I felt intense pain in my foot. As I limped to my room, my parents were doing everything they could to keep a straight face. Larry, who had been sworn to secrecy by my parents, finally confessed. In the meantime, if I got out of line, my mother would threaten me with, "Do you want us to put your foot back in the piranha tank?" No!

Between both of my parents, my father was the one who disciplined us most. Still, my mother was the one who delivered most of the teaching moments. For example, she was a fierce anti-drug advocate. She began talking to us about the dangers of drug abuse at an early age. One day, she took Larry and me with her to run some errands in the neighborhood. As we passed by a random storefront, there was a filthy Black man in stained clothing sitting on top of a nearby garbage can. He was nodding, almost to the point of tipping over. He would catch himself each time and sit back up, never opening his eyes. He had snot dripping from his nose. This man looked disgusting! Instead of ignoring him, my mother walked us right up to the man. He wasn't even aware that we were standing right in front of him. She said to us, "You see him, he's a junkie." That was the slang term used for a heroin addict. She then said, "If you take drugs, that's how you're going to look. Ok, let's go." That was all she said. She never said, "Don't use drugs" or anything like that. She showed us a real live junkie, and that was all I needed to see. At six years old, I vowed never to become a junkie. The image was so vivid it shook me to my core. I have never taken an illegal drug in my life.

As a six-year-old, I can recall being a very curious...ah, nosey kid. I was always eavesdropping on adult conversations. Even though I couldn't comprehend most aspects of it, I still wanted to hear everything. I was a mini "Big Brother" collecting information, trying to understand the adult world. I began to overhear problems in my parents' marriage of three years. At first, they decided not to argue in front of us children, but I could still tell when there was tension between them. Soon the spats became full-blown arguments, complete with shouting and threats. During one heated exchange, my father pulled out a handgun and put it to my mother's head. He yelled, "I will blow your head off!" Larry and I stood there, watching the whole drama unfold, not knowing what to do. After they finished arguing, my father called me over. I don't know why he singled me out. I looked upset. He said, "Come here, I wanna show you something." It was a gun. He said, "One day, I'm gonna show you how to use it." I was conflicted. My father pointed a firearm at my mother's head. Even at six years old, I understood he could've killed her. At the same time, I was curious to see a real gun. As a kid, this was amazing. My father also pulled out a rifle and showed it to me as well. I remember him opening the rifle from the middle to show me how to load it. I found it odd that a rifle bent in half to load. What was more strange was how my father used this incident as a teaching moment for his son. Right on cue, my mother came into the living room and yelled, "What are you doing? Don't show him that!" John put his firearms away, and concluded the evening.

After that, the shouting matches began to occur at a more frequent rate. My father devised a new strategy to inflict maximum emotional damage on my mother. He would say something to hurt the children. After one heated argument, my father came into our room and said, "Guess what, kids? There is no such thing as Santa Claus. It was us who brought you the gifts." What? There's no Santa Claus? How can that be? We loved Christmas and Santa Claus. Our mother had to come into the room and explain to us that our father spoke the truth, Santa Claus was a hoax. I was crushed. He didn't stop there. After another argument, he came into our room and declared, "There is no Tooth Fairy! That was us putting money under your pillow" and walked out of the room, leaving us dumbfounded. Our mother had to follow his outburst with the truth behind the Tooth Fairy, a personal favorite. I couldn't understand it.

As it turned out, my father saved his best trick for last. Following another fight, he stormed into our room and proclaimed, "Hey kids, guess what? I'm not your real father; you were adopted!" Oh, my God! This one dropped like a nuclear bomb. I can remember his announcement as clear as day. This one couldn't be true. He's the only man I've ever known. My mother entered the room from what must have been a long walk and said, "He's right; he is not your real father." Her face had a certain sadness to it but also resolve. This news was a lot of information for my young mind to process. I thought I was better than the other kids in Harlem who didn't have a father. I thought I was special. I had to swallow the tough pill that I wasn't special after all. My mother gathered us together and said, "Here's the truth, John is not your father. When John and I got married, he adopted both of you and changed your last name to Parker." Wait a minute! My last name isn't Parker? Every word out of my mother's mouth hit like a sledgehammer. I had so many questions. I wanted to know everything now. She continued, "You kids have a real father. His name is Sheffield, and he's from Barbados. He was living illegally in the United States and got deported when I was pregnant with you, Kenny. He's never seen you before." Wow!! The story went from shocking to fascinating. My mind was spinning in circles. That's a lot for a six-year-old to process. One aspect of the story did add a tremendous amount of clarity to my limited understanding. I now realized why John was able to beat us like that; he wasn't our real father. In my mind, our real father would never beat us like that. My mother also revealed she married John partly for her children's security. She was explaining the whole situation to us like we were grown, men. Somehow, it all began to make sense. There were still many unanswered questions about our biological father. For now, this was all I needed. All my feelings of hurt and disappointment directed themselves towards John. His dubious plan to hurt us, children, with information had backfired. He became the enemy. John was now a separate entity living in our home outside of the family. My heart turned to stone; I had no love for him. As you would expect, my parent's fragile marriage was in severe trouble.

 Shortly after the paternal revelation, there was another serious discussion. My mother sat both Larry and myself down and said, "I'm leaving John, and I'm moving to a new place. You kids can either stay here with him or come with me." She explained that if we chose to come with her, money would be tight because she would be the sole provider. I didn't care. For me, it was a no-brainer...I'm leaving with my mother. I had no feelings for this imposter, John, anyway. The thought of receiving far fewer beatings was too enticing. Larry shared my sentiment. She said, "Ok, I'm going to look for a place for us to live, but you can't say anything. It's a secret." It became a game for us. There was no way I was going to be the one who cracked and spilled the beans. All this cloak and dagger was exciting to me. My mother found a beat-up, dingy apartment on University Avenue in The Bronx. The people who previously lived there left the apartment filthy. She needed to scrub the entire place before taking possession. The stage was now set.

On December 23rd, 1972, the Parker family sat down at the dining room table for dinner. Everything was proceeding as it would on any random night. As we were eating dinner, my mother looked right into my fake father's eyes and blurted, "John, I'm leaving you. I'm taking the kids with me." Whoa! It was going down right here over dinner! Larry and I were sitting right there. Without hesitation, John said, "Fine, you can go but the boys are staying with me." The feeling was mutual. This marriage was over. My mother looked right and then to her left at both Larry and myself and asked, "What do you kids want to do?" Before we could answer, John said, "You wanna stay with me right?" In unison, we both said, "No, we wanna go with Ma." John was furious. He yelled, "You've brainwashed my sons." I remember him using the word brainwash because, in that most serious moment, I found that word funny. I understood what it meant, though. I thought to myself, "She didn't brainwash me, you're the one who said you weren't my real father!" After that, there was nothing else left to say.

The following day, on Christmas Eve, we moved to The Bronx with nothing. My mother's marriage of three years was over. On Christmas Day, Larry and I discovered an entire room full of new toys, including the gift we coveted the most, a 'Big Wheel.' My mother stated that she wanted us to have the same type of Christmas we would've had before. She overcompensated with a cache of gifts. But, there was no Christmas tree. She explained how she couldn't afford to get both a Christmas tree and the number of toys she wanted to buy for us. She figured we would rather have more gifts than a Christmas tree. She was correct! We didn't know at the time what the future of the Christmas tree would be moving forward. At that moment, the future didn't matter. It was a celebration! Despite the end of the doorman, the cars, the trips, the fish tank, and the cable, I was ecstatic. My whole life changed completely overnight. It didn't matter; everything I had known up until age six was a lie anyway. There were no more illusions now, only reality. We were now living in a low-income, single-parent household.

Larry and I soon began asking more questions about our biological father. My mother revealed more details. After she became pregnant with me, Sheffield learned of his deportation. He was already an absentee father who only visited his son Larry once since he'd been born. Sheffield claimed the expulsion back to Barbados was only temporary. He promised to write her until he was able to get back into the country. Soon after, things became tough for my pregnant mother, who still had a newborn baby to feed. Every single day she would wait for a letter from Sheffield. She would meet the mailman right in front of her Park Slope, Brooklyn apartment building. The mailman would say, "I'm sorry, miss, no letter for you today." Day after day, the same thing. Finally, after about six months, she ambushed the mailman as he delivered the mail. She grabbed him and began shaking him, screaming, "Why won't you give me my mail? Why are you doing this to me? Where's my letter?" The mailman looked at her and said, "Miss, it ain't coming." My mother broke down in tears as the reality of what she was facing set in. Sheffield wasn't coming back; she was on her own. My mother's situation became dire. The landlord evicted her from the apartment with two brand new babies. Thankfully, a friend agreed to take her in until she got back on her feet. Three years later, she married John. I don't know how much she even knew about Sheffield. My mother met him around age seventeen, and by twenty, he disappeared. Back in the 1960s, a woman being pregnant outside of wedlock carried a social stigma. My mother was well aware of Sheffield's immigration status and lack of credibility. Knowing this, her decision to give birth to me was a questionable one at best. I am grateful for her poor decision-making, though. Ha!

About a month after we moved out of Lenox Terrace, my mother informed us that John had requested to see us. We told her to tell him, "No, thank you." We never saw John again.

CHAPTER 2
BIG WHEELS

"**A**nd remember...No matter where you go, there you are" - Confucius

The new Parker family, sans John, now resided in a Bronx apartment on University Place. Our stay in the new place was temporary, as my mother had a promising lead on a better apartment in a high-rise building about a mile away. The majority of our belongings remained unpacked. Most experts would agree that discovering our true father's identity and the abrupt separation of our parents was grounds for psychological counseling for both Larry and myself. Instead, it became a part of our lives we would have to accept. My mother did her best to help us adjust, but she must have had her own personal issues dealing with her three-year marriage collapse.

The only memorable thing about University Place was the roaches! As a kid who had never dealt with roaches, it was shocking to enter the kitchen at night, cut on the light, and see dozens of roaches scatter for cover. The roach problem reached a point where it forced my mother to visit the hardware store and buy something called a 'Bomb.' It was an aerosol can that, when opened, would send a poisonous mist in the air that would cover an entire room. This fog was so potent that all apartment inhabitants, including pets, had to leave the premises for at least two hours. My mother activated the bomb, and we evacuated the apartment. When we returned, there were hundreds of dead roaches in the kitchen. It made my skin crawl. The bomb was successful for a while, but after a couple of weeks, the roach problem returned. Another bomb was needed to combat the infestation. I wondered if this was how those kids from the tenements across the street were living? We were a long way from Lenox Terrace.

Luckily, our fortunes would change in the nick of time. After three months, the new hi-rise apartment my mother was waiting for became available. We were moving once again to a two-bedroom apartment on the 24th floor. Our new address was 1600 Sedgwick Avenue in The Bronx. I thought it was the world's tallest building, comparable to The World Trade Center (which I happen to see during construction). The new building featured a playground built next to it. Perfect! This section of The Bronx had a similar demographic to Harlem. The majority of people were African-American and Hispanic. Unfortunately for Larry and myself, the bullying started right on cue. The same problems continued but with a different twist. One day, my mother gave Larry and me $1 and sent us to the store to get two pizza slices for lunch. In 1973, a slice of pizza cost fifty cents. We went to the pizza shop, ordered two slices of pizza, and gave the cashier one dollar. When we received our slices, Larry chooses to take a nibble of his slice right away. As we left the store, there were a couple of older kids loitering in the front. Without warning, they walked right up to us and said, "Yo! Give us your pizza!" We were so scared that we handed over our pizza with no questions asked. This type of act wasn't bullying anymore; it was a straight-up robbery. What kind of foul individuals would steal an already bitten slice of pizza anyway? We were so sad. I remember turning to Larry and saying, "Dag, at least you got to bite yours." I had experienced my very first robbery at the age of six. It wouldn't be my last.

One of the unique things about having a sibling so close in age was I always had someone to play with me. Larry was my best friend. We had a special kinship. We didn't need to rely on other kids to have a good time. Our fun could turn mischievous at times, but the ratio between Larry's transgressions and mine appeared lopsided. He always seemed to be getting into trouble. One day my mother struck up what appeared to be a random conversation with both Larry and myself. She said, "You know, I've been hearing a lot about this place called 'The Bad Boys School'." Huh? Her statement sparked our curiosity. What kind of place is this? She explained that when boys don't behave or follow their parent's rules, this school will find out and send for you. It was like a jail for young boys. When you arrive there, they beat you with a whip every day, and all you eat is bread and water. We thought this Bad Boys School sounded terrible. She warned us, "If y'all don't watch out, The Bad Boys School is coming for both of you." I wanted no part of this institution; thank you very much.

About two days later, my mother comes home from work, and she has the daily mail in her hand. She says, "Larry, there's a letter here for you" and hands it to him. What? A letter? He's only seven years old. Larry took the letter, stamped and addressed to Lawrence Parker. My mother said, "Open it. It's your letter." Upon further inspection, Oh My Goodness! It was from The Bad Boys School! She said, "They must have heard about you." I began freaking out so much that I don't even remember Larry's reaction. My mother took the letter and began reading it aloud.

"Dear Larry Parker, we have heard about all the things you've been doing lately. We summon you to The Bad Boys School."

She began reading off his list of infractions and the corresponding punishments. Larry didn't do his homework = 10 lashes. Larry didn't clean his room = 10 lashes, and so on. By the time she finished reading the list, Larry was due about 50 lashes per day! I lost my mind, and I hadn't received a letter. I began crying and pleading, "Please don't let him go to The Bad Boy School!" She said there was "nothing she could do. Once they write to you, your parents can't save you." I couldn't believe what was happening. My mother said, "Come on, Larry, pack your stuff. You're leaving tonight." We were both distraught by this point. She helped Larry pack a bag and stated, "OK, go downstairs, sit in front of the building and wait. They'll be coming in a brown truck." That was the longest elevator ride of my life. I went downstairs with Larry to wait with him. For all I knew, this was the last time I was ever going to see him alive. Our building sat right next to The Major Deegan Expressway. There was plenty of traffic flowing right in front of our building, including many trucks. Every time a brown vehicle would turn the corner, we would start screaming and crying, "OH MY GOD, THAT'S THE TRUCK!" The truck would drive by without stopping. "No, that's not it," and we would exhale.

This false truck scenario went on for some time. It reached a point where I decided, "This can't happen, I gotta go upstairs and beg." I rode that elevator back up to the 24th floor, determined to change my brother's fate. I confronted my mother teary-eyed, "Please, Ma, you gotta do something. You can't let this happen!" She said, "Why should I try to intervene in this? They're right! Look at all the stuff Larry's doing; He's not going to change." I began pleading, "He'll change! He'll change!" She said, "I don't know. I don't believe it." I ran back downstairs and told Larry what she said. He pledged to change his ways. I began navigating my way up and down the twenty-four floors acting as Larry's negotiator. I had to convince my mother to call off the Bad Boys School. Finally, after about three trips, she relented, "Alright, it doesn't look like the truck is coming. Let me see what I can do." Yes! My begging worked. Still, she warned, "Next time, I'm not gonna get involved." Larry came back upstairs. We were proud of our mother for defying The Bad Boys School's summons. Months later, we found out it was once again a very creative ploy she devised. It struck fear in both of her children even though I wasn't in trouble at all. Good one! To this day, if I mention 'The Bad Boys School' to my brother, he will fall out laughing.

"No matter who you are, no matter what you do, you'd like to witness history" - *Richard Sherman*

Up in The Bronx in the summer of 1973, right in my neighborhood, something very unique was brewing. A young eighteen-year-old Jamaican DJ named Kool Herc was making a name for himself in our area. This guy was different from the other DJs of that era who would play the records of their chosen genre. They didn't mix songs the way a DJ would today. They played one track after the other in its entirety as a Spotify playlist would. Kool Herc played many different genres of music at the same time. He would mix them in at his leisure instead of waiting for the song to finish. Kool Herc discovered that certain songs would sometimes have a small musical breakdown. This section usually occurred in the middle of the song. People would wait for that part of the song to arrive and dance extra hard. This part of the song became known as "The Break." Kool Herc began searching everywhere for songs with significant breaks for people to enjoy. He would then mix several of these "Break" records consecutively. He was creating a little niche for himself and became very popular. Kool Herc also possessed one of the most booming sound systems in The Bronx. This combination made Kool Herc a DJ like no other. Herc happened to live at 1520 Sedgwick Avenue. That was the next building over from our family. The playground in which Larry and I played every day was what separated the two buildings. We ran up and down that street often during that summer. It would have been impossible for us not to have crossed paths with Kool Herc several times. We had a routine of mounting our Big Wheel right in front of his building. We would cruise down the hill to the opposite corner. Now I'm not saying Herc would have acknowledged two nappy-headed kids darting past him daily, but we were definitely in the same place and time absorbing the same environment that gave him his inspiration.

On August 11th, 1973, DJ Kool Herc threw a party at 1520 Sedgwick Ave. The event was a fundraiser for his sister Cindy. Herc wanted to raise money to buy her new school clothes. Herc distributed a crude, makeshift flyer for his "Back To School Jam" in the recreation room. The party was from 9 pm until 4 am and cost fifty cents for fellas and twenty-five cents for ladies. The party was a success. Kool Herc enlisted a master of ceremonies (MC) to assist him in entertaining the crowd. Kool Herc combined his DJ style, the sound system, and an "emcee" on the microphone. This particular party became the official birth of what we now call Hip-Hop. Rap is the #1 selling and most popular form of music in the world today. Its birthday is August 11th, 1973, and DJ Kool Herc is the undisputed Father Of Hip-Hop.

Talk about being in the right place at the right time. This monumental event in music history took place 100 feet away from us in the next building. Who could've imagined that? Let's speculate for a minute. On that historic day, the weather forecast was 84 degrees with 75% humidity and a 0% chance of rain. On such a beautiful day in August, the probability of Larry and I seeing Kool Herc was pretty high. More than likely, we rode our big wheel or ran past his building dozens of times that day. My mother could've attended that very party if she wanted to. She must have seen the flyer. The next logical place for Kool Herc to post flyers after his building would've been our building. My mother was twenty-seven years old at the time. She most likely wouldn't have been partying with an eighteen-year-old Kool Herc, but hey, who knows? Let's take the speculation further. What if, on that memorable day, Larry or myself ran into Kool Herc with our Big Wheel causing him an injury? What if that injury caused Herc to cancel the party? He might not have needed to reschedule since the party was a fundraiser for back to school, which was days away. What if this injury caused Hip-Hop to have never existed or at least been altered in some way? Would it be a stretch to say that thanks to my expert Big Wheel maneuvering, we now have Hip-Hop today? Ha! OK, I pushed it... Let's move on.

Larry & Kenny at 1600 Sedgwick Ave

"Sometimes, The Devil is not quite what we expect when we meet him face to face" - *Nelson DeMille*

The winter of 1973 arrived, bringing with it the dreaded New York City cold weather. It also brought a rare guest to our home. My mother returned from work one evening accompanied by a slender-built, clean-shaven man. He was dark-skinned with a short haircut. He smiled as my mother introduced us. Let's call this gentleman Joe. The introduction felt awkward. We had lived there for about eight months and hadn't received any visitors. It was apparent my mother liked him by the way she was acting. She was smiling a lot and speaking to us in a softer tone, almost like she was on her best behavior. As soon as Joe opened his mouth to speak, an unfamiliar accent emerged. What kind of accent is this? I grew up in New York City, AKA "The Melting Pot." By seven years old, I had heard several different accents before, but Joe's accent was new. Being the curious kid I was, I asked him, "Why do you talk like that?" He proclaimed with pride in that unique accent, "I'm from Jamaica!" Now I'd heard of the country of Jamaica before, but I'd never met a real Jamaican.

As the night progressed, Joe lets his guard down a little and becomes more comfortable. He begins speaking more. I heard him say, "Yeah, mon." He pronounced certain words that start with the letter H, but he wouldn't pronounce the H sound. So instead of saying "house," he would say "ouse." Instead of "help," he would say "elp." I will swear to you right now, on my life. At the age of seven, I thought to myself, "What kind of man has my mother brought into the house?" Joe stayed for a little while, then left. We immediately began asking my mother some rather intrusive questions. How did you meet him? Do you like him? She explained to us that she met him several weeks earlier on her lunch break. He worked at a midtown Manhattan shoe store called Lord & Taylor. He would see her every day and try to speak to her, but she would ignore him. One day she agreed to have lunch with him and soon found herself liking him. They'd been seeing each other for a few weeks before she finally decided to bring him home. Joe received a green card when he moved to The USA from Jamaica. He was living with his family in Queens, New York. She also told us Joe had a tough time growing up in Jamaica. Not only did he not graduate from high school, but he didn't finish the 8th grade! Immediately I'm like, "WHAT?" My mother has brought home a guy who didn't even finish the 8th grade? I was already disappointed by her choice. Something in my little gut told me this wasn't good. I felt she could do better, but hey, what did I know?

Joe began to visit the apartment often. He seemed OK. We would have little conversations here and there. I was having difficulty understanding what he was saying due to his accent. He kept having to repeat himself over and over and would get frustrated. One day, he told me, "Damn man, a muss-ghetto bit me." I said, "What?" He repeated himself, "A muss-ghetto bit me!" I said, "What is a muss-ghetto?" He yelled, "A muss-ghetto boy, a muss-ghetto!!" I had no idea what a muss-ghetto was. I was looking at him in utter bewilderment. He finally says, "Ya know, the little bug that flies around, and it bites people." I said, "Ohhh...a mosquito?" He said, "Yes, mon...a muss-ghetto!!!" I was like, "Wow, OK, this is gonna be a real adventure." LOL!

Christmas arrived but with a different tone than the previous year. There was no anticipation of a Santa Claus; we were too old for that now. Besides, John already ruined that aspect of Christmas for us anyway. The whole "freedom from bondage" theme of the previous year was absent too. But, like last year, there was no Christmas tree. We didn't mind not having a tree last Christmas because of the overabundance of toys. This time though, there were no toys either. I can recall an excuse about money being tight and bills being behind or something like that. Fair enough. My mother promised gifts during the next pay period, which would be after Christmas. They never came. I remember a feeling of jealousy following the Christmas break.

I had to listen to all the other kids brag about all the gifts they'd received. Oh well. Life goes on.

Meanwhile, my academics were exceptional. I was once again at the top of my class. Even so, an odd new dynamic arose during school that didn't exist the previous year. Every morning, our teacher took attendance. Each student would line up from the shortest to the tallest. That's when I made my discovery; I was the tallest kid in my class. We did the same line up during the auditorium assembly. I discovered that I was the tallest second grader in the entire school! Out of nowhere, I was considerably tall for my age. How did this happen? Well, my mother stood at 5'11" so she was tall for a woman. I guess that's where I acquired my height. My father was allegedly shorter than my mother. Of course, my newfound height caused the other kids to single me out, and the jokes began. There used to be a popular television show called 'The Adam's Family.' The program aired twice daily on channel 5 in New York City. One of the main characters was a tall butler named "Lurch." Some of the kids began calling me Lurch, and I hated it. Unfortunately, I was too timid and not savvy enough to do anything about it. More derogatory nicknames followed. What could I do? I wasn't going to get any shorter. Who could I complain to anyway? People didn't consider this type of verbal abuse bullying back then. It was kids being kids. Adults would quote that old cliché "Sticks and stones will break your bones, but words will never hurt you." That's not true. Words can hurt more than sticks and stones sometimes.

Meanwhile, my brother Larry was having the same problem and more. He was the tallest kid in his third-grade class, and he continued to underperform in school. To make matters worse, Larry was still wetting the bed at eight years old. My mother took him to the doctor for a complete physical examination. The doctor determined nothing was wrong with him. We had no idea why Larry continued to wet the bed. Was it because he didn't feel like getting up at night? Beating him didn't solve the problem. My mother would question Larry, but he gave no real answers. One would assume the next logical step would be a psychological evaluation. That never happened. Larry exhibited poor behavior and subpar academic performance. If you factor in the bedwetting, something was not OK with him. I would eavesdrop on my mother's conversations about Larry. His teachers were saying he was "a little different" than other children. My mother told me, "There's nothing wrong with your brother you hear me? He's eccentric." It was the first time I'd ever heard the word eccentric, and my mother used it to describe Larry. I felt like she was trying to sugarcoat the truth by describing him that way, even though I didn't think he was weird. Larry was a regular kid. He was my brother. I was around him more and knew him better than anybody. Larry had already experienced a tremendous amount of psychological and physical trauma. He was only an eight-year-old child. Still, the adults categorized Larry as "different" in some way.

March of 1974 arrived, and our one-year lease was up for renewal. My mother broke the disappointing news. We were moving for the third time in a little over a year. The new rent increase made our hi-rise apartment too expensive. I liked our building and didn't want to move. Our financial situation forced us to move into a small two-bedroom apartment in of all places, East New York, Brooklyn. By comparison, East NY was more impoverished than Harlem and more dangerous than The Bronx or almost anywhere else in New York City. East New York was THE HOOD!! Our new, crime-ridden area had guys walking around wearing denim gang jackets. Their names were menacing, like The Savage Skulls, The Young Skulls, and The Tomahawks. These were real street gangs, not television; this was bad. I had grown accustomed to living in high-crime areas. East NY was still somewhat of a culture shock.

New York City, nicknamed "The City That Never Sleeps," is always active, day or night. But, if you were poor, your recreational options were minimal. In my neighborhood, almost every summer event was of the makeshift variety. You went outside and made up things to do with your friends. The most popular summer pastime was playing in front of the fire hydrant. Someone would get a wrench, turn on the water and let it blast onto the street. People of all ages would assemble in front of the water, some wearing bathing suits. They would splash in the middle of the road, despite oncoming traffic. My mother decided it would be better to send us to the free local public swimming pool. Great Idea! There was a pool within walking distance of our apartment called 'The Betsy Head Pool,' but there was one problem. That location was the neighboring section next to East New York called Brownsville. This section of Brooklyn was the only area in New York City considered worse than East New York. Brownsville was the official crime capital of New York City. That distinction would make it one of the worst areas in the entire country. When Larry and I arrived, there were packs of wild kids running around, causing all sorts of mayhem. They were pushing other kids into the water, which was against the rules. Some were beating kids with wet towels and fighting amongst themselves. Everything not secured in a locker was missing. The lifeguards were powerless to stop this band of young hoodlums. This pool wasn't the place for kids like Larry and myself; they would have eaten us alive. We never got undressed. We fled Brownsville for the "safety" of East New York. When we arrived home, my mother asked us, "How was the pool?" No comment.

Since my earliest memory, my mother kept us informed of important family decisions. The majority of those decisions were not subject to debate. Information and opinions flowed in one direction, from the top down. Late in the summer of 74', we received two pieces of blockbuster news. First, she asked her now-boyfriend Joe to move in with us. I don't know if this decision coincided with Joe losing his job as a shoe salesman. I wasn't overjoyed to hear this news because I was still suspicious of him. I didn't know why; I couldn't quite put my finger on it. The next bit of news was even more significant and came shortly afterward. My mother was pregnant! That revelation was a lot for an eight-year-old to comprehend. I didn't know how a woman became pregnant, but I understood Joe was now going to be a significant part of our lives. My mother confided in us that she didn't want to have a baby. When she first found out about her pregnancy, she cried, saying, "I already have two kids to feed." She told us Joe was the exact opposite. He was thrilled. Joe said, "Don't worry, I want you to have this baby, I'll take care of you, and I'll take care of Larry and Kenny too." Based on his enthusiasm and financial promises, my mother agreed to have the baby. She had known unemployed Joe for less than a year.

For me, there wasn't much thought. A new sibling was on the way, and that was it. During the first trimester of her pregnancy, I overheard her say, "This will be my last baby. After this, I'm getting my tubes tied." I became confused, so later on, I asked her what does that mean? She explained how it was a medical procedure done to ensure she wouldn't become pregnant again. Although I didn't know how they conceived a baby, I internalized her explanation. The way I rationalized it, having children wasn't a good thing. Was the possibility of having another Kenny that terrible? Was I so awful that she wanted to have an operation to make sure she could never have another child like me? That hurt my feelings, but I never said anything. An eight-year-old needed more clarity. I wasn't mature enough for this type of subject matter at all, to be honest. Still, it bothered me for a long time.

"The truly evil and deliberate men are a very small minority. It is the appeaser who unleashes them on humanity" - Ayn Rand

The summer of 1974 came to its conclusion. My mother's early-stage pregnancy allowed her to continue working. That meant unemployed Joe would be home alone with both Larry and me after school. I didn't think much of it. It was business as usual. One day, Larry and I were in our room, playing with our collection of miniature toy soldiers. Without notice, Joe began yelling at us in a way that he'd never addressed us before. What is this? The next thing I knew, Joe took off his belt and began beating me. I couldn't believe this was happening. Joe paused and diverted his attention to Larry, who he began striking. We hadn't received a beating like this since my mother left her husband, John. What was going on? We knew this guy for less than a year, and now he's beating us? I was beside myself, screaming from the beating's pure shock and from whom the lashing was coming. This man is not my father; he can't beat me! While Joe was still beating Larry, I ran to the telephone and called my mother at work. When she answered the phone, I began screaming, "Joe's beating us!! Joe's beating us!!" She said, "Put him on the phone. I can't have this aggravation while I'm at work!" I handed Joe the phone, and he stopped his assault.

Larry and I went to our room, dazed and confused by what happened. We stayed in our room motionless until my mother arrived home from work. When she returned, she sat both of us down on the couch. She said, "Look... Joe mentioned to me that you boys need some serious chastising. Y'all are running around here very undisciplined, so I'm allowing Joe to beat both of you from now on." My heart sank. I thought Joe was behaving that way because my mother wasn't home. Come to find out; the whole ordeal was a deliberate plan. I can only describe my feelings as shaken to my very core.

I felt like my mother sold us out to appease her new boyfriend. The hatred Larry and I had for this man became solidified that day. From that moment on, Joe took his license to beat us at will to heights John never imagined.

Christmas of 1974 arrived with a whimper. Once again, there was no tree or any gifts exchanged. A proper Christmas celebration became the least of our worries. After living in our apartment for several months, a new problem arose. This issue didn't seem to exist when we first moved in...a rodent problem. I'm not talking about mice, but rats!! I began to overhear my mother and Joe talking about spotting them in our apartment. My mother said she saw one at the top of the window structure, near the ceiling. Once, I was going to get something from my closet, and when I opened the door, I saw something slide under the wall. It was a long tail. I was like, "Wow! That was a rat!" It caused me some anxiety because I'd never seen or been anywhere near rats before. I was too young to understand the full gravity of the situation. My mother feared rodents. She declared it was time for us to move. No kidding!

Right around this time, Joe changed his "profession." With the financial help of my mother, he began driving a taxicab in Manhattan. Joe's new schedule had him arriving home very late at night. When my mother was about six or seven months pregnant, she was lying in bed, preparing to sleep. In no time, a swarm of rats began coming out from the walls and everywhere. Maybe the smell of her breast milk attracted them. Who knows? She froze up and went into shock as they began closing in on her. Thank God Joe came home right in the nick of time. When he opened the bedroom door and turned on the lights, he saw rats everywhere. He stomped one of them right there on the floor as the rest of them scattered. Joe had to take my mother to the hospital for observation. We moved out right after that. A few weeks later, we received some news about our former building. The New York City Board of Health came to inspect the building and chose to shut it down. Everyone needed to vacate immediately. They condemned the premises because it was "uninhabitable for human beings." One could only imagine what the inspectors must have seen to make that determination. Our building was so rodent-infested that extermination was not an option. Instead, they boarded up the entire building. We were living there less than a month earlier. Crazy!.

What an eventful and traumatizing year it had been for me—first, the "Bad Boys School" episode, then my first robbery. My classmates taunted me about my height. We met my mother's new boyfriend, who beat us. Then, there was the shocking announcement of my mother's pregnancy. We fled at rat-infested tenement. I moved three times in one year, including changing schools each time. Could things get any worse?

Our new family was on the move again for the 4th time in two years. We settled in the Flatbush section of Brooklyn. Flatbush was not as rough as East New York but was still considered a high crime area in its own right. We moved to 2617 Foster Avenue. It was a four-story, 24 unit apartment building on a pretty nice block. Unfortunately, this new place was mice-infested. I guess it was better than rats but still disgusting. My mother's pregnancy reached the stage where she could no longer work. Joe's taxi income became our only means of support. With Joe now the acting head of the household, his behavior began to change. He started to reveal more of his Jamaican/ West Indian heritage. He began speaking with a broader Jamaican accent than ever before. He started using Jamaican slang words like "Blood Clot," "Bumba Clot," and "Ras Clot." I was like, "What the hell is he talking about?" It became clear that Joe had been acting more Americanized while courting my mother. He had been on his best behavior, but now that he was in the door, his real personality began to show. We all had to learn the Jamaican lingo to understand and better communicate with him. When Joe would leave the apartment, he would say, "Soon come," which meant he'd be right back. The word "Chuh" meant "Ugh," and when something shocked or amused him, he would say, "Blouse & Skirt!" None of this made any sense to me. Joe began to change his appearance as well. He was no longer the well-groomed man with a short haircut. Joe proclaimed to be a follower of the Rastafarian religion. He no longer shaved his facial hair. Joe announced he was letting his hair grow into the dreadlock style that was popular with the "Rasta's." My pregnant mother remained silent. By this time, the beatings increased in both frequency and severity. Joe beat us almost daily. One day he made a declaration in his now thick Jamaican accent. "Ya know what? This belt I've been using isn't working. From now on, I'm gonna use an extension cord!" Joe displayed the extension cord he bought from the store. This cord was to be his new weapon of choice, and it struck terror in our young hearts. The most challenging part was the fact that my mother was standing right there when he said it. How could you allow your children to receive this form of punishment? What were we doing at eight and nine years of age that required this level of discipline? Were we making too much noise? Did we not wash a dish? Did we break something?

The first time someone beats you with an extension cord, it will alter your perception of life. Getting beat by a belt was terrible. Each slap of the belt would sting. Some of the hits would feel different than others depending on if the belt hit you square or not. Afterward, you were able to recover in a few minutes and try to resume your day. Although it still hurt, the belt's psychological effect was more significant than the physical. An extension cord is different. There is a distinctive feel when it hits your skin. There is a burning, cutting sensation like your skin is being ripped off. Each lash of an extension cord is consistent; it doesn't matter how it lands; the pain will be the same. Even the sound of the wire traveling through the air was different than a belt. Whoosh! It was way more menacing and memorable. Of course, you should not use an extension cord in this manner. It became a crude whip, if you will.

The aftermath of the thrashing lasted longer as well. The cord would leave welt marks on your skin that would be visible for days and sensitive to the touch. Taking a shower or putting on a shirt would remind you of the previous beating. As horrifying as this act was, Larry and I were only in the infancy stages of understanding what Joe was capable of doing. He had a twisted rationale for his slave-like treatment of us children. Joe felt that if you don't discipline boys in this manner, they won't grow to become proper men. My mother bought into his "parenting style." She never said ANYTHING about its brutality. The problem with Joe's medieval approach was, he never actually taught us any lessons. He never guided us. He never passed down the so-called ancient wisdom a father teaches his son. Joe never showed us what becoming a man entailed. He had no answers, only one question, "Why didn't you do what I said?" After that, a beating would follow. My mother loved to toss around that old cliché, "Don't do as I do, do as I say." I hated that quote. As a child, I watched my parents make several questionable decisions. Each one was contrary to what they were trying to "teach" us. There were times when they should've gotten a beating too.

"Sometimes it's not the people who change, it's the mask that falls off" - Anonymous

The bold transformation of Joe continued to manifest itself as the weeks progressed. He now strutted around the house with his chest poked out. He flaunted all his Jamaican bravado in front of his "step-children." Meanwhile, the "honeymoon" period between my mother and her boyfriend began to fade. Joe's confrontational tone and total disregard for others crept into her direction. I guess she needed some chastising too. Arguments between the two of them began to erupt as the days progressed. During one of these heated exchanges, I heard scuffling coming from their bedroom. What is this? Were they having a physical altercation? I heard a thump, and then my mother cries out, "The baby!! The baby!!" I came running out of my room to see what was going on. I peeked into their bedroom. I saw Joe standing over my eight months pregnant mother, with a scowl on his face. She appeared to be in pain. He backed away. This incident was the worst thing I had ever seen. I wanted to do something, but what could I do against this man? If I entered the room, I would've received the extension cord or worse. I felt powerless. It was upsetting to know this man had thrown my mother to the ground. His reckless actions could have caused her to go into premature labor or lose the baby. Unbelievable! How did things become this bad so quickly? It now appeared that we were all living under the rule of a new oppressive tyrant. Every aspect of our lives changed. Later that day, everything seemed to return to "normal." Which meant us walking around on eggshells trying not to invoke the wrath of the king.

On April 15th, 1975, my mother gave birth to a baby girl. She named her Chanele (my suggestion) after her favorite perfume, Chanel no. 5. I was pretty excited. It was a joyous occasion. The summer of 1975 arrived, my time of year! It was time to hit the streets and get familiar with my new surroundings. There was a grammar school (PS 269), which Larry and I would be attending in September, about three blocks away. There was an enormous playground connected to it. Perfect! My mother formed a friendship with our neighbor who lived below our apartment. She had a son named Alex, who was similar in age to Larry and me. We would run back and forth between each other's apartments having fun. Unfortunately, the volatility existing in our apartment was always brewing below the surface. Any peaceful moments were short-lived. One day, my mother and Joe got into another heated exchange. This one was worse than ever before. Alex's mother was present during this argument. She ordered both Larry and me to "Go down to my apartment and stay there!" It was a tense moment. What could be happening so drastic that we couldn't even be in the apartment? After a while, Alex's mom came down to check on us. Her eyes looked red and puffy like she had been crying for hours. Ah, man!

We spent the entire night at Alex's house, and the next morning returned to our apartment. Joe wasn't home, but my mother was there sitting on her bed, wearing shades. Immediately I knew something was wrong; she rarely wore sunglasses. My mother gathered both of us together and said, "I want you guys to know that Joe hit me" and took off her glasses. Her whole face was bruised. One of her eyes was black and swollen shut. Oh, my God!! There are no words to describe how it feels to see the person who you love most in the world have her face look like that. I tried not to stare at her, but it was unavoidable. She put her shades back on and continued, "We were arguing, and I walked away from him and sat on the other side of the room. I began talking to Alex's mother when Joe snapped. He said, 'You think you can come over here and talk about me?' Then he punched me in my face and began beating me. Alex's mother dragged him off of me." I was both shocked and not surprised. I knew this guy was bad news from the beginning. I knew it! I knew it! I knew It! What I didn't realize was how awful he was. He was capable of anything. My childhood intuition was correct. My mother had allowed the initial violence to take place via her children. Joe became more emboldened after that. The saddest part for me was that her sons should have defended her, but we were powerless. We were no match for this grown man. What an absolute feeling of helplessness and shame.

The question became, what was she going to do now? My mother told us that after things calmed down, Joe apologized (of course). He vowed never to hit her again (typical). She said to us, "I'm going to forgive him this time, but I won't forget. I told him if he ever puts his hands on me again, I'm going to leave him." Is that what it's going to take? Next time he might put you in the hospital or worse. By my count, this was the second time Joe assaulted her already. On another note, what about us kids? Joe puts his hands on us almost every day. I was too young to understand the dynamics between a man and a woman. I had a limited understanding of the financial responsibilities of having a newborn baby. Still, I felt like it was time to leave, now! What did I know? My mother wore her shades whenever she went outside for about two weeks. After that, it was back to our routine, go to school, return home, and get beat by Joe's extension cord.

Despite the nonstop physical abuse, Larry and I continued to search for ways to have fun. During an errand run with my mother, we noticed a small shop on Flatbush Avenue and 4th Street. They only sold comic books. It looked interesting. We asked our mother if we could check it out. She agreed and left us in there for about thirty minutes while she continued to run her errands. It was like entering a whole new world. The heroes, the villains, the stories, the artwork, the colors, I loved it. From that moment on, this became my new favorite pastime. Soon I would be spending every coin I had on comic books. Larry fell in love with comic books too. He was the same kid who wouldn't read in school but would spend hours reading any comic book he could get his hands on. Comics also gave us another interest we both had in common. We would share comic books. It became our escape from reality. We began searching for the older comic books from the 1960s, The Golden Age of Marvel Comics. Marvel comics were our favorite, but we liked DC comics too.

I also believe comic books helped to expand my vocabulary, especially Marvel. The writing style was for both kids and adults to enjoy. Sometimes I would look up words I didn't understand in the dictionary. Other times, I could figure out what a word meant by its context in the story. Comic books took my reading comprehension to another level. Larry and I studied the comic book's credits too. We enjoyed the work of the now-legendary duo of Stan "The Man" Lee and Jack "King" Kirby. We began to seek out their work.

Besides reading comics, our other favorite pastime was going to that school playground. This park had swings, monkey bars, and seesaws. There were handball and basketball courts, even a baseball field. Unfortunately, on the other side of the field were the infamous projects called, 'The Vanderveer Houses.' Larry and I were newcomers, so we learned about Vanderveer's notorious reputation the hard way. Most of the kids that played in the park were cool, but unfortunately, there were a few bad apples. As usual, it didn't take long for them to sniff me out. There was this one boy in particular named Marcus. We were the same age, but he was one of those tough street kids from Vanderveer. He appeared to be friends with a group of older boys. They assembled on a bench near the playground about 30 feet away. They never played in the park, only hung around. I was about to be a 4th grader, but these bench dwellers were about to enter the 6th grade. Compared to a 4th grader, a 6th grader could be a real problem. I stayed as far away from them as possible. In no time at all, this kid Marcus began harassing me every day. He pushed me, slapped me around, and took whatever money I had in my pocket. I was terrified of Marcus. One day, I found a handball on the street. Handball was very popular in this park. Everyone played using a standard, light-pinkish colored handball. This particular handball I found was bright orange! I had never seen one that color before. When I took that handball to the park, everyone was like, "Yooo, you got an orange handball!" I started playing with this orange handball. When I turned around, Marcus was standing there. Damn. He yelled, "Whose handball is this"? I said,

"Mine." Marcus said, "It's mine now." He put it right in his pocket and left. I was devastated, but there was nothing I could do. Day after day, Marcus continued to bother me. This behavior went on for about a month, all the way until September and the beginning of 4th-grade classes.

    One of the main features of this particular playground was these metal swings. They allowed you to stand on them and swing very high. Some kids would swing so high that it looked like they were going to go all the way over the support pole. These kids were like circus acrobats. They would do death-defying tricks on the swings with no helmet or padding of any kind. There was no padding on the ground either, only concrete. They would lay on their stomachs while swinging without using their hands. They would go under the swing and come up on the other side while it was still moving. Sometimes on one leg! Incredible! The ultimate trick was "The Spider-Man." There was a chain-linked fence about fifteen feet away from the swings. One of these flying daredevils would jump from the swing in mid-air and try to land on the gate. If you were able to do this AND still be able to cling to the gate like Spider-Man, you were the best. Only a few kids were able to pull off The Spider-Man stunt. They were jumping from a swing moving at about 25 mph and catching on to a gate fifteen feet away with their bare hands! These kids were Lebron James level athletic at nine years old. Sheesh!! One day Marcus decided, "You know what, I gotta new Spider-Man that's better than what everybody else is doing. I'm not gonna land on the gate anymore; I wanna land on a real person!!" He turns to me and says, "Yo, I want you to stand right there and wait. I'm going to jump off this swing and land on you! It's going to top everyone's Spiderman." I was so terrified of him that I agreed to stand there! Everyone in the park was watching this historic event. Marcus gets on the swing and begins pumping. He goes higher and higher, gaining momentum. When he reaches his greatest speed, he leaps off the swing with both feet out for added effect. I stood there with my eyes closed like a crash test dummy awaiting impact. Luckily, he miscalculated his jump and landed right next to me. Marcus became pissed. He said, "Shit!" Marcus then takes me by the shoulders and adjusts my position a little to the left where I needed to be. He was now confident that he placed me in the right spot. Marcus looks at me and says, "You better not fuckin' move!" He gets back on the swing and starts pumping again. All the other kids were gawking at me, and I was standing there like an idiot. Everything seemed to be happening in slow motion. I could visualize the entire scenario. Out of nowhere, something came over me and said, "You can't do this. I don't care how scared you are of Marcus; you cannot let him jump off that swing with his two feet and hit your body at 25 mph." At the exact moment, I took a look at Marcus' face. I could see the sheer determination in his eyes as he was taking his final pump. Marcus jumped from the swing with all his might. At the very last second, I moved over. Marcus fell and busted his ass! He jumped up, furious, "I told you don't fuckin' move!!" The same spirit that told me to move gave me the courage to cock back and punch Marcus right in his face, POW!! I don't know where this sudden bravery came from, but we began fighting right there by the swings! All of a sudden, I could feel other fists hitting me. It was the 6th graders from the bench. They were his boys. They saw what was going on and came to his aid. I don't know how many of them there were. They beat my ass from the swing to a makeshift hole in the fence that someone had cut about twenty feet away. As I was fleeing, trying to get through this opening, someone drop-kicked me through the hole in the fence. I flew through the gate and landed on the other side. I was screaming and crying. They kept pummeling me outside of the park and onto the sidewalk. One of them yelled, "Don't you ever come around here no more!" I ran home. My lip was bleeding, and my nose was bleeding. I was sure I had a footprint on my back from getting drop kicked. I was in bad shape. I saw my mother in the kitchen cooking, and I began crying. All I wanted was to hug her. I said, "Ma, they beat me up in the park." She turned around and said, "Damn! I'm so sick of you, every day it's something. Go to your room and leave me alone!!" I slumped off to my room, sat on my bed, and cried, wishing for a hug that would never come.

 The next morning, I had no choice but to cut through that same park to enter the school building. I retraced the same agonizing steps from the previous afternoon's beatdown. Who was the first person I saw as I entered the park? None other than Marcus. Ah, man! My heart sunk. He spots me immediately and begins coming straight towards me. "Well, this is it," I thought. He could've done whatever he wanted to do at that point; I felt demoralized. Marcus could've made up a new game called "The Aquaman" and peed on me; I would have stood there. I had my head down, looking at my shoes as he approached me. In a very calm manner, he says, "Hey, man, how you doin'?" I didn't say a word. To my utter surprise, he goes, "Guess what, man? I'm not gonna bother you anymore. We're friends, right? We can be cool, right?" What? I couldn't believe it. Of course, I accepted his olive branch, "Sure! We can be friends." He said, "OK cool," and walked away. What the hell happened here? Don't get me wrong, I was ecstatic by the sudden turn of events, but still, I felt confused. I know I lost the fight? Or did I?

It took me years to figure out what happened the previous afternoon. Meanwhile, I would see Marcus around the school, and he would always speak to me with a smile. It was so weird. I'll let you ponder this riddle yourself for now as we will revisit this topic a little later in the story. In the meantime, all I cared about was Marcus wanted to be my friend, and the bullying was over. It was one of the weirdest things I had ever experienced.

Dealing with bullies was trying for a kid with my particular temperament. That became the least of my problems. Larry and I began getting robbed while going to the grocery store. My mother would send one of us to the store with a few dollars and a list of items to buy like bread, milk, and eggs. Tough street guys would be outside roaming around looking for trouble. As soon as they spotted one of us, they would pounce, "Give me your money!" We would hand over our mother's change without delay. It reached a point where these guys would see one of us and immediately empty our pockets.

Going to the store or park became very stressful. My mother would get angry. She would ask, "Where's my change?" I would have to tell her, "These boys took it." She would get disgusted and say, "Get out my sight!" These incidents happened countless times. We were easy victims. Somehow these thugs would be able to sniff us out in a crowd of people. Most of the time, I didn't have any money on me. They would be skeptical and actually stick their hands in my pockets and turn them inside out! These crooks had creative ways of robbing you, "Yo! You got money?" I would say no. They would say, "Jump up and down!" If they heard any spare change jingling in my pockets, they would take it. How embarrassing and demeaning was it to be in the middle of the sidewalk, jumping up and down? Getting mugged at nine years old became a regular part of my life. I developed a zigzag route to the grocery store based on the blocks I felt were safe. It would take me twice as long to run simple errands. Joe didn't volunteer to teach us how to defend ourselves, either. Instead, he would just ridicule us for losing the money. Robbery added to my daily stress list, along with bullying and getting teased for being too tall or too dark-skinned. Joe's extension cord topped it off.

As the fall of 1975 became the winter of 1975, our low-income reality began to set in. My mother was still tending to her newborn baby and remained unemployed. Joe's taxicab income was all that sustained our family of five. Of course, there would be no Christmas gifts again this year. Somehow we always managed to have dinner on the table and adequate clothing. There was little money for anything else, except music. My mother would buy all the hottest R&B singles in vinyl 7" format called "45's" because of their rpm speed on the record player. Larry and I listened to all of her songs, but Joe had his particular taste in music. One day, he returned home from a visit to his family's house in Queens, holding his favorite album. The title was 'Natty Dread.' Joe declared, "This guy right here is the best; his name is Bob Marley." Who is Bob Marley? Bob Marley was the most prominent artist in Jamaica. His style of music is called Reggae music. I never heard of Reggae music, nor did I care. Joe began playing Bob Marley so often, Larry and I learned all the words to the songs. We didn't understand his message very well, but we liked his smooth melodies and soothing voice. No one else in our neighborhood appeared to be playing Bob Marley. Joe predicted, "One day, this guy is gonna be big in America, wait and see." Larry seemed to take a liking to Bob Marley even more than I did.

One day, the superintendent of our building offered Larry $10 to sweep the entire building. That sum of money wasn't a lot compared to the size of the job (it took him all day). Still, for a ten-year-old living in Flatbush circa 1976, it was plenty. After that grueling day, Larry mustered up the energy to say, "I'm going to the store to buy me some records." I was like, "You're gonna spend your hard-earned money on some records?" He sure did! Larry went to the local record shop and bought the brand new Bob Marley album, 'Rastaman Vibration.' What a shocking decision! To put this in perspective, Larry would otherwise have not had $10 to spend in total for the entire year. If you combined both of our yearly spending budgets, it still wouldn't have equaled $10. Larry chose to spend almost his whole unexpected windfall on a Bob Marley album. It showed how much he connected with "The Tuff Gong." Even Joe wasn't aware of the new Bob Marley album yet. Larry caught everyone by surprise.

The winter of 1976 had been another brutal one both inside and outside the home. Our apartment was always kept clean. Thanks in part to my mother's diligence and her ability to delegate chores to her two sons. Still, we spent the entire winter without heat. Our "Slumlord" took the boiler out of the building to install it on another property. We would have to get dressed for school in the morning, sit in front of the oven at 400 degrees, and wash up—this required boiling water. In fact, I thought the word radiator was pronounced "Rat-tiator" because that's how the rats entered the apartment. The heat never came from the heater, only rodents. It confused me why it was even present in an apartment. Speaking of rodents, we sure had plenty of them. The mice were everywhere! I used to stay up at night and watch several of them run around our living room like a playground. Larry would be sound asleep (as usual), but these creepy intruders would keep me awake with their scratching and squeaking. Once, I was taking out the kitchen garbage as instructed by my mother. We used paper grocery bags as makeshift garbage bags. As I was taking the trash downstairs, a mouse jumped out of the garbage. Right past my face! I screamed and threw the garbage bag up in the air. Trash landed everywhere in the hallway. My mother yelled, "What is all that noise?" I told her what happened. I had to clean up the mess in the hallway to boot. I acquired a deep hatred for these little critters. Larry and I once sat and watched a small group of mice gather around and eat a tray of rat poison. They even had one mouse positioned off to the side like a lookout or something. Unbelievable! I couldn't help but find myself reminiscing about living in Lenox Terrace with the fish tank and the doorman. That was a long time ago.

Despite all the daily distractions, I was still excelling in school—my brother, not so much. One day I was sitting in class doing my school work when there was a knock on the door. My 4th-grade teacher opens the door. To my surprise, in walks my brother's 5th-grade teacher from down the hall along with Larry. What is going on? My entire class was silent. The 5th-grade teacher said, "I'm sorry to disrupt your class, I needed to prove a point." He then takes Larry by the hand and brings him over to my desk. He says to me, "Will you please give your brother a pencil! He comes to school every day unprepared." Of course, I had several pens & pencils inside of my desk. I gave Larry the pencil. The teacher remarked, "I knew you would have a pencil, that's why I brought him down here." It appeared that both of our teachers were well aware that we were related. They were also familiar with both of our scholastic approaches. They must have had quite a discussion amongst themselves about the two of us. How frustrated did Larry's teacher have to be? He abandoned the rest of his students and walked down the hall to my class to embarrass him. Larry didn't look like he cared one bit. It was confusing because we both walked to school together that very morning. He didn't appear unprepared. I know for a fact Larry had pencils at home. If my parents ever heard about this episode, they would have beaten him. Joe had recently announced to us children that he found a new weapon of choice, a rubber hose. He dared to tell me to my face how he felt the extension cord was leaving too many identifying marks. Joe decided to use the rubber hose because it would be less traceable (more silence from my mother).

True to his word, Joe tested the rubber hose on me shortly after that. He decided it wasn't as effective as the extension cord, so he switched back. Anyway, based on the known outcome, how could Larry put himself in a position to deal with my mother's yelling and Joe's extension cord? Larry's behavior even had me baffled. I guess another one of those timeless clichés applies here, "You are who you are." Speaking of Joe, the rocky relationship between my mother and Joe appeared to level off. Which was good considering Joe's penchant for violence and our family's financial strain.

One day, I came home from school and my mother looked distressed. Once again she sat both of us kids down for a very mature discussion. She told us how Joe had gone to visit his family in Queens and returned with a new declaration. He stated that there was no reason why he should be working this hard to care of "these boys" who weren't his children. Joe should only be responsible for his daughter, period. He added that my mother needed to get on welfare until she was able to find a job. Joe blindsided her completely. She felt betrayed by him. She said, "I've worked my whole life since I was sixteen years old. Now that I'm in this position, with a young baby to take care of, he comes with this?" Joe had done a complete 180-degree flip on his promise that if she had the baby, he would take care of us. What did she expect?

They say, "Hindsight is 20/20." Still, why would anyone risk the financial security of themselves and their children? Especially for a person who they had only known for eight months? Was she that confident Joe would do the honorable thing and stand by his word? My mother was in a tight spot now. My sister was still too young to be alone without competent infant care. There wasn't enough money for a proper nurse if my mother chose to work full time. So for the immediate future, she needed to stay home with the baby. Somewhere, during early 1976, my mother applied for and received welfare benefits. This included food stamps, medical insurance, and housing. Now, I know what you're thinking. After Joe's double-cross, she was definitely considering leaving him right? Wrong. That possibility was never mentioned at all. In fact, with the new government help, my parents agreed to move from our mouse-infested apartment. In the spring of 1976, we were moving once again, for the fifth time in four years.

CHAPTER 3
THE DEVIL IS IN THE DETAILS

"**A***s your kids grow, they may forget what you said, but won't forget how you made them feel." - Kevin Heath*

In the bicentennial year of 1976, our family moved into a two-bedroom apartment about 1.3 miles away. Our new address was 170 East 35th Street, in the East Flatbush section of Brooklyn. The new apartment looked clean, with no mice or roaches anywhere. The block was quiet and there were several kids our age who lived on the block. None of them appeared to have a bully mentality. It was a much-needed breath of fresh air.

The summer arrived, and so did my birthday. I was finally ten years old. I watched my one-year-old sister Chanele take her first steps. It was amazing. My mother assigned Larry and me the added responsibility of babysitting Chanele. She now felt confident enough to take on a new part-time job. Unreported income violates NYC welfare regulations, but hey, who's going to tell? Larry and I spent the summer exploring our new neighborhood together. My mother allowed us to travel by ourselves to the 526-acre forest known as Prospect Park, which was 1.2 miles away. It was the second-largest public park in the borough of Brooklyn. Larry and I couldn't get enough of Prospect Park and walked over there every chance we could. We would spend hours there and return home so filthy my mother would ask, "What did you guys do? Bring a piece of the park home with you?" On our block, Larry and I played the popular playground board game 'Skelly' and hung out with our new friends. If you add reading comic books, we had the best summer of our young lives.

Larry and Kenny at Prospect Park

Classes resumed in the fall of 1976. On the first day of school, some kid named Dee wanted to fight me for no reason. He sized me up with a single glance; I was a pushover. Once again, I was the tallest kid in the entire 5th-grade class. Larry was also tall for a 6th grader. He was only eleven years old and already wore a size thirteen shoe! One day, Larry's teacher summoned him over and said, "I want you to run an errand." He gave Larry a note to take to another teacher down the hall. Larry walked over to the other class, knocked on the door, and handed the teacher the note. The teacher took the letter, opened it, looked down at Larry's feet, and started laughing. Larry peeked at the message in the teacher's hand, and it read, "Look at his feet!" Larry became very upset by this inappropriate prank pulled by his teacher. He later told my mother what happened, and she was furious! She called the school and yelled at them, "How dare you humiliate my child like this?" They were very apologetic, "We're so sorry, that joke was in poor taste. He never thought your son would see the note"...blah, blah, blah. It was bad enough dealing with the other students, but now the teachers were joining in on the fun?

After about a month, I outgrew all my clothing. My pants and shirts were too small. Unfortunately, there was no money for new clothes. The jokes were endless. "Hey, Kenny, are you expecting a flood? No? Then why are your pants so high?" I had to stand there and absorb their verbal abuse. The nickname for pants that were too short was "High Waters" or "Floods." I could hear them laughing as I entered the school, "Hey Kenny, pull up your shoes!" I wanted to hide, but I couldn't, I was too tall. Adding to our woes, neither Larry nor myself had received a haircut since 1972 when we lived in Harlem. It had been over four years and counting without a haircut! While everyone else had shaped-up afros, we had "nappy" unkempt hair. More jokes followed. Even in a neighborhood where poverty was the norm, our appearance looked subpar.

As I reflect on my life at this point, I would consider this period, "The calm before the storm." Everything you've read so far is the warm-up to the main events which were about to unfold in our lives. I will pause my life right here, at age ten, and speculate. What could I have done at this moment in time to change the course of my life? Since I was a young child with limited options, the answer to that question is; not much. No one knew what the future held anyway. Still, seeds already got planted that I was yet unaware of. I would've had to do something drastic to make a ripple in my future timeline now. I traveled along as a passenger, strapped into a moving car, destination unknown. My only consolation would be that I wasn't taking this journey alone. I had my partner in crime with me, my brother Larry.

The 1970s were a tough time for my hometown of New York City. Statistics showed the city's poverty rate rose during the decade. By 1977, one in five residents, or 20%, lived below the poverty level. That number was 8% higher than the national average. The data showed many New York families dealt with the same financial hardships as ours. That may have been true but, I couldn't tell. Every kid in my area appeared to have more of the necessities of life than Larry, and I did. Even our family receiving welfare had an awkward dynamic to it. For my mother to qualify, she had to establish that she was a single parent, requiring government help to care for her children. That was true for Larry and me, but not for my sister. There could be no evidence of her father, Joe, living in the apartment. A social worker could drop by at any time to inspect the children's living conditions. If they found so much as a man's shoe, it could pose a potential problem for my mother's welfare benefits. Every six months, Brooklyn's main welfare office required my mother to appear in person and show evidence that she used the allotted welfare money to pay her bills. They called this interview a "Face To Face." This interaction was a very stressful event. If the meeting didn't go well, she could lose her benefits.

How must my mother have felt hiding in her apartment the very man who forced her to get on welfare in the first place? Anyway, speaking of Joe, his behavior was becoming more volatile. The rate of our beatings increased to now daily. Joe would enter our room and concoct some trumped-up charges against one or both of us. After that, the whipping would begin. He seemed to enjoy it now, like a form of recreation. He even developed a new technique. Instead of beating us at a steady pace, he decided to alternate the lashes' speed to make us squirm even more. Joe would hold the extension cord over his head with both hands like a matador. He would then swing the wire downward with great force. It was hard to try and block the extension cord when he did this. This technique was so brutal that I would cry hysterically, watching him beat Larry. He would yell at me, "Why are you crying? I didn't even hit you!" We were in the clutches of a sadistic maniac, and no one could save us now.

One spring afternoon, I arrived home from school, as usual, to find no one home. That was odd since Larry usually beat me back from school. Laying on my bed was a handwritten note addressed to me from Larry. Inside the letter was a bombshell. Larry had run away from home!! What? I couldn't believe what I was reading. He wrote that Joe called the house and told Larry he was going to beat him when he returned home for no reason at all. Larry stated that he had enough of the beatings. He left before anyone could arrive. I felt crushed. My brother, who was my best friend, was gone. Some part of me understood his decision, but I didn't see it coming. When my mother came home, I showed her the note thinking she would be concerned. Wrong! Her first words after reading the letter were, "Oh, he thinks he's grown? Well, he can stay out there then!" I couldn't believe her attitude. He's wasn't grown; he was eleven years old! Larry stated in the note that he left because he was sick of the beatings. Did she even read that part? I had to do something. I told her, "I know where he is; I'm gonna go look for him." She didn't seem to care at all. Her stance remained tough. I was the only one who knew where he would go anyway, Prospect Park. I immediately left the house and walked the mile-plus trek to the park. There was a zoo there with a bunch of cages, minus the animals. There was also a food court located in this section of the park. When I arrived, there he was. I greeted him, "Yoooo… What's up?" Larry repeated his claim, "Joe's gonna beat me; I can't take it anymore." Although I understood, I still needed to state the obvious, "Where are you gonna go? You can't live out here." Larry says, "I'm gonna live out here and sleep out here!" The temperature was somewhat warm for a late spring day. I asked him, "Well, what's gonna happen when it gets cold?" He didn't answer. I then asked, "Well, what are you gonna do for food?" Larry says, "Let me show you something." He brings me over to the food court and says, "You see all those people eating? Look at how they eat. Some of them don't throw away their food; they don't even finish it. I can go over there, pick it up and eat it." What? I couldn't believe my ears. I said, "Nah, man, you can't be eating other people's food scraps; you gotta come home." He said, "No!!" I pleaded with him to change his mind. After begging for a while, Larry softened his stance to about a 70/30 possibility of returning home. Well, at least he wasn't 100% against my proposal; I could work with that. I said, "Ok, I'm going back home and talk to Ma." I walked another mile plus back home to convince my mother to allow her son back into the apartment.

    I reached home and told my mother I had found Larry and spoke to him. I asked her flat out, "Can you please let Larry come back home?" She said, "NO! Wherever he is, let him stay there. You go get in the tub, and that's it!" I became very emotional. I couldn't believe this was happening. Joe was there by this point, but he was quiet. I sat there in the tub, crying in disbelief. My mother must have heard me crying. She knocked on the door and yelled, "Are you alright in there," and I said, "Yes, I'm fine." When I came out of the bathroom, she said, "Go get your brother and tell him he can come home. You can also tell him things are going to be different around here! He can't come back here thinking he can act the way he did before! He don't pay no bills around here!" I didn't care about her ranting. I ran the mile-plus back to Prospect Park to get Larry. It was around 6 or 7 pm by now. Luckily, Larry hadn't left the area yet. I told him, "They said you could come back!" Larry was less than enthusiastic but agreed to return home. He asked me if they mentioned the initial beating threat, which caused him to run away in the first place. I said, "They're not gonna beat you; come home." We walked the mile together back to our apartment. When Larry returned home, he didn't receive that beating, but he wasn't welcomed with open arms either. With an attitude, my mother opened the door for him. Larry went to his room, crisis averted.

    Once again, I became the mediator between my brother and my mother. I was initially thrust into the mediator role at six years old when the 'Bad Boy School' was coming for Larry. This time the situation was real. At ten, I managed to inject myself into a battle between these two strong-minded individuals. During the spring of 1977, at age eleven, Larry ran away from home for the first time. It wouldn't be the last.

    The summer of '77 approached. Joe had now evolved into a full-fledged Rastafarian right before our eyes. He completed his transformation with the introduction of marijuana use. Joe didn't smoke in the house, only outside. Still, Joe was so bold that he would send me to the store to buy marijuana. There was a record shop nearby, which was a front for a weed spot. Joe would send me to buy a "Dime Bag" ($10) or a "Nickel Bag" ($5) for him. The guy at the counter would say, "You're Joe's son, right? This weed is for Joe?" I would say yes, and then he would sell a ten-year-old boy a bag of weed. "Money was tight" was the explanation given to Larry and me about why we couldn't receive anything extra. We couldn't even get pants that fit, but somehow there was extra money for "Ganja."

    My mother instilled in us from an early age that any form of illegal drug use was unacceptable. I didn't know the smell of marijuana until Joe started smoking it. How could a woman who never smoked anything, not even a cigarette, condone this? My mother rarely drank. She was never, ever drunk. Somehow, this behavior was ok for Joe, though. In 1977, most of society didn't accept marijuana. It was also considered a controlled substance. Sending a ten-year-old child to buy a controlled substance is a felony. That was one of several which Joe had already committed since he began dating my mother. Somehow, it didn't matter. Instead of trying to curb Joe's behavior, my mother found a way to encourage it. She purchased him a light blue, eight-passenger Chevrolet van as a gift. I don't know if she used the money from her part-time job or some kind of credit, but the vehicle was real. Joe drove it 90% of the time. The van featured a large sliding door that made a distinctive sound when it opened or closed. We were so terrified of Joe that we would panic if we heard the van door slide open from outside our window. Oh My God! Joe is home! Our whole demeanor would change. We would immediately start doing homework or cleaning up. We would do anything to make it appear like we were doing something positive when he walked in the door. You didn't want him to have to speak to you.

When my mother was working, we would be home alone with Joe after school. He would do outlandish things. For example, Joe would exit the shower nude and parade in front of us while we were watching television. We would have no choice but to observe his naked body. What was he trying to prove? On one occasion, I was home alone with Joe, reading a comic book in my room when he summoned me to the living room. Joe yelled in his Jamaican accent, "Ken-ay, come 'ere!" I jumped up and ran to see what he wanted; I knew Joe wouldn't tolerate any slow responses. When I arrived, he said, "From now on, when I call you, I want you to say 'yes' from your room first and then come see what I want." Huh? I became confused by his new rule. I said ok, returned to my room, and resumed reading my comic book.

About fifteen minutes later, Joe yells, "Ken-ay, come 'ere!" I jumped up and ran into the living room. When I arrived, without warning, Joe slapped me in my face, Pow! I immediately began wailing in pain. He said, "I told you...When I call you, say 'yes' from your room first!" I returned to my room, crying and shaken up. I sat on the edge of my bed, waiting for the next time Joe would summon me. Sure enough, about ten minutes later, I heard, "Ken-ay, come 'ere!" I screamed at the top of my lungs, "Yes!" and then proceeded to the living room. I wanted to be 100% sure Joe heard my response from my bedroom. When I arrived in the living room, all he said was, "Get me a glass of water." I spent the rest of the afternoon in terror, awaiting the next time Joe would call me. This little random psychological game was typical of Joe and his unpredictable behavior. Larry and I lived under constant fear that at any time, for any reason, we would get abused.

On occasion, when my mother wasn't home, Joe would invite his friends over, more Jamaicans. His West Indian accent would become even thicker when his friends came around. He would blast his Reggae music and summon us from our room so he could show off in front of his friends. He would yell for us to come to the living room, but he wouldn't use our names. Instead, he would yell…YOUTH!!! In his Jamaican accent, it would sound like YUTE!!! (rhymes with flute). "COME 'ERE YUTE!!!" We would come running out of our room at top speed. He would say, "Come over here and take off my shoes, Yute!" I felt like a slave. We would have to get down on our knees in front of him and take off his shoes. Next, he would command,

"Now take off my socks." We would take off his socks. "Now, go get me some juice, Yute!" He would only talk to us like this when my mother wasn't home and in front of his Rastafarian friends. As time progressed, he became even bolder. One of the central doctrines of the Rastafarian religion is wearing one's hair in a dreadlocks style. Joe had announced earlier that he would no longer cut or comb his hair. He quoted the Bible, Numbers 6:5, which claimed no man should put a razor to his scalp. Now it was his prerogative to practice his religion anyway way he saw fit. Yet, Joe decided to take his dominance to another level by declaring that both Larry and myself would become Rastafarians too. "I want you to (dread) lock up your hair," he said to us. Huh? Is he serious? I didn't want to be a Rasta. We had no choice in the matter; his word was the law. The way our hair looked at the time, I doubt anyone would have noticed the difference. We spent the entire summer learning how to be young Rastafarians. My mother raised us Christians. She also took us to church with her on occasion. Still, she said nothing of our newfound religious conversion. Not a word.

"Divide and Conquer" definition: To make a group of people disagree and fight with one another so that they will not join together against one.

One random day, I happened to be home alone with Joe. He wandered into my room with a confession, "Ya know Kenny…You are my favorite. I don't like your brother." Huh? I tried not to look at him while he spoke; I stared at my shoes and shook my head up and down. Why is he telling me this? Does he even have a clue how much I despised him? I used to wish he would die all the time. Joe continued speaking, "I don't even like the way he looks. Some people say Larry looks like your mother; no, he doesn't! He looks nothing like her!" Still, I didn't answer him. I nodded my head, trying to avoid making him angry. After that, Joe gave me an assuring pat

Larry, Joe, Chanele and Kenny

on the back and left the room. I immediately put that nonsense out of my mind. I was young, but I could still see what Joe was trying to do. Drive a wedge between Larry and me so he could isolate him from the rest of the family. It would be much easier for Joe to break him if I wasn't always there crying and trying to influence my mother. Joe appeared to have unique plans for Larry, and he was beginning to set the stage. I didn't tell Larry what Joe said to me. It didn't matter. There was nothing he could do to break our bond. I hated this man.

The summer of 1977 kicked off with a bang. My mother and Joe decided they were going to be entrepreneurs. They hatched a plan to open a small business, a fruit & vegetable store. I have no idea how they acquired the money to invest in their new venture. We were still on welfare. The funds must have originated, once again, from my mother's side hustle. Joe proclaimed himself to be an excellent carpenter. He wanted to build all the store shelves himself. The store's location was two miles away on Clarkson Avenue between 94th and 95th street. This area is the notorious Brownsville section they called "The 90's." Ruthless Jamaican drug gangs controlled this turf. One crew was called "The Shower Posse." They got the name because they would spray an entire area with machine-gun fire to kill one rival gang member. They didn't care who got hit in the crossfire. Now I know what you're thinking; Why would they pick an area like this to open a fruit & vegetable store? Your guess is as good as mine.

Joe focused all his attention on building the store. Of course, Larry and I were his assistants. Joe brought his "favorite son" to work with him every day. In fairness, Joe was pretty good with his hands. He built all of the shelves and the counter. I even handled a saw and did some woodwork from time to time. During one break, Joe decided to review the storefront sign, which he was designing himself. I noticed it was taking him a long time to draw up the simple lettering. After a while, I finally realized what the problem was; he couldn't spell the word 'vegetable.' I looked at his sketch and corrected it for him, mentally shaking my disappointed head.

July 13th, 1977, was four days after my birthday. It was that weird time of year when both Larry and I would be eleven years old at the same time. NYC was in the grips of an oppressive heatwave. It was a little after 9 pm, and our parents weren't home yet. All three children were sitting on the couch watching the hit television show, 'Charlie's Angels.' The next thing we knew, all the lights went out in the entire apartment. My first reaction was Con Edison had shut our power off due to lack of payment. We ran to the window and noticed that all the lights on the entire block were out too. It was apparent that this was a significant outage.

About two minutes later, we heard a loud SMASH!!! Someone had busted the window of the musical instrument store around the corner. We saw two guys running down the street carrying a couch with two televisions resting on the cushions. We were gasping, "Yo! They stole that couch!" Chaos had erupted in Brooklyn in less than five minutes. It was an official blackout. My mother arrived shortly afterward. She had exited the train in the nick of time. Joe came home still in possession of his cab. He said, "I had to ride over the Brooklyn Bridge from Manhattan in the dark. It's crazy!! The lights are even off in New Jersey." My mother became concerned about our store, which was still under construction. They decided to ride to Brownsville and check on the store. When we arrived downstairs, people were running around everywhere. The man who owned the corner grocery store had positioned his car in front of his store. He was sitting on the hood of his car with a shotgun! The radio newscast described how widespread the blackout was, and Con Edison had no timetable for restoring power. As we traveled through the streets of Brooklyn, I couldn't believe my eyes. Thousands of people were outside, many of them looting stores. Dozens of stores were already looted and destroyed. Every liquor store got robbed. Every grocery store had smashed windows with people pushing carts of food over the glass. The most surprising thing was that it wasn't only young people and criminals doing the looting. I saw older men and women out there, acting as lawless as the young people were. Every race and nationality had representation. The police were overwhelmed and powerless. New York City was already the crime capital of America. With the lights out, Brooklyn was in anarchy. We arrived at our store and found everything intact. No one bothered to waste time on an empty store. We drove back through the chaos and returned home.

Observing the aftermath of the blackout in the morning was even more shocking. Brooklyn looked like a war zone. There were miles of looted stores, and debris was everywhere. Many buildings and cars were smoldering from random arson fires. In all, there were 1,037 fires reported and 1,616 stores damaged. The police recorded the most significant mass arrest in New York City history, with 3,776 people arrested. Estimates put the damages at three hundred million dollars. That is equal to 1.2 billion today. As night fell, Con Edison restored the power. The people of New York City returned to their "civilized" behavior.

The fruit & vegetable store opened for business during the middle of July 1977. Everything started well as customers began to patronize the store. Sometimes Joe worked the counter; other times, my mother operated the counter. Sometimes Joe would leave me alone to run the store while he went around the corner to hang out with his Jamaican friends. At eleven, I felt like a grown-up because I was able to talk to customers and give them change after they paid me for their groceries. One day, Joe closed the store a little earlier than usual and said we weren't going home yet. I followed Joe around the corner and into a dark building on East 95th street. He knocked on an unmarked door. A deep voice with a Jamaican accent answered the door, "Ooo (who) is it?"..."It's Joe." The Jamaican guy slid back a homemade peephole, saw who it was, then opened the door to greet us. Joe said, "This is my son," as I walked through the door.
There were a few guys in the apartment, and weed was everywhere! It was a marijuana wholesale operation. They had pot in different stages of production lying on a long table. Some of it was still in leaf form connected to little stems. Some of it was already crushed and spread out on the table. A guy was sitting at the end of the table, separating the crushed leaves from the seeds that mixed in. We stayed for a little while then left. Even I knew right away we had been in an illegal operation. I also knew marijuana was illegal and you could go to jail for possessing it. These guys were well beyond owning it; they were preparing for distribution. I was well aware that no kid should've been in there. Of course, I had questions. For one, how does Joe know these types of people? I wouldn't dare ask him a question like that, but I did ask him, "Why were they separating the seeds from the weed?" Joe replied, "No one wants to smoke the seeds mon, only the herb."

The summer of 1977 began to wind down. Unfortunately, like most small businesses, the fruit & vegetable store failed. It only lasted two months. My parents cited the location as one of the main reasons for the downfall. Brownsville didn't exactly have a booming economy. Also, neither of my parents had experience running a business. It was a recipe for disaster.
Still, my parents pushed on. Rumor had it that there was work to be had

"Down South." They devised a plan for Joe to drive down to Florida, find employment, and then send for the rest of us. We were all relocating to "The Sunshine State." Joe left New York with a part of the welfare money. After about a week and a half, Joe phoned home, claiming that he didn't find work. He also spent all the funds allocated to him for the "business" trip. Even my mother, who appeared to believe anything this man could conjure up, was not happy. She complained to us children about Joe's blatant irresponsibility. Somehow, my mother scraped together enough money to get Joe back to New York. This trip added more financial strain on the family. Still, two weeks without Joe was fantastic! Money well spent if you asked me.

When Joe returned from his job search, he greeted my mother with a kiss. He then opened up his suitcase and said, "Look what I bought!" Laying right on top of his clothes was a brand new gun! What the Hell? I was looking right at it, as was my mother. It became evident that the whole trip was a farce. Joe couldn't find time to secure employment, but he found time and money to buy a gun? He could've never purchased a firearm in New York City with its strict gun laws. Regardless, Down South had plenty of gun shops eager to sell anyone a pistol. This purchase was all the world needed; another lunatic, wannabe thug, in possession of an illegal handgun. Once again, my mother said nothing.

The very next day, I was alone in my room reading a comic book. Without warning, Joe kicks open my room door and fires a live round from his gun into the closet door! POW!!! He fired the gun less than two feet from where I was sitting. The sound of the gunshot in my little room made my ears begin to ring. The bullet pierced the closet door and traveled right through Larry's coat sleeve into the wall. Now, Larry had a bullet hole in his coat sleeve. All because Joe decided he wanted to be a cowboy and bust off a shot for no reason. That bullet could have gone through the wall and killed somebody next door or outside. Joe was giggling like a kid. He picked up the cartridge, which fell on the floor, and handed it to me. He said, "Look, Kenny, this is a real bullet cartridge." I was excited to see a real bullet cartridge. That sure topped the little plastic cap guns our friends used to have. Of course, when my mother found out what Joe had done, she didn't say much. She stated how dangerous it was to fire a gun in the apartment with young children around (duh!), and she agreed to fix Larry's coat sleeve (didn't happen), but wait…A couple of days later, he did the same thing! Joe kicked open my room door like he was Starsky & Hutch. He fired his weapon into the wall, leaving another large bullet hole. Unbelievable!!

The arrival of fall meant back to school. I enrolled at Walt Whitman Junior High School (I.S. 246), which was bigger than my grammar school. Entering the 6th grade in a new school was intimidating. Walt Whitman housed grades 6, 7, and 8. As I mentioned before, anytime I found myself around older kids; things would go south. The bullying began immediately upon my arrival. I was sitting in the cafeteria on the very first day of school, minding my own business. This 7th grader named DJ, who happened to be sitting across from me, says, "Yo… Don't you owe me a dollar?" I'm like, "No, I've never seen you before in my life." He said, "Yes, you do. You better have my money by tomorrow, or else I'm gonna fuck you up!" Fear engulfed me. I hadn't even completed my first day of school, and I already had a debt. Where was I going to get a dollar? My only source of income was the occasional spare change I received from my mother. Of course, the next day, I didn't have DJ's money. He slapped me in the back of my head and threatened, "You better have my money tomorrow."

The following day I gave him a quarter. Later, I was able to scrounge up another quarter, which whittled my deficit down to 50 cents. In true loan shark fashion, DJ said, "Nah, you're taking too long. You still owe me a dollar!" He was relentless, hounding me every day. It took me about two weeks to pay DJ off. I ended up giving him $1.50 in total. After that, DJ never extorted me for money again. He would continue to hassle me throughout the school year. I soon discovered that DJ was small potatoes compared to some other students.

A week after settling my debt with DJ, I made my routine exit from school at 3 o'clock. There were hundreds of kids filing out of the school at one time. I noticed this one, reckless guy, on a bicycle riding through the crowd of exiting students. He seemed to be around my age and about average height. He was dark-skinned with very dark lips. People used to call them "Reefer Lips" because people who smoked a lot of weed developed this shade of lip color. How could someone so young have reefer lips?

While he rode his bike through the sea of students, he notices me as well. This guy immediately veers his bicycle right in my direction and tries to hit me at top speed. I don't think I was his initial target, but something about me was too enticing. But, he misses me, hits the curb, and falls off of his bike. He gets up, furious, and says, "Yo! Why did you do that? You made me crash!"

What? I barked back at him, "I ain't do anything to you, man!" As I was responding, four or five guys who were with him approached us. I was pissed off because I knew he was trying to hit me. One of his friends said, "Yo, what happened?" This liar said," That guy made me fall!" I said, "Man, I ain't make you fall; you were trying to hit me!" As I was saying this, more of his guys arrived. They started circling me, and now my heart was beating. One of them said, "Wait a minute! Look over there! Ain't that those White Boys we robbed last week?" They all turned and started running in that direction. I began walking away. I knew I had dodged a bullet right there.

I remember thinking how strange it was for some White Boys to be in my area anyway. I hadn't seen one at my school in three weeks. As I walked away, the whole crew that left me less than two minutes earlier came running past me. They looked like they had done something terrible down the block. I thought to myself, "Those poor White Boys." One by one, they ran past me until one of them stopped short right in front of me and, POW!!! He sucker-punched me right in my face. It was the hardest punch I ever felt. It was like a reminder, "Oh, we didn't forget about you." I burst out crying and screaming in pain. The school security guard, standing there doing nothing, comes over to me and says, "Hey! Do you want to press charges? We know exactly who that is, his name is Eugene Baker, and we're sick of him! We're sick of him!" I didn't want to press charges; I wanted to go home. I started walking home, still crying when these two girls came over to me and said, "We'll walk with you. I hate that boy. He beat up my brother the other day." Now I'm thinking, who is this guy Eugene Baker?

As it turned out, he was at the next level in juvenile crime. I was "used to" getting robbed by random older dudes, a bully like Marcus, or even getting extorted by DJ. Those all seemed like isolated, random acts, but this guy Eugene was different. He was the leader of an organized gang. Eugene and his crew terrorized my junior high school for the entire three years I attended. I found out Eugene had a bunch of family members who went to nearby Erasmus Hall High School. Erasmus was one of the worst high schools in the city. Eugene had connections to the hoodlums that ran amok in Erasmus Hall.

Eugene already possessed a notorious reputation when I encountered him for the first time. He couldn't have been older than eleven or twelve years old. Before classes, all the 6th graders had to line up outside of the school around 8:30 in the morning. Eugene would be out there at 8 am every morning like clockwork. He and his crew would check every kid's pockets looking for money as they entered the building. The school safety officers did nothing. Eugene was always loitering in the school hallways but never attended any classes. Was he even a student? Our school had a strict staircase policy. Every student had to stay on the right side of the staircase when they walked up or down. One day, Eugene was roaming the stairs using the wrong side. Of course, the rules didn't apply to him. Our favorite gym teacher, Mr. Morgenstern, saw Eugene and told him to use the staircase's proper side. Somehow they got into an argument and then a scuffle. Mr. Morgenstern ended up smashing Eugene's head into the wall, and Eugene left the school. At 3 o'clock, there was an angry mob outside of our school. Dozens of Erasmus Hall students were waiting for Mr. Morgenstern. The police had to escort Morgenstern out of the school for his safety. He took a leave of absence for a few weeks until all the commotion died down.

Everyone was afraid of this kid, Eugene. There were hordes of students, many of whom knew each other, that could have banded together. We could have taken a stand against Eugene, but no one dared. Contrary to popular belief, the vast majority of kids in my neighborhood were good kids. They displayed typical childhood behavior—no one prepared for the likes of Eugene. Everyone in our school had a Eugene story. He became a sort of mythical figure. He didn't commit every crime his name became associated with, but he sure did most of them. Unfortunately for me, I got to experience his antics up close and personal.

As far as school work, I had no problems with the 6th grade. My grades stayed in the A/B+ range. I took the Board Of Education's citywide reading and math tests. It indicated I was reading at almost a high school level in the 6th grade. But, my math scores were only satisfactory at best. I excelled in every subject except math; it was my kryptonite. I would get C's in math on my report card. Report cards were a very stressful time because of my mother's educational standards. A bad report card was grounds for a beating and punishment too. A bad report card for me was different than a bad report card for Larry. I could get all As and Bs, but if I got one C, that was a lousy report card. Larry would get all D's and F's with one C on his report card. My mother would go, "Well, I see that you're trying; it's a little better than your last report card." What? That used to piss me off more than anything.

Why was there a double standard when it came to academics? Larry had a label as some troubled kid who had a hard time learning in school. Bullshit! Nobody knew him better than I did. We were together every single day of our lives. He didn't have a learning disability; he was bright. We would talk about a variety of topics daily. He would often teach me things. Larry would read the books that HE felt like reading with no problem. Sometimes, there would be a comic book I hadn't read yet. Larry would describe to me everything that was going on in the story arc. It reached a point where Larry started creating comic books. He taught himself to draw by studying the art style of comic legend Jack Kirby. Larry would illustrate his comics and then create a storyline as well. He produced heroes, villains, everything. Larry would draw and color them with accurate detail. Then he would come home with all D's and F's on his report card, and my mother would accept that, but I would get a beating? That wasn't fair.

The "experts" in school concluded something was wrong with him. Something WAS awry, but it wasn't his ability to learn. One time my mother went to the mid-semester parent/teacher conference at his school. She returned home after speaking to his teacher. My mother said, "Larry's teacher says he stares out of the window the entire day while class is in session." He had no interest in school.

One random day, I arrived home from school to find no one around. An empty apartment was rather odd because Larry would be home by that time. The sound of my mother's favorite Jazz singer, George Benson, would usually be playing. As I entered the apartment, there was silence. Even unemployed Joe might've been lurking around, but he was missing too. I was home alone for quite a while before the door opened, and everyone entered the apartment at the same time. Larry was wearing some kind of sling or soft cast on his hand. What is this? Larry seemed to be in good spirits, but as soon as we got into our room, I asked him what happened?

Larry told me they had returned from Kings County Hospital. Ah man, this wasn't good. Larry began to reveal the horrifying details. Joe started to beat him with the extension cord when he arrived home from school. Who knows for what this time. That wasn't news, but Joe's behavior was. Larry said the way Joe was swinging at him was different, more savage than before. The first lash Joe hit him with was so forceful that it ripped the skin right off of his arm. The gash was so deep that it left a permanent scar. Larry was bleeding. The second swing was so ferocious that when Larry tried to block it with his hand, it dislocated his thumb! Larry screamed in agony. His yell startled my mother, who had never said a word to Joe in over three years of him brutalizing us. She ran over and pushed Joe off of Larry. Seeing his dangling finger made her scream, which in turn made Joe stop whipping him. Even my mother realized what was going on and had to intervene. She risked her safety to stop this maniac. Joe's history showed he had no problems hitting a woman either. Something was different this time. Even for Joe, this was a new level of brutality. One could only conclude that he was trying to cause Larry serious harm, even death.

The law states that assault and battery on a child under the age of fourteen, which causes injury, is a felony. Joe's hatred of this twelve-year-old boy reached criminal levels. The only question now was, what did my mother do next? Did she call the police? Did she throw this loser out in the street? Did she try to find a haven for her son? No. Instead, she instructed Larry to lie to the hospital staff upon arrival. When the doctor asks him how he dislocated his thumb, Larry said it was a bicycling accident. They all rehearsed the bogus story before they arrived at the hospital. Larry did what they demanded of him and lied to the doctor. I was speechless. Not only was an aggravated felony assault committed against a minor, but there was also a cover-up, "accessory after the fact," which is another crime. I felt relieved to know my brother was "ok." It would take weeks before his hand would heal.

Years later, I would reflect on this particular incident. The most unbelievable part of it all had to be my mother's behavior. Joe's brutality towards us had been consistent throughout the relationship. Yet this time, my mother saw the whole thing. She was so disturbed by what she observed that it compelled her to take action. Still, she chose to protect her man despite him being wrong. She could have agreed to spare Joe with some newly added stipulations. For one, he couldn't beat us anymore. That would have at least been a start, though still inexcusable. She definitely didn't make that suggestion because the beatings continued. She elected to turn a blind eye and try to act like everything was "normal" afterward. What would it have to take? The next incident could be far worse. I have always wondered what would have happened if Larry went to the hospital and told the truth? How different would our lives have been? What kind of criminal charges would they have brought against Joe for his actions? Would they have removed all the children from the household? What if The Welfare learned of this abusive man living in a state-sponsored apartment? How would the Immigration Services handle a green card holder assaulting children? It's all speculation because, in reality, life went on.

The holiday season of 1977 arrived with a new declaration from my mother. We were no longer celebrating the traditional Christmas holiday. Instead, we were now celebrating the African-American holiday called Kwanzaa. We received an entire history lesson on how this was better for our people than Christmas. It sounded great. In reality, there was no real difference in our household; we still didn't exchange gifts. The holiday season came and went as usual. Not long after the holiday season, I arrived home from school to find Larry sitting on his bed, messing around with one of Joe's belts, and Joe wasn't there. Bothering Joe's stuff was both unusual and dangerous. Joe's clothes were off-limits. I asked Larry, "What are you doing with Joe's belt? Are you crazy?" The answer to that last question was debatable as Larry told me what happened. He said, "When I came home from school, Joe was gonna beat me again…This time with this belt. You know Kenny, I've had enough of this. When he swung the belt, I grabbed it." I said, "Wait! You, WHAT??" Larry responded, "Yeah, I grabbed the belt." I couldn't believe what I was hearing. I asked, "Then what happened?" Larry explained, "I caught the belt when he swung it, and we both began pulling the belt and the buckle broke." This story was too farfetched for me to comprehend, but I knew Larry was telling me the truth. That would explain why he had possession of Joe's belt.

I still couldn't understand how Larry was still alive? I needed more information. I began badgering Larry for answers, "Joe didn't try to punch you or anything?" Larry said, "No, he told me, 'You better fix my belt!' " That's it? I couldn't believe it. "That's all he said?" I asked. "Yeah, then he left," Larry concluded. I was in shock. This man was a living nightmare. His stature was that of a giant invincible figure, but in reality, he was a regular, average-sized man. Larry was 12 years old but tall for his age. He was close to Joe's height by this time. I don't know what went down in that room, but somehow Joe was the one who backed down. Larry finally had enough.

I was waiting to see what would happen when Joe returned home. I mean, this man owned a gun and all. To my surprise, nothing happened. Larry didn't fix his belt buckle either. It was a game-changer in our lives. After that, all the beatings stopped. Larry was my absolute hero. He stood toe to toe, eye to eye with the beast, and the beast blinked. It was a new day for us, an independence day! I remained cautious, though. I couldn't help but think that the other shoe was going to drop sooner or later. I was right, except it wasn't the shoe I was expecting.

A couple of months after the revolution, my mother sat us down for a quick meeting. She stated that Joe had broken his promise and put his hands on her once again. This time, she told him to get out. Well, for crying out loud. Is that what it finally took? It didn't matter what he did to us, as long as he didn't hit her? It was still a joyous occasion, regardless. Who needs to be analytical at a time like this? My mother met Joe in the fall of 1974. It was now the spring of 1978. Joe packed his stuff and left. Twice that week, he came by the apartment, begging my mother to take him back (I was eavesdropping), and she refused. A few days later, Joe returned in a predicament. He said the place where he was going to stay wouldn't be ready for a few days. He asked to leave his stuff at our apartment for the time being. I was standing right there, watching him negotiate with my mother. She agreed to help him. As soon as he brought all his stuff back into the apartment, the real Joe emerged again. He professed, "I'm not leaving, I'm back!... You can't put me out; everyone around here knows we both live here together." Oh no! How could this be happening? I looked at my mother's face when she said, "I'm calling the police!" Joe says, "Call them...You can't prove I don't live here." He was right. My mother responded with, "Yes, I can, and I will...TRY ME!" I was a nervous wreck. How could she fall for this trick? To be honest, I didn't see it coming either.

Joe left the apartment, leaving all his stuff piled up in the living room. I asked my mother straight up, "How are you gonna prove he doesn't live here?" She said, "You know what, every single rent receipt for this apartment is in my name only. This apartment is in my name. The electricity and gas are in my name. His name couldn't be on anything because of The Welfare." She then pulled out a little box containing every single rent receipt. I was like, "YES!" She had finally done something smart when it came to this man. Joe came back and got his stuff a few hours later. He chose not to call her bluff and finally moved out. Hallelujah!!

Joe moved into a studio apartment about a mile away on Rogers Avenue in Flatbush. My mother revealed to us that Joe had a new girlfriend too. Her name was Jane. I found this very suspicious. A month earlier, he lived with my mother, and now he's in another full-blown relationship? I was too young to know anything about relationships but, that seemed a bit fast to me, almost overlapping. To make matters worse, Joe was still trying to rekindle his relationship with my mother. He was telling her that he would leave Jane in a heartbeat if she would take him back. I was praying my mother wouldn't be dumb enough to go back down that road again. Joe had the nerve to dedicate a new R&B song to my mother called 'Used To Be My Girl' by The O'Jays. Quick! Somebody break out the violins!! I hate that song to this day because of him.

The summer of 1978 blew in. Chanele was three years old; I was turning twelve, and Larry was turning thirteen. I got promoted to the 7th grade, and Larry managed to escape to the 8th grade. Joe would still stop by the house to visit his daughter and speak to my mother. He had found work as a freelance messenger. Joe would use his van to pick up packages from one place and drop them off at another location in Manhattan. He approached me with a business proposition. "Kenny, do you wanna work with me? I'll pay you some money to do this messenger job with me." Damn. Now I had a dilemma. I didn't want to be around him at all. I also needed money to buy the things I wanted, like comic books, junk food, and a pair of sneakers. My mother was encouraging me to be mature and give the job a chance. Welfare was going to be our only source of income for the foreseeable future. Who knows if I would have a single dollar to spend for the entire summer. Things might be different now. He can't beat me anymore, and he doesn't live with us either. I agreed to accept the job.

The first day of work was super awkward because there were only two of us and a lot of small talk. Immediately there was a problem. Joe didn't know how to fill out the order slips detailing what address to bring the packages to. He also couldn't do the bookkeeping at the end of the day, either. I could do both of those things. We made a good team. I would help him lift boxes all day and do all the paperwork at the end of the shift. Our relationship changed, as well. One day, we were riding down the street, and Joe spots a girl. He says, "Look at her, doesn't she look good?" I didn't say anything. I didn't know what to say. Joe barked, "What? Don't you think she's pretty? Don't you like girls? What's wrong with you?" I liked girls; only I wasn't used to having a conversation like that with him. We weren't friends. I despised him. What is he saying?

On the second day of work, we stopped at a red light, and a few girls were standing on the sidewalk. Joe says, "Look at them, they're prostitutes." I'm like, "Wow!" I had never seen a prostitute before. That was pretty exciting for a twelve-year-old boy. Joe goes, "Watch this," and rolls down the window. A girl comes right up to the van…"Hey Daddy, Hey Daddy," and puts her hand in the car. It looked like she was feeling around for his wallet. Her aggressiveness did not faze Joe. I'm sitting there thinking, "Why is she feeling around for his wallet?" All of a sudden, Joe grabs her arm and says, "I'm THE POLICE!" Her whole face turned red, and she starts begging, "Oh my God! Please don't do this, please don't do this! Please don't arrest me!" Joe then says, "I'm not the police" and bursts out laughing. She starts cursing him out, "You fuckin' asshole!!" and she storms off. Joe was grinning from ear to ear as we pulled off.

Here I come with the questions...."How did you know she was a prostitute?" Joe says, "You can look at them and tell." Huh? I grew confused. She looked regular to me. I asked, "What do you mean, you can tell?" Joe said, "You can tell by looking at them, the way they dress. You didn't see her grab my dick?" I said "Nooo!! I thought she was reaching for your wallet." Joe said, What? No boy, she was trying to turn me on, what's wrong with you?" I had no clue. Joe then says, "You know Kenny, once, in a while, I may wanna pick up a prostitute and bring her in the back of the van. If I do, you need to go and take a walk for a while. I'll do the same for you if you get a girl." I'm like, WHAT?? First of all, I wasn't close to having sex with any girl at twelve years old. Second, a couple of weeks ago, Joe was begging my mother to take him back. Now he's here with me talking about prostitutes in the back of a van? How could he be that casual talking to me like this? I soon realized Joe had most likely been indulging in this whole prostitute thing all along. That also meant he'd been cheating on my mother the entire time. That's how my young mind saw it anyway. I could've been wrong, but I doubt it.

After working with Joe for one week, I was anticipating my pay. We never discussed the exact amount, but I knew how much money we made since I kept the books. Joe netted about $140 that week. I felt like I had done a large percentage of the work, almost equal to him. Our workload was at least 60/40. Joe handed me my pay; $8, and I was not happy at all. Now I know that it was HIS van, he was the driver and the adult, but I still didn't think it was fair. Without me doing the accounting, Joe would've had a tough time doing that job. Meanwhile, Larry was telling me every day how much summer fun he was having with the other kids on the block. He even discovered a special program called "Free Lunch." It served meals to children 13 and under in low-income areas. I began feeling like I was missing out on my summer vacation. Was it worth it for $8 a week? Plus, I didn't want to spend all my time around Joe anyway. I told my mother I didn't want to work with Joe anymore. I was too scared to tell him myself.

Joe arrived the following week to pick me up for work. My mother blurted out, "Guess what, Kenny doesn't wanna work with you anymore." Joe looked at me, thoroughly disappointed. He said, "Ah, man, you're not a real man. You're supposed to be my favorite." Yeah, whatever. What does he know about being a real man? I made the right decision. I should have never taken that job in the first place. Nothing positive would've resulted from being around a loser like that anyway. I spent my one-week salary on a new pair of Pro-Keds sneakers. After that, Joe was out of our lives, for now.

What an eventful fifteen months it had been for me. My brother ran away from home at age eleven. Joe fired live rounds from a gun into my room on two occasions, and I experienced The New York City Blackout of 1977. I got extorted by a fellow student and assaulted by another. I bought marijuana on several occasions. I went inside an illegal weed distribution operation. Joe beat me with an extension cord at least 200 times (conservatively). My brother got beaten to the point of hospitalization. I also saw him rise up and challenge our tormentor. I saw a real prostitute first hand. I was a Rastafarian for a while. Most of all, I finally saw the demise of Joe and his four-year reign of terror. For most adolescents, that would be enough to warrant some serious counseling. For us, the drama was only getting started.

CHAPTER 4
THIS IS NOT A TEST

The summer of 1978 was fantastic! Joe's long overdue dismissal removed the dark cloud that hung over our heads, like a never-ending four-year storm. I was able to rejoin Larry and the other kids on the block. We would raid all the free lunch spots in the area. Larry and I would begin with the hot lunch at P.S. 181. Then, we would race to one of two other places to get the cold lunch as well. We even found a free dinner spot for kids that served dinner around 6 pm. It reached a point where we had too many miniature cartons of milk in our refrigerator. They would start to spoil because we couldn't drink them fast enough. My mother seemed happy; it meant less money she would have to spend on us. During that summer, a new kid named Marlon moved around the corner from us on Linden Boulevard. Everyone liked him right away. Marlon also brought something new and unique to our block, his cassette tapes. But, his music was a little different. By 1978, Disco music, which originated in New York City, had exploded. Disco was not only prominent in our neighborhood but globally. R&B music was still popular, but the style changed. The Motown sound was gone. What replaced it was an up-tempo, less soulful, dance-orientated form of music called Disco. Names like Donna Summer, The Bee Gees and KC & The Sunshine Band took over the charts. For the first time, White artists made songs that played in my neighborhood.

Marlon's cassette tapes were different. His tapes were not of high audio quality. I recognized the backing music. They called this form of aggressive drum and bass line R&B music "Funk." The groove made your head nod upon hearing it. However, the artists on Marlon's tapes weren't singing over this music. They did something different. They dubbed it "Rap." These guys were talking and rhyming over the Funk music while staying in rhythm with the beat. The tape Marlon played sounded like it originated from a live recording. The way most Rap tapes originated during this time was simple. Someone went to where rappers were performing live. They would cut on their portable radio and record the show onto a cassette. Sometimes, the party would be indoors. There would be so many people in attendance that some guys were unable to get inside the party. They would hold their radios up to the window of the building and try to record the events inside.

This crude technique made the tapes very difficult to hear. The quality of the recordings wouldn't be that great. To make matters worse, Marlon would only play a little of his Rap tape and then cut it off. He would only tease you with a small taste for some reason. He definitely wouldn't let anyone borrow his tapes either. Both Larry and I loved this new Rap music...what little of it we could hear anyway.

As it turned out, Rap music had grown in popularity up in The Bronx. Rap had evolved since DJ Kool Herc created it on that very same block in which we shared in 1973. Guys like Grandmaster Flash and Afrika Bambaataa added their unique innovations. In 1978, Rap music found us again after five years. Unfortunately, if you didn't live in The Bronx, Rap music was hard to get. It was still only available on dirty cassette tapes. It took a while for Rap music to make its way to the other boroughs, but now it finally arrived on our little block. Still, in Brooklyn, even Reggae music was more popular than Rap due to the influx of West Indian people. Rap wasn't an official music genre yet. Marlon's stay around the corner was short-lived. He moved away before the summer ended. Our Rap connection disappeared, for now.

Being a member of a family whose sole income was being provided by the government was very difficult. Welfare offered enough money for the essentials, nothing more. There was little money available for new clothing.

Any form of entertainment was definitely out of the question. Neither Larry nor myself had been to a movie in three years! Free lunch, started as our pleasant little juvenile discovery. Soon, it became an absolute necessity. Many families in our area relied on government assistance. Still, no one chose to volunteer that embarrassing information. The only way a family could get exposed was through Food Stamps. Every month, the welfare office sent two envelopes via mail. One contained a check to pay your rent and utilities, and another included Food Stamps. These stamps or coupons were the same sizes as standard money. They came in different colors and denominations. One note featured a former president's picture on the front. Most grocery stores in our area accepted food stamps. When my mother would send me to the store, I didn't want anyone to see me spending this "poor peoples" money. I would walk to a store further away from our apartment, so no one on the block would catch me.

The worst thing about using Food Stamps was none of the local stores would give you real coins back as change. There was no such thing as "Welfare Coins." The store clerk would rip off a brown paper bag and write an IOU in pen for the amount of change they owed you. After a while, we would accumulate several strips of paper from three or four different bodegas. We wouldn't know which strip was for which store. I would have to go into a store and show the clerk my collection of IOU strips. We would attempt to figure out which one belonged to that particular store. Sometimes, they couldn't figure it out themselves. What a mess!

To make matters worse, someone in our building began breaking into the mailboxes. They would steal people's mail. This act was common in tenements. If they took our welfare check, it would have disastrous consequences for the family. To combat this, I sat in the hallway like a cop on a stakeout. I would intercept the mailman and take the check right out of his hand. It was the only way to be sure.

On the first day of school, we didn't receive any new school clothes, not a single thing. Shopping for new clothes was a back-to-school tradition in every household except ours. You wanted to look sharp on the first day of school, at least. Not us. Almost every kid enrolled in my 7th-grade class was also a former 6th-grade classmate. They immediately noticed I was wearing the same clothes I wore the last time they saw me in June. Of course, the jokes commenced. I was wearing the same pair of sneakers I bought in early

July with my messenger salary. They already looked worn down by the first day of school in September. Since I grew over the summer, I only owned one outfit that fit correctly. I had no choice but to wear the same clothes to school every day. What difference did it make? Poverty became the norm. Larry was experiencing the same clothing drought as I was. It seemed like we were the two most impoverished kids within a five-mile radius. Oh, and by the way, we still hadn't received a haircut since 1972. That was six years ago.

Meanwhile, the dreaded Eugene was still outside doing what he did best, robbing kids in front of the school. Around this time, Adidas and Puma sneakers had become quite popular. They were around for years but not in the hood. Everyone wore Pro-Keds or Converse All-Stars, made of canvas material. However, Pumas were suede, and Adidas was leather with a rubber shell toe. Adidas and Puma sneakers retailed at $40 each compared to Pro-Ked's at $8 each. Because of their luxurious status, these sneakers became a target for criminals. They would take them right off your feet.

Kenny at Prospect Park, 1979

Eugene always wore a fresh pair of Adidas, and you knew he didn't pay for them. Eugene would stand in the hallway of our school during recess. He would stick his foot out further than necessary, trying to bait someone into stepping on his foot. That gave him an excuse to beat them up. Stepping on somebody's new sneakers was very disrespectful in my neighborhood. Stepping on Adidas or Puma's was dangerous. If someone had given me a free pair of Adidas, I wouldn't have worn them anyway; it wasn't worth the hassle.

That wasn't a problem I needed to worry about. My mother might have bought us two pairs of sneakers per year. That's two pairs of sneakers to play in and wear to school in twelve months. The problem with Pro-Keds was, the soles of the shoe would wear down fast. An actual hole would appear at the bottom of the shoe. No matter how careful you were, under normal wear, a kid would need a new pair after two or three months. We had to wear our sneakers for about six months at a time. I can recall having a hole in my sneakers for the majority of my junior high school years. Sometimes, the hole would get so big, almost half of the sole would be gone! Kids would see our sneakers and tease us to no end. Having a hole in our sneakers during the winter months was particularly brutal. Our feet would be freezing most of the time. When there was snow on the ground, it would be tough. Sleet? Forget about it.

Still, Larry and I persevered. Our fanaticism with Marvel would cause us to walk 2.3 miles in the snow to our favorite comic book store. Our feet would be so cold that they would be completely numb by the time we arrived. We would have to stay inside the store for an extended period to allow our feet to thaw out. Sometimes we would only have 25 cents each, enough to buy one comic book. After our feet melted, we would turn around and walk another 2.3 miles back home. Most of the time, our socks would have holes in them as well from scrapping the sidewalk while we walked. Sometimes, you might step on a little piece of glass on the street, and it would make your foot bleed. We began cutting up pieces of cardboard and putting them in the bottom of our sneaker to create a makeshift sole. My mother wouldn't buy us a new pair of sneakers until our current sneakers reached the cardboard stage. People could hear us walking down the street because the cardboard would make a dragging sound. It was so embarrassing.

Sometimes, my mother might not give us enough money to buy the Pro-Keds we wanted. Instead, she might give you $5 and order you to "Go to the bin and find something in your size." The bin was a big barrel in the shoe store with casual sneakers thrown in there. Some of the sneakers would be irregular or defective. Others were two-year-old sneakers they couldn't sell for the full price anymore. They also sold generic no-name sneakers. In the hood, they called these sneakers "Skips." Wearing Skips when everyone else wore Pro-Keds sucked! None of this adversity stopped us from going outside and playing with our friends. We got accustomed to being the laughing stock of the neighborhood.

Around my way, what we called "Hard Rocks" committed the majority of robberies and muggings. A Hard Rock was a tough guy with a violent reputation, usually associated with a group or gang. Of course, neither myself nor any of my friends were Hard Rocks. Eugene was a Hard Rock. I would estimate that 90% of the guys I encountered daily were not Hard Rocks. Of course, you had your wannabe thugs who were all talk. Sometimes, you couldn't differentiate between the common loudmouth and a very dangerous individual. Any miscalculation could cost you dearly.

The vast majority of the people in our area originated from low-income households. Lack of funds created a feeling of desperation. It also gave specific individuals a penchant for lawlessness. This combination created an atmosphere where anyone could get mugged for almost anything. I can recall earmuffs becoming popular. Yeah, the fluffy ones. Before the emergence of earmuffs, knit skully hats were popular during the winter season. Some clown might try to snatch your hat and run. However, wearing earmuffs increased your likelihood of being robbed considerably. This criminal behavior sounds petty by today's standards, but not in 1970s NYC. A mugger would say, "Yo! Run them earmuffs!" You now had the option of giving them up or choosing to get your head knocked off. Some robbers would seem rather "polite." They would walk up to you, look at your feet, and say, "Hey man! What size are those sneakers? They are BAD!" Some poor unsuspecting guy would say, "Oh, they're a size nine." The Hard Rock would say, "Oh... That's my size! Take them shits off!" Sometimes a crook would walk up to you and say, "Yo, you got some money?" If you responded with "No," they would say, "All I find I keep?" Only in the hood would you hear a ridiculous question like that. I've come across that particular line several times.

Months of wearing the same run-down clothes to school every day began to take a toll on my psyche. Despite having a good relationship with most of my classmates, I felt like I was on an island all by myself on many days. My self-esteem was at its absolute lowest. One day, during class, a male classmate came up with what he thought was a brilliant idea to pass the time. He decided to collaborate with a couple of other guys and rank all the girls from the "prettiest to ugliest." The goal was to write down every girl's name in order of attractiveness. There were thirty total students in my class, fifteen boys and fifteen girls. After completing the survey, the guys debated the accuracy of the list.

Of course, the girls got wind of this prank and countered with, "Ok, we're gonna rate the boys too." Oh no! That was the last thing I wanted to hear. I was 100% sure I would finish last on that survey, number fifteen. It was going to be humiliating seeing my name at the bottom of the list. Why did I have to get dissed? I didn't have anything to do with the first list. Some of these girls were my friends, but now they would have no choice but to degrade me. Every girl in the class participated in this revenge survey too.

They were mad. As they huddled together, working on the list, my anxiety level was peaking. At long last, they released the survey. I ranked number eleven. I was so happy! From my perspective, this result was fantastic news. I couldn't believe four guys in my class ranked lower than I did. How was that possible? I was the worst-looking kid in the entire world. No one in human history could've been happier to finish number eleven in a fifteen-person race than I was. I wanted to go around the room and thank the voters like a politician.

Now that Joe was gone, more of my mother's personality began to show. She took the bold move of furthering her education. She enrolled in night school at The Borough Of Manhattan Community College (BMCC). Her decision to attend college increased my already taxing workload. We had to clean the bathroom, the kitchen, the living room, our bedroom, take out the garbage, do laundry, go grocery shopping, and take care of Chanele. My mother demanded perfection and inspected our chores daily. If any of our duties didn't meet her satisfaction, she would become enraged and break into screaming fits. Despite the added workload, our grades had to be maintained. I felt overwhelmed most of the time. We received a small piece of good news that eased my pain for a brief moment. My mother announced she was giving us a Christmas gift. This offering would be the first time we were receiving a present in six years! She handed both of us envelopes containing $5 each. Nice!

During my life, I've learned some great lessons. One is, sometimes, small events or suggestions seem trivial at first but end up having an enormous impact on your life. Case in point, my mother announced, "I'm taking you guys to get library cards. There's a big library not far from here. There's no excuse not to take advantage." The Central Library was near Grand Army Plaza in the Park Slope section of Brooklyn. It is one of the largest libraries in the country, with over one million books. It was also right across the street from Prospect Park, so we were familiar with the location. To our surprise, we loved it. We would walk to the library often and spend hours there reading free books. It was like Brooklyn's version of Google. I was in official "Nerd Heaven." While there, Larry began to take an interest in the complex study of Metaphysics. Was this the same learning impaired Larry now reading Philosophy books? Go figure. I knew it was odd for twelve and thirteen-year-olds from our neighborhood to hang out in the library. I didn't care. Robbing from people who are less fortunate than yourself was strange too. Yet, plenty of people in my area did it with no problem, but I digress.

Anyway, all the goodwill and higher learning came to a crashing halt at the end of the school year. Larry came home with his report card and a shocker. He got left back!! The NY Board Of Education required Larry to repeat the 8th grade. This news marked a new academic low, even for him. For a public school to hold back a student in the 8th grade was uncommon. They had to determine that the student didn't meet the minimum requirements by a long shot.

I had no idea Larry was performing that poorly in school. He was a complete enigma. Even more surprising was my mother's reaction. She didn't seem upset. No yelling, no punishment, nothing. What was there to say by this point anyway? Everyone was treating Larry like a learning impaired student. Once again, I begged to differ, but there was an undeniable problem here. Not only was his academic performance abysmal, but Larry was still bedwetting at age thirteen. That is a sure sign of some sort of trauma gone untreated. In the end, nothing happened. We accepted it and moved on as a family.

The summer of 1979 was upon us. Larry and I planned on having a continuation of the previous summer's fun and games with the same kids who lived on the block last year. It was going to be a virtual block party every day. This time, the party had an added twist when a new kid named Nookie (New-Key) moved around the corner. This wannabe Hard Rock was approximately our age but burly in size. He might have suffered from a personality disorder. Sometimes he would be calm and then without warning, would flip and start bullying kids on the block. We hated to see him come around the corner.

One day Nookie came on the block agitated and looking for trouble. He was acting very aggressive, challenging everyone present to a "Slap Boxing" contest. Slap boxing was like conventional boxing. Instead of throwing punches, you kept your hands open and tried to slap your opponent. I hated slap boxing! This "fun" competition would ALWAYS turn into an unnecessary fight. Who needed that? No one volunteered to slap box with Nookie, so he decided to pick an opponent anyway. That unfortunate person happened to be Larry. Ah man, this was not going to end well. Nookie immediately began swinging at Larry, who had no choice but to defend himself. As expected, the impromptu slap boxing match became real in no time.

All of the kids on the block gathered around. They were anticipating Larry's defeat at the hands of the more experienced Nookie. I was standing right there watching. I also foresaw Nookie beating up my brother. Larry didn't share my nervousness. In fact, to my surprise, he didn't back down either. After a quick exchange, Nookie came in close to yoke Larry by the neck. Right when Nookie grabbed Larry's neck to choke him, Larry picked Nookie up off of the ground with ease. He then body slammed Nookie right there in the middle of the street!! Boom! Larry jumped on top of Nookie about to punch him when Nookie started yelling, "Get off me. Get off me!!" WHAT?? We couldn't believe our ears. Everyone in The Hood knows that once you yell, "Get off me" in a fight, you were admitting defeat. No Mas? It was over for you after that.

Larry climbed off of Nookie, who got up and walked home embarrassed. The whole ordeal took less than a minute. Everyone gathered around Larry now, congratulating him like a conquering hero. I was proud of him too. He pulled off a colossal upset on our block. In reality, Larry was equal in physical size and strength to Nookie. It was Nookie's demeanor and stature on the block that made him appear way bigger. Larry was mild-mannered, but when he decided to stand up to Nookie, he defeated him in no time. Nookie asked for it too, which made his defeat even sweeter. Nookie lost all his juice after that. He was a regular guy now.

A few days later, fresh off of his stunning defeat, a much friendlier Nookie came around the corner. He carried a small radio. Nookie walked right up to Larry and me and said, "Yo, check out this tape I made." Did we have a choice? He pressed play, and a familiar tune came through his little speakers. It was 'Don't Stop 'Til You Get Enough' by megastar Michael Jackson. This song couldn't be what Nookie interrupted us for, could it? All of a sudden, Nookie's voice appeared on the tape. He overdubbed his voice on top of Michael Jackson's instrumental intro. What is this? It was a tape of Nookie rapping.

The streets of Brooklyn were now all a buzz about this new Rap music. But, an actual Rap tape was still hard to get your hands on. Nookie's homemade dub tape was the closest we came to one of these tapes since Marlon moved away. 'Don't Stop' has a long instrumental intro before

Michael Jackson begins to sing. Nookie rapped during the intro part, but what baffled Larry and me was Nookie kept rapping as MJ's vocals began to play. He rapped right over the singing. Did he think no one would notice Michael Jackson's overpowering voice? It was both weird and cool at the same time. Although Nookie's tape was a mess, he became the first person we knew who rapped.

The fall of '79 arrived, and so did my final year of grammar school. I was entering the 8th grade, as was Larry. Some things changed, but most remained the same. There was no money for new school clothes once again. Instead, my mother sent us on an excursion to The Salvation Army Thrift Store. We scrounged around to see if we could find some clothing in our size. I indeed found some pants that were actually in style, three years ago. I still hadn't received a haircut, seven years and counting. Eugene and his crew were still outside, terrorizing students on the very first day. My music instructor selected me as an official member of the school band. I had been taking trombone lessons in band class for three years. I was mediocre at best but still good enough to be in the group. We traveled to different schools and performed contemporary songs for the students. I skipped out on a few band dates because I didn't own proper shoes or a dress shirt. The band instructor didn't know the reason for my absences and threatened to remove me from the band.

A month after school resumed, my mother returned home from a long day in the city with some fantastic news. She found a job as an administrative assistant in Manhattan. Hallelujah! No more Welfare. No more "Face to Face" and no more food stamps! Our family had been on welfare at different times for almost five years. Three of those years were consecutive. In the 1970s, most families who relied on aid for that long a period rarely left the system. Welfare dependency would become your inheritance, like a family heirloom. Someone should have commended my mother for her perseverance. She broke the cycle before it started.

Despite her new job, my mother continued to pursue her college degree at night. We were home alone for large portions of the evening by ourselves. One evening during the early fall, we were alone in the apartment waiting for our mother to return. We finished all of our chores and were listening to an indie AM station called WNJR. At about 9:30 pm, they premiered a new song. It began as a random instrumental. After a few bars, the song switched into the familiar music of the smash R&B anthem 'Good Times' by the Disco group Chic. All of a sudden, something different and unexpected happened. Right when the singing should have begun, a guy started rapping instead. Wait! What is this?

Larry and I had heard rapping before, but never this crystal clear and never on the radio. My heart was pounding. The rapper said, "This is not a test." It felt like he was talking directly to us. The new song continued for fifteen minutes straight. Three different rappers took turns rapping and telling funny stories. When the song ended, Larry and I were staring at the radio in total shock. We knew at that exact moment that we had just heard music history. You could sense that a new genre of music had arrived. Every other music genre became secondary to Rap in my eyes. I HAD to hear more.

The next day, I told some of my classmates my experience. I said, "I heard a song with some guys rapping over 'Good Times' on the radio last night." They rolled their eyes and said, "No, you didn't. You're lying!!" I pleaded with them, but I couldn't convince anyone of what I'd heard. The next night, Larry and I clung to the stereo in the living room, listening to WNJR. Sure enough, at the same time, the song comes on. We turned the volume up super loud and rocked out for the entire fifteen minutes of the song. This time, the radio DJ gave the name of the song. It was 'Rapper's Delight' by The Sugarhill Gang. When my mother came home from school, we begged her to buy us this song. She must've seen the overwhelming excitement in our eyes because she vowed to find the record for us. The next night, she came home with the 12" single of 'Rapper's Delight.' Wow!! She found it in one day. We were the first people on our block to have this record.

The next day, we listened to the song from when we arrived home at 3:30 pm until my mother arrived at 6:30 pm. That became our daily routine, come home from school, and listen to 'Rapper's Delight' for hours. We became so obsessed with this song that one day the man who lived downstairs knocked on the door. We opened the door, and he said, "The music!" I said, "I'm sorry; we'll turn it down." He said, "No, I don't care about the volume, play something else besides that same song!" Ha!

About two weeks later, a new R&B FM station called WKTU announced that they were premiering 'Rapper's Delight.' They were claiming to be the first in the country to play it. I was like, "Hell, no! WNJR played this song weeks ago." Regardless, when WKTU played 'Rapper's Delight,' the song exploded like a nuclear bomb. It became the talk of the town. Soon the other radio stations followed. The record stores couldn't keep the vinyl on the shelf. 'Rapper's Delight' took off worldwide. It sold six million copies, making it the biggest-selling 12" single of all time. Rap music had arrived in 1979.

Larry and I were listening to 'Rapper's Delight' one day after school. I mentioned how I couldn't wait to hear another new Rap song. Larry replied, "You know what, I wanna make a Rap song. I want to be a rapper." WHAT?? I asked him if he was serious, "What the hell are you talking about?" is what I said. Larry told me that he felt like he could do it. I had never seen him so adamant about anything before in his entire life. Outside of comic books, Larry never seemed to care about anything else. His entire existence had been very carefree. Now, out of the blue, he believed that he could be a rapper? I was looking at him in utter disbelief, but I could tell this was different. It was like he'd been going through the motions of life waiting for a sign, some sort of inspiration to appear. He seemed to find it when he heard Rap Music on the radio.

Who knows how long Larry was contemplating this? Rap Music had been on our radar for over a year now. I always knew he liked Rap, but this time something was different. I could see it in his eyes. Larry didn't mention his newfound inspiration to anyone but me. To say I was skeptical would be putting it mildly. Saying I thought he was out of his mind would be a more accurate description. By this time, other rappers were emerging in The Bronx that we hadn't heard of yet. Still, there were only a small group of guys thought of as professional-level rappers at the time. None of them had recorded a record yet. For someone to choose "Rapper" as their future occupation was a farfetched idea. To be fourteen years old made it even crazier. To be living in Brooklyn and not The Bronx made it harder. To be living under the conditions we lived in made it even more ludicrous. I could go on and on. If Larry would've said he wanted to be an astronaut, that would have made more sense. In fact, there were more astronauts than rappers in 1979. I thought he was nuts. Larry got left back in the 8th grade; he needed to focus on his schoolwork, not some pipe dream.

Right around the same time as Larry had his epiphany, I saw an advertisement on the school gymnasium door. The flyer announced tryouts for a new school basketball team, the first in 25 years. I had never been on a basketball team before. I decided to make the bold decision to try out for the team. As I should've guessed, so did every other boy in my school. At this point, I was a decent basketball player at best. I wasn't even the best player in my class. I didn't know all the rules of basketball. I had only played half-court pick-up basketball with my friends. On the day of the tryout, overcrowding in the gym resulted in each player only having a short time to display their talents. I played ok in my brief stint on the court. But, what I did discover was, I had one advantage over everyone else trying out. I was now the tallest kid in my entire school. I was thirteen years old, and I stood a shade under six feet tall.

At the end of the tryouts, they posted the boys' names who made the team on the gymnasium door. I read the list with nervous anticipation. Wait... that looks like my name. Yes! I made the team! I was beyond happy. Trying out for the Walt Whitman Junior High School team was the first thing I'd ever attempted to do. I felt like I had accomplished something extraordinary. My classmates disagreed. The backlash was immediate and vicious. They bombarded me with, "How did you make the team over me?" "I'm better than you"... "You ain't all that." The best one was, "You only made the team because you're tall."

In reality, that last assessment was accurate. There's an old basketball saying that goes, "You can't teach height." All things being equal, you'd chose an inferior tall player over a shorter superior player. If you teach him how to play the game, it'll pay off in the end. Our coach was trying to build a basketball team. He needed to have some tall players on the squad, so he had to pick me. Making the final cut was the first time in my life being tall worked to my advantage. All the guys who laughed at me for being too tall were now jealous. My attitude was, I didn't care how or why I made the team, I was part of something special in my school. I chose not to focus on jealousy.

Basketball practice began, and all the guys who made the team were pretty good. One of them was light years ahead of everyone else. His name was "John-John." He could shoot, drive the ball, pass, play defense; he excelled at every aspect of the game. Everyone on the team practiced in a regular t-shirt, but John was different. He practiced in t-shirts from various basketball tournaments in which he played. He wore a different team shirt every time we practiced. One shirt I remembered, in particular, was from a league called 'City-Wide.' It was the best tournament in New York City. They held it in every borough during the summer months. In the end, they would crown an NYC City-Wide champion. Different teams wore different colored t-shirts. John would come to practice with a different colored City-Wide t-shirt every time. How many years has he played in this tournament already? He was only thirteen years old. I desperately wanted one of those City-Wide t-shirts. The coach gave us a playbook with a few routine plays that I found challenging. I didn't know all the rules of basketball, much less how to run a play. I struggled. After a few short weeks, it was time for our first exhibition game versus the teachers. They had some talent. One of the teachers previously played college basketball.

The packed gymnasium overflowed with students for the first exhibition game. Of course, I didn't start the game. I waited on the bench for my chance to play. The entire first half went by, and I didn't get in at all. Midway through the third quarter, the coach finally called my name. I was so nervous. I had never played full-court basketball with a referee before. On my first trip down the court, I didn't follow the play call. I ran and stood under the basket. The referee blew the whistle, a three-second violation on me, a turnover. What is a three-second violation? I had no idea. I ran down the court on defense. After the teachers scored a bucket, my teammate threw me the ball on the inbound pass. I turned around and shuffled my feet. The referee blew the whistle, traveling. In only 30 seconds, I had two turnovers.

The next thing I knew, the coach subbed me out of the game. I could hear some of the students heckling me, saying I was terrible, as I walked off the court. At first, I dared to be mad at the coach for subbing out of the game. Then, I felt relieved because I was so nervous. After a while, I regained my composure and had the nerve to ask the coach when he was going to put me back in. He told me, "I'm gonna put you back in during the 5th quarter." I said ok and waited for the end of the 4th quarter. After the 4th quarter buzzer sounded, everyone began shaking hands with each other. What? Is the game over already? I turned to a teammate and said, "Coach told me I was playing in the 5th quarter." He looked at me and said, "You stupid!! There is no 5th quarter!"

Damn, the coach lied to me. The whole experience did not turn out how I envisioned it. We lost the game to the teachers despite 31 points from John. I decided I was quitting the team. I came home, sad, and dejected. But, after analyzing the situation, I realized giving up was not the best solution. I decided to give it one more try and see how it goes. There were another two weeks of practice before our first real game. Meanwhile, Lefferts asked

Larry to join his school basketball team as a late addition. He was very tall as well. Once again, "You can't teach height."

After two weeks, it was time for our first official game. Our Walt Whitman Junior High School basketball uniforms arrived right before tip-off. We looked legit. Once again, our gym had a packed crowd, along with our very own cheerleader squad, who decided to make up nicknames for all the players. Damn, what are they going to say when my turn comes around? They were cheering for every player as we made a lay-up during warm-ups. When my turn came, I heard "Gooo Spaghetti Go!" What? I guess my legs looked so skinny in my shorts that they felt I resembled spaghetti. Ha! It could've been worse. This time around, I understood the plays better and felt more prepared to play. Somewhere during the 2nd quarter of the game, the coach subbed me in.

About two minutes had elapsed, and everything was going well. I received a pass about fifteen feet from the basket, and I was wide open. I took my first official shot, and I made it! Swish!! I was ecstatic. Everyone was cheering. I was so happy that I ran down the court, clapping like the fans on the sidelines. It was hilarious. During halftime, the coach said, "Kenny, you're starting the second half." Wow! I was getting real playing time in a real game.

As soon as the second half began, on the first play of the third quarter, I somehow got my hands on the basketball. Once again, I was wide open. I was feeling confident now. As I turned to take my shot, I could hear the coach yelling, "Nooo!!!" Why is he yelling NO to me? I was wide open. Unbeknownst to me, at the start of the second half, the two teams switched baskets. The basket I was shooting at during the first half, was no longer my basket. That's why I was so wide open. I still didn't know the rules of basketball very well. This match was only my second organized basketball game. Regardless, I shot the ball with confidence, at the wrong basket! Luckily, I missed it. Everyone started laughing and screaming. I was so embarrassed. All the jealous guys who didn't make the team were on the sidelines, pointing at me and yelling. They were happy to see me fail. The coach didn't take me out, though. I played most of the second half and even hit another jump shot. We won the game, and I scored 4 points. It was the best and worst day of my young basketball life all at once.

Lost in the hilariousness of my ill-advised shot attempt was the improvement I made over the two weeks. I started out waiting for the 5th quarter to get into an exhibition game. Now I was receiving significant playing time in a real game, and I scored 4 points. We played the game on a Friday afternoon. By the time I arrived for classes on Monday morning, I was the talk of the entire school. Everyone was saying, "Yo, he shot at the wrong basket." Everyone was laughing. When I arrived at my homeroom class, my teacher said, "Hey, I heard you shot at the wrong basket." I became "The guy who shot at the wrong basket." Even so, right before the next game, the coach inserted me into the starting lineup. I was now the starting center on my junior high school basketball team. I was an official ballplayer now. At that moment, I no longer cared about anything else, not even comic books. I found a new love, basketball.

One day, I decided to attend one of Larry's basketball games at Lefferts. He didn't start the game, but the coach put him in pretty early. He played for a few minutes and then got replaced. Larry wasn't happy about his substitution. During a time out, Larry sat at the very end of the bench all by himself. The rest of the team was in the huddle listening to the coach. He appeared uninterested. This exchange was the first time I'd seen Larry interacting with people his age that I didn't know as well. I was able to observe Larry's body language from a distance. He was there physically, but mentally, not a part of the team. He was in another world. I recognized the look on his face too, and I knew he wouldn't be on that team much longer. I was right.

Approximately a year earlier, I had met and befriended a classmate of mine named Neville. He only lived one block away from me on East 34th Street. Neville was an only child. His mother worked as a nurse and spoiled him with gifts. He owned all the latest clothes, several pairs of sneakers, a television, and a portable radio with a cassette deck in his bedroom. Neville had all the cool board games and an Atari game system connected to the television in his bedroom. Neville's mother bought him everything a kid could want. After a year of hanging out, Neville became my closest friend.

One day, Neville approached me with a business proposition. He had started a newspaper route delivering for The New York Daily News. Neville wanted to expand and asked me to work for him. He was already earning about $20 per week. That was an enormous amount of money to me. I didn't have $20 to spend for the entire year of 1979. Neville calculated that with my help, he could double the size of his paper route. He offered me $10 per week to work for him. I accepted the offer. We split the work 50/50, but

Neville made $30 per week, and I only made $10. I didn't care because it was his route. He was responsible for bringing the money to the Daily News distribution office. $10 per week was fine with me. My mother declared; since I was now working, I would have to give her $4 per week out of my salary. The remaining $6 would be mine to spend as I pleased. In no time, my family and Neville's family became good friends. Larry and Neville hung out together sometimes without me.

January arrived, and Walt Whitman released the mid-semester grades. I made the Honor Roll. Still, my mother was growing more frustrated with Larry and me as the days progressed. Her emotional outbursts were becoming more intense. Nothing we did seemed to please her. Any mistake would result in long screaming fits, which caused me anxiety. Larry didn't seem fazed by her at all. Even when I made the honor roll, it wasn't good enough. What could I have been doing that was so unacceptable? I was a thirteen-year-old kid living in crime-ridden Brooklyn who never broke the law. I delivered newspapers in the morning and was a top student. My school selected me for both the band and the basketball team. All my chores got completed daily, and I never spoke back to her, not once. Most parents in America would've signed up for that. My mother acted like she couldn't have had a worse child. I couldn't understand it.

Meanwhile, my junior high school basketball season was progressing nicely. One day, after practice, I was having a friendly conversation with my basketball coach. He mentioned that he also taught at another junior high school. I asked him where did he teach? He said Lefferts Junior High School. What a small world! I told him my brother attended Lefferts. He asked, "Who's your brother?" I said, "Lawrence Parker." The coach said, "THAT'S YOUR BROTHER??" I said, "Yeah." He began to interrogate me. He asked, "Are you guys, blood-related?" I said, "Yes." He then asked, "Do you have the same mother and father?" I said, "Yes!" I became confused. He said, "I can see the resemblance now, but do you two live in the same household?" I answered him with a resounding "YES!!" Coach shook his head and walked away. I didn't understand what that whole exchange was all about until I thought about it later on. This man happened to be in a unique position. He knew both of our personalities and behaviors pretty well. Given that information, he found it hard to believe Larry and I could have any relation. What kind of hell was Larry raising in Lefferts Junior High School?

The Walt Whitman Junior High School basketball season concluded in March. I ended up starting every game and averaging about 4 points per game. My appetite for basketball was now insatiable. Up until that point, I had never watched a basketball game on television before. I started watching every game possible (when Larry wasn't hogging the tv), including NCAA college basketball.

One day, out of the blue, my mother returns home from work and says, "You boys come here and sit down. I have something I want to tell you." We sat down on the couch, awaiting her announcement. She said, "Guess what? I ran into your real father Sheffield on the street today, right here in Brooklyn." What? Well, that was a surprise. It had been over thirteen years since she last heard a peep from him. She told us that they had a brief conversation, and she asked him flat out what happened? How did he get back into the country? Why didn't he ever try to locate his children? Sheffield told her that he was able to return to America with the help of another woman. However, the woman gave him a warning. She said, if Sheffield ever tried to contact my mother or his two children, she would have him deported back to Barbados. My mother then told us that they exchanged numbers and asked us if we wanted to meet him. In unison, we both said, "NO!"

It wasn't the fact that his "explanation" sounded utterly bogus and raised more questions than it answered. I didn't care what his story was. In my mind, the definition of a father was a man who had the authority to beat me. Even though I was thirteen years old now, I couldn't go through that experience again. I had almost zero curiosity about this man. I didn't know what Larry's reasoning was, but it was a no-brainer. She asked us one more time, "Are you sure?" We said, "Yeah, we're sure." She never mentioned him again. Larry and I didn't talk about it afterward. It was a non-issue.

During the early spring of 1980, my mother called a family meeting. She informed us that her co-worker had a litter of kittens, and she was thinking about adopting one of the cats. Huh? A cat? Why? She declared that there would be a vote on whether she should accept the cat or not. The election would be between her, Larry, and myself. Before we cast our votes, she gave us a warning. If we decided to get a cat, caring for the cat would fall upon Larry and me. What? Another added chore? I felt it was an easy decision. I immediately voted no! Larry voted yes (What the Hell?) as did my mother. They outvoted me. A couple of days later, my mother came home with a small black and white male cat named Pepper. I had no choice but to get accustomed to having a cat running around the apartment now. Oh well, I guess we won't have any mice.

The cold NYC weather finally broke, and we were able to hang outside once more. One day, Larry and I strolled together down Church Avenue and walked past a new record shop near Bedford Avenue. They had set-up speakers outside and were blasting music. It was customary for record stores to advertise new music this way. On this particular day, they were playing a new Rap song. Once again, the backing music was familiar. It was an interpolation of the hit R&B song "Bounce, Rock, Roll, Skate" by (R.I.P.) Vaughan Mason. The rapping style of this song was unique. The rapper was telling funny stories while using different voices and personas. It was incredible! The song's name was 'The Adventures Of Super Rhymes' by (R.I.P.) Jimmy Spicer. The record store kept playing the song over and over again. We stood there, mesmerized. Larry became more energized after hearing 'Super Rhymes.' He now began acting like he WAS a rapper. He was writing rhymes and calling himself "Larry Gee." Of course, I had to challenge this, "Why do you call yourself Larry Gee when there's no G in your name? Shouldn't you be Larry Pee?" He said, "No, I like 'Larry Gee' better." I couldn't understand him at all. My brother had lost it!

April arrived, and the days were moving along without incident. Until one day, I came home from school to find the apartment door unlocked. I was usually the last to leave in the morning and the first one home in the afternoon. I always locked the door whenever I left for school. Once inside, I discovered the apartment ransacked. Someone burglarized our home! The crooks searched every room, with my mother's bedroom being in the worst shape. They dumped all her dresser drawers onto her bed. Our stereo was gone. I called my mother at work, and she rushed right home. She was agitated. When we called the police, all they did was make a report and left. It didn't seem like there was any forced entry. "Did you lock the door when you left for school today?" She asked. "Yes," I said. "ARE YOU SURE?" she asked. "Yes, I'm sure," I said. We went door-to-door asking if anyone saw or heard anything. Of course, no one saw a thing. We felt like it had to be a tenant in the building, someone who would say hello to us every day. My mother no longer felt safe living there. She decided it was time to move. The hunt for a new apartment began.

After a quiet beginning to spring, things were beginning to happen one after another. One day, I was walking home from school with Neville when a lady approached us with a frantic look. She claimed she locked herself out of her apartment. She needed someone to climb up the fire escape, open the window, and enter her apartment. Once inside, they can open the front door and let her in. Our initial response was no. She then offered one dollar to whichever one of us would help her out. Now she was speaking our language. We assessed the situation and realized the ladder wouldn't be easy to reach. That ruled Neville out. Luckily for her, I was 6 feet tall and athletic. I jumped up, grabbed the ladder, and pulled myself up onto the second-story fire escape. In my haste to earn the dollar, I brought some unwanted attention to myself. Neville looked up at me while I was climbing the ladder and said, "Yo, man, I can see a hole in the bottom of your sneaker." He burst out laughing. I felt embarrassed, but, since I was already on the ladder, I pushed on.

I climbed the fire escape to her third-floor apartment window and began attempting to pry it open. No sooner did I raise the window one inch, a man came to the window from inside the apartment. He yelled, "What the hell are you doing? Oh, you're trying to rob me? You wait right there!" I froze. The man returned to the window and pointed a gun at me!! I screamed, "Don't Shoot!! Don't Shoot!!" With the speed of an auctioneer, I blurted, "There's a lady downstairs who told me she got locked out. I was only trying to help her out!" My heart was pounding. He said, "That bitch ain't locked out, I threw her out. Fuck that bitch!!" I yelled, "I'm sorry! I'm sorry!" and hustled back down the fire escape.

When I got back down to the ground level, the lady had a stupid look on her face. I was furious. That man could've shot me. Only the fact that he was composed and chose to listen to my explanation prevented him from killing me. I wanted to get away from there as soon as possible. I turned to leave, but Neville, forever the businessman, said, "Wait." He turned to the lady and said, "You still owe him the dollar." She handed me the dollar, and we left. I will consider this foolish incident my second brush with potential death.

The hunt for a new apartment was taking longer than expected. My mother couldn't seem to find anything suitable on the housing market. At long last, she finally found a place about two miles away on Coney Island Avenue. I went with her to inspect the apartment. The block was excellent, and the building looked well kept. After finalizing with the realtor, she agreed to accept the apartment. The only thing left to do was give the landlord the deposit. At the very last minute, the landlord called my mother and asked if she had any children? My mother told him she had one girl and two boys. He asked, "How old are the boys?" She said thirteen and fourteen years old. He immediately claimed the apartment was unavailable and hung up the phone.

The landlord's response infuriated my mother. She directed her frustration towards me, "You see, this is why I can't find a place. As soon as I mention that I have teenage boys, they turn me down." She then began ranting about how easier her life would be if she didn't have children. She then launched into her new theme, "I can't wait until you both turn eighteen so y'all can move out." My mother had expressed her feelings about Larry and me moving out as soon as possible several times. Now, it became a full-blown talking point. It was like she started a countdown in her head. Our eighteenth birthdays equaled zero on the clock.

Not long afterward, she finally found a place willing to accept a woman with teenage boys. It wasn't too far from where we currently lived, 1.3 miles away. Once again, I went with her to inspect the apartment. It was on the corner of East 21st Street and Regent Place in the Flatbush section of Brooklyn. We arrived on the block. I immediately noticed hordes of guys hanging out all over the place. They were on the corner, in front of the buildings, and even in front of the corner bodega. These guys looked rough too. As we approached the building, there was graffiti all over the outside walls. What is this? When we entered the hallway of the building, there was more graffiti on the inside walls. There was so much graffiti that it looked like a subway car, not a residential building. We met with the super and went into the apartment. The whole building had a funny smell like a combination of mold, roaches, and piss. I had a bad feeling about this place. My mother confirmed with the super that we would take the apartment.

As we left the building, I had an overwhelming feeling of impending doom. Is this happening? Were we both looking at the same place? My mother must've seen the look on my face and asked me what was wrong? I asked her why were we moving there? That place looked terrible. She flew into a rage, "It's the only thing I could find. It's the only place that will accept me because of you two. This apartment is where we are moving, and that's it!" There was nothing else I could say. I kept my mouth shut.

Moving day was a sad one. It wasn't only because of the new building's condition, but I liked living on East 35th Street. We had many friends there, and I was going to miss them. I completely understood the necessity to move after the burglary. Still, I didn't want to go, and I surely didn't want to move to that new place. Damn.

CHAPTER 5
MILK CARTON

"Life is hard, and it gets worse and worse and worse" - Cat Power

The spring of 1980 arrived with the New York City crime rate at an all-time high. NYC was the crime capital of America. The total number of murders now averaged more than 1,700 per year. To put that into perspective, the total number of murders committed in NYC in 2018 was less than 300. Violent crimes such as robbery, burglary, and rape also soared to record heights. The NYC subway system was no better. It was one of the most dangerous places in the entire city. Violence, muggings, and sexual assaults were routine. There weren't enough police officers to patrol the trains, especially at night. Straphangers were on their own. New York was under siege.

There were three major crime sections in New York City. The northern part of Manhattan, which was Harlem and above. The southern part of The Bronx or 'South Bronx' and Brooklyn (from the middle sections moving east). Brooklyn was the clear frontrunner. Our family had resided in all three of these sections, the literal ground zero's of crime in the city. Out of all the places we lived so far, it was clear that the corner of East 21st Street and Regent Place was the worse. The wall-to-wall graffiti and the smell only scratched the surface. I counted at least a dozen guys hanging out in the hallway when I entered the building. They loitered there every day, and none of them lived there. It was terrifying, coming into that dark hallway. I would try not to make eye contact with any of them, but I could feel them checking me out as I walked by.

Immediately upon moving into the apartment, the superintendent propositioned my mother. He told her, "If you have sex with me, I will fix up this apartment and make sure everything gets done around here." She refused his advances. As a result, he neglected to make any repairs in the apartment. When he did agree to fix something, he was very slow to get around to it. We lived on the first floor. The guys hanging out in the hallway were right around the corridor from our front door, about 25 feet away. They were always smoking, drinking, and making noise. We were in for a long summer.

As far as academics, things were proceeding as expected. I graduated from junior high school with honors, and now high school awaited. Students usually attended a "zone school" nearest to their home. Mine was Erasmus Hall, the same institution that Eugene's older crew attended. There was NO WAY I would step foot in that school. Luckily for me, New York City faced an overcrowding problem. Students were allowed to enroll in high schools outside of their zone if they agreed to enter a lottery system. The Board Of Education would select a high school for you to attend.

I decided to take my chances with this lottery. It was a risky gamble. There were other terrible high schools in Brooklyn, located near Brownsville or East New York. The school chosen for me was Abraham Lincoln High School. I never heard of that school. Where is it located? The answer was way out near Coney Island in the Brighton Beach section of Brooklyn. I had never been out there before. Some of my classmates were like, "Oh, you going to Lincoln? That's where all the White Boys are. They're gonna chase you every day. They have race riots. Black people don't go out there." Well, that was great! Did I go from Eugene and his crew to the Ku Klux Klan?

Larry was also entering high school. He "graduated" from junior high school despite having similar grades as the previous year. I guess there's only so long they can hold a kid in junior high school. Larry entered the lottery as well. The school chosen for him was William E. Grady High School. It happened to be about a ten-minute walk from my new high school in Brighton Beach. Out of all the high schools they could have chosen, they placed us very close to each other. We would both take the subway to school every morning. The NY Board Of Education partnered with The MTA to supply free train passes for eligible high school students. The commute would be 45 minutes each way. That sucked, but it still beats attending Erasmus Hall, a five-minute walk from my apartment.

Meanwhile, I was still delivering newspapers, but things had changed. Now that I lived over a mile away, I could no longer work with Neville. I decided to start a paper route closer to where I lived. I knew where the newspaper distribution center was because I used to go with Neville to drop off the money. I knew all the ins and outs of his newspaper operation. I went to the office and told them I wanted to start a paper route. They were delighted and gave me a job right on the spot. I also submerged myself deeper into basketball; my life revolved around the sport. I decided that the only way I would get better was to play every day. My former junior high school, Walt Whitman, had a park next to it. Guys would play basketball there. I used to be afraid to walk past the courts when I was younger (a few months earlier). Now, I felt confident to go in there and play ball.

I took the seven-minute walk to Walt Whitman park, wearing my basketball team jersey to give me extra clout. Along the way, I saw a couple of guys in their backyard playing basketball. I immediately recognized one of the guys; his name was Darrell Bailey. We were former 5th-grade classmates, but we didn't like each other. We were both members of the school band at Walt Whitman, and we both played the trombone as well. We sat right next to each other for three years and rarely said a word to each other. The only time we ever spoke was during our final year. I was third-level trombone (the lowest), and Darrell was second-level trombone. Our music instructor would place all of the sheet music on the music stands before class began. I arrived a little early to class one day and thought, "You know what, let me take a look at this second-level trombone music and see if I can play this." I leaned to the left and began playing the more advanced musical arrangement when Darrell darted over, snatched the sheet music from me and, barked, "You're not on second trombone, you're on third trombone, stick to your music." What an asshole! That was our only conversation in four years.

Now it was June of 1980. I'm walking past this guy Darrell's house; he says, "Yo what's up? You played for the team, right? Come over here and play with us." I agreed. It seemed like a genuine invitation, and I was dying to play some ball. Darrell and his older brother Kevin, who was a year older than the both of us, were there. Kevin was tall, around my height. Darrell was only about 5'5". As it turned out, both Darrell and Kevin were excellent basketball players. I suspect they invited me to play with them because I was wearing my basketball jersey. They wanted to test their skills against someone from the team. I had a good time playing ball in their backyard and began stopping by more often. Darrell turned out to be a decent guy. His brother Kevin, AKA "Chilly Kev" because of his laid-back demeanor, was the most popular. Darrell was the wise guy with all the smart-ass comments. It didn't bother me, Darrell wasn't malicious, only annoying.

Darrell's family appeared to be living the American dream. They owned their own house, complete with a backyard, two-car garage, driveway, and car. Darrell's parents appeared to have a healthy marriage. Darrell and Kevin wore stylish clothes, and they always had a haircut. Darrell was also an excellent student. We shared several teachers who taught advanced classes. I found out Eugene terrorized him too. Because Darrell lived on the same block as our school, Eugene hung out directly across the street. Darrell would leave his home for school and walk around the block in the opposite direction to avoid Eugene. Darrell also refused to attend Erasmus Hall despite living around the corner from the school. We had a lot in common. He seemed like a quality person, but there was one problem; Darrell was West Indian. After my whole ordeal with Joe, I did not like or trusted West Indian people at all. I asked Darrell, "So, you're Jamaican?" He said, "No, I'm Trinidadian." I said, "It's the same thing. All West Indians are the same." He would say, "No, they're not!!" I'm like, "Whatever." We would argue about West Indian culture all the time. I had a lot to learn.

I discovered that there are several differences between Trinidadian and Jamaican people. Their accents are different, along with their food and music. Everything about them is different. Luckily for me, Darrell didn't let my ignorance force him to ban me from his home. We became good friends in no time. I would tell him, "You know, I used to think you were an asshole, now I KNOW you are an asshole!" It was hilarious. Darrell had extended family living with him. They were a cousin named Avalon and her fiancé Gerard, who was about ten years older than we were. Gerard would play basketball with us and lecture us about how we should conduct ourselves as young men. The atmosphere was great, no bullies, no drama, only fun. I hated leaving Darrell's peaceful block to return to my "thugged out" neighborhood. Soon, Larry began coming with me to hang out with my newfound friends. By this time, Larry was telling anyone who would listen that he was a rapper. They greeted him with the same reaction I had given him, skepticism. It didn't faze Larry. He wanted everyone to share his enthusiasm. Larry faced quite an uphill battle.

1980 was a pivotal year for music as the landscape had changed. Disco was dead. Most of the stars of the Disco era were fading. A new bass line-driven R&B sound influenced by the group Chic emerged. Meanwhile, the growing music sub-genre called Rap exploded in my neighborhood. The hottest rappers from the streets of New York were all releasing songs now. You had Grandmaster Flash & The Furious Five, The Funky 4+1, and The Treacherous Three. There were also solo rappers like Spoonie Gee and Kurtis Blow; it was becoming hard to keep up.

Block parties with live deejays also began popping up everywhere. These deejays/electricians would bring their equipment outside. Someone would connect the plug right into the light post on the street corner. On occasion, they used a long series of extension cords to power their sets. We weren't allowed to hang outside after sunset when the best block parties were happening. Luckily for us, someone decided to throw a block party right around the corner from our building. Larry and I ventured over there to hear the music before it got too dark. It was going to be my first time seeing a real live DJ in action.

People of all ages packed the block. The DJ was mixing and scratching records using two turntables. It was amazing! I can recall hearing a funk song with the most memorable horn riff for the first time. The song was 'Get Up And Dance' by the group Freedom. It blew me away! As we enjoyed the music and the atmosphere, I bumped into one of my friends from my 8th-grade class named Dino. He began as an outstanding student but somehow fell astray during the school year. After a while, Dino started rolling with Eugene and his crew. I wonder if he graduated from the 8th grade? Anyway, we were happy to see each other at the block party, but soon his tone became serious. Dino said, "Yo, they are about to shoot up this block party and rob the DJ." What? Why would anyone want to ruin this awesome party?

Dino warned me, "When I tell you it's almost time, GO HOME!" I said ok, but now I was on edge. Was he sure something was going to go down? About twenty minutes later, Dino came over to me and said, "Go home!!" We immediately left the block party and went inside our apartment. I don't know if anything terrible happened, but I sure wasn't sticking around to find out. I never saw Dino again after that evening.

As my eventful June came to an end, I found myself in Walt Whitman Park playing ball. A basketball coach named Mr. Screen entered the park and began hanging up flyers announcing a tryout for a basketball team in one week. The age requirement was fourteen and under to play. I felt confident I could make this squad. The very next day, I was walking home when I ran into another former classmate. I wasn't thrilled to see him. Our relationship was cordial, at best. He immediately began making unprovoked, derogatory comments about my appearance. That pissed me off. The next thing I knew, we were in a full-blown fist fight right in front of a grocery store. This fool grabbed a discarded soda bottle on the ground, broke it against the wall, and came at me. I kept flailing away, unconcerned about the bottle. Some bystander who was walking past broke up the fight. Afterward, I wandered into the grocery store to buy some water and compose myself. There was an Asian man behind the counter. He looked at me and said, "You're bleeding!" I said, "What do you mean?" I looked down at my chest, and there was blood. The store clerk handed me a mirror. I saw a gash on my chest from where that idiot cut me with the bottle. Now I felt the pain. I realized I needed medical attention. I went to the hospital and received two stitches from the gash. The doctor advised me not to do anything strenuous for two weeks until he removed the stitches. Ah, man! Basketball tryouts were in a few days. Because of my injury, I sat on the sideline and watched guys I felt were inferior earn a spot on the team. I became frustrated and disappointed—life in Da Hood.

When the doctor cleared me to play basketball, I resumed my mission to become a better player. After a grueling day of balling, I departed Darrell's house a little early to make my nightfall curfew. I had plenty of time. The sun was setting, and the walk was only seven minutes to my apartment. I arrived at Flatbush Avenue, which was about three minutes into my journey. A black man with cornrows and large eyes walks up to me and says, "Hey man, you wanna make twenty dollars? We're moving some boxes, and I need help. It'll be real quick." Of course, I wanted the twenty bucks, but accepting his offer would cause me to miss my curfew. I needed to make a spontaneous decision. I decided my mother would understand my lateness after I showed her the money I earned. The building's location wasn't too far away. Perfect! I agreed to do the job.

I Immediately made a detour and began following this guy down the street. As we were walking, he begins to make small talk. He asks me, "So, how do you feel about gay people?" Huh? That was a very random and awkward question. I said, "I don't feel anything about gay people; I don't have any feelings towards them one way or another." He says, "Yeah, cause one of the guys helping us is gay." I'm like, "Alright cool, whatever." My focus was on the $20; I didn't care about the other guy's sexuality.

We arrived at our destination; a three-story house with a "stoop." He told me the boxes were in the basement; we would use the lower entrance. I said, ok. Right before we entered the lower level, he says, "Let me talk to you for a second. Before we do this, let me ask you a question; Can I pay you some money to suck your dick?" WHAT?? I said, "What are you talking about, man? Nah!" Despite being very naive, I knew this situation had taken a wrong turn. He continues, "It's no big deal. You know, it's like regular sex. You've had sex before, right?" I said, no. He goes, "Oh. How old are you?" I told him I was thirteen. He said, "Well, you know, it's like jerking off then." Now I'm annoyed. I said, "Nah, man!" I wanted to move the boxes and get the hell out of there.

He then pulls out a big roll of money from his pocket and shows it to me. He says, "Ok, how about I give you five dollars, and you let me touch it." He peels off $5 from the roll and offers it to me. Now I finally comprehend what's going on. I asked him directly, "So we're not gonna be moving any boxes, right?" He's says, "Nah, come down here behind the steps and let me touch it for five dollars." Now I'm pissed when I realized there was no $20. I said, "Fuck this, I gotta go." He was still trying to convince me as I was walking away, "Are you sure? Damn, what a shame; You're so big! Are you really only thirteen?" I hustled home in time for my mother not to notice my slight lateness.

The sad reality of this story is; I could've disappeared off the face of the earth. Thousands of minors disappear every year without a trace. I was somewhere I NEVER should have been. I should have called my mother from a payphone and asked for her permission. Instead, I thought I was mature enough to make that decision on my own. This man was a sexual predator and a pedophile. Any number of horrible scenarios could've unfolded in that basement. The police would have done an investigation. All they would have been able to piece together was, I left Darrell's house at a particular time, walked in the direction of my apartment, and disappeared. That's it. The window of opportunity would have only been seven minutes. There were no security cameras or video footage in 1980. Would the police have suspected foul play? I could've decided to run away from home. You see stories on the news about kids who disappeared or got lured away by a stranger. How could they be that stupid? Well, I was THAT stupid. My mother lectured me plenty of times about strangers. I thought she prepared me, but I was so naive that it took me way too long to figure out there were no boxes. The unthinkable could've happened to me only a few blocks from my home, on busy Flatbush Avenue. I never told anyone about this incident.

    July couldn't have arrived any sooner. I was glad to see that crazy month of June end. Good riddance. One warm evening, my mother sent me to the store to pick up dinner. We had only been living in that wretched building for less than two months. I would see the same group of guys posted in the hallway every day, but I never said anything to them. I would be nervous walking by but so far, so good. My mother sent me to pick up a pizza. This was no ordinary pie, but a new pizza style called a 'Meat Pizza.' It contained crushed ground beef on top of a cheese pizza. My mother would splurge every so often. It was definitely worth the extra money. I walked to the shop, picked up the pie, and returned home. As I was entering the building holding the pizza box, someone yelled, "Yooo! This nigga got pizza!" The next thing I knew, they rushed me! Somebody started choking me from behind while I was still holding the pizza box, trying not to drop it. Another guy held my left arm while a third accomplice snatched the pizza box from my hand. He ran up the staircase while yet another guy blocked me from following him. The guy who was choking me released my neck. The remaining guys took off up the stairs following the guy with the pizza. They left me standing there alone in the hallway. After regaining my composure, I had to go into the apartment and explain to my mother that I'd got robbed of the pizza. As expected, she became enraged. Here we go again.

This incident wasn't the first time I'd gotten robbed when she sent me to the store with her hard-earned money. She didn't even ask me if I was ok, only "Who did it?" I told her I only recognized one dude from the crew who lived in the building. She asked, "Where does he live?" I had seen him enter an apartment on the first floor a couple of times, so I assumed he lived there. My mother and I walked over to his apartment and knocked on the door. A woman who presumably was his mother answered. The guy in question had already returned to his apartment. He was peeking from the background. My mother immediately said, "Your son and his friends stole a pizza from my son!" The lady at the door became angry and turned around to face her son. He put his head down in shame. The lady then said, "Ok, I get paid on Friday, I'll give you back your money then" (which she did). My mother said ok, and we left.

When we got back to our apartment, my mother was still fuming, yelling to no one in particular, "We don't have any dinner! We're going to have to go to bed without food. Kenny lost dinner, so no food for us!" I felt terrible. I knew I should've defended our pizza better, but no less than fifteen of them were in the hallway. To make matters worse, I still had to walk past them every day.

July hadn't started off the way I would've liked at all. Adding to my miserable summer of 1980, Joe reappeared in our lives. My mother hadn't mentioned him at all since their relationship ended about two years ago. They must have kept a line of communication open during that time. Joe decided to request visitation with his daughter, my little sister, Chanele. My mother agreed to let her visit him on some weekends, moving forward. Joe didn't live too far, only a couple of miles away. He was now living with the same mysterious girlfriend, Jane. She was the one Joe allegedly met "right after" he broke up with my mother. Joe never visited our home (Thank God). My mother would drop Chanele off at his house on Friday evenings and pick her up Sunday afternoons. Three weekends in a row, Chanele stayed at her father's apartment. Nothing appeared unusual about this new custody agreement.

Shortly after the third week's visitation, my mother made an announcement. Joe was asking for permanent custody of his daughter. He wanted Chanele to live with him and his girlfriend now. It was honorable for Joe to volunteer to take responsibility for his daughter. Still, his request seemed absurd to me. By law, if the parents were never married, the mother has sole legal and physical custody. Only a court order can change that. The unmarried father has no legal rights to custody or visitation of the child. The ball was in my mother's court. I was confident she would reject the man we had come to know and some other woman, raising her daughter. I asked my mother what her response would be? She said with a straight face, "I'm gonna let Chanele decide for herself." WHAT? She's only five years old. Chanele wasn't capable of making a life-changing custody decision like that. I couldn't comprehend how my mother thought that was possible. In a proper court proceeding, the courts wouldn't weigh the child's wishes until they could understand the situation. This age is usually around twelve or thirteen. My mother couldn't be serious?

The following day, my mother announced the verdict. She stated that Chanele decided she wanted to live with her father. There were more kids on his block to play with than there were on our block. I couldn't believe my ears. Of course, a five-year-old would make a decision based on the ratio of kids on her block. What a disaster! I felt like I couldn't take it anymore. I had to speak up. My mother made 99% of all family decisions. We lived under a totalitarian regime, but this time was different. I could not let my sister grow up under the same abusive conditions Larry and I endured for years.

After some soul-searching, I finally mustered up the courage to confront my mother. This encounter would be the very first time I challenged her in my almost fourteen years of life. I asked her, "How could you let Chanele go live with Joe? You know what kind of man he is." As one might expect, my mother exploded! "How the hell could you ask me that? You don't know what it's like to raise children! I have three mouths to feed, and I don't have any help. It's hard for me!" She continued yelling, "Look at you! You don't have a job! Are you going to help feed her? You can't even feed yourself. All you do is eat, sleep, and play basketball!"

After that, I felt defeated. There was nothing else I could do or say. I retreated to my room. Everything in my physical being knew this was a bad idea. Almost immediately, Chanele got shipped off to go live with her father. The new arrangement had my mother traveling to Joe's apartment to visit her daughter on the weekends. A few weeks later, my mother placed her weekly call to Joe to schedule her visit. The number was not in service. What is this? Did Joe not pay the bill? My mother went over to his apartment anyway to see what was going on. There was no one there. Joe packed up and moved away without giving any advanced notice. Still, we remained optimistic. Joe must have recently moved; he will call once he gets himself situated. That call never came.

After about a month, the grim reality began to sink in. Joe had no intention of revealing his whereabouts. He kidnapped my little sister. Joe was already preparing to move; that's why his custody request was so hasty. Joe knew all along that he was going to pull this unforgivable stunt.

My mother never called the authorities or any investigative agency of any kind. We didn't talk about it at all. It was like my sister never existed. Like Chanele hadn't been a part of our family for the past five years. I was heartbroken. Not only because I missed her, but I wondered what kind of upbringing she would have with this madman. Larry and I didn't even talk about it amongst ourselves. He had to feel upset. Larry was even closer to Chanele than I was. He all but raised her, and now she was gone. We would not see her again for many years.

By this point, the only thing that seemed to make any sense was basketball. My 14th birthday came and went with little fanfare as usual. The start of high school was only weeks away. I was anxious about how I was going to look on the first day. We rarely, if ever, wore new clothes on the first day of school. I wanted to at least make a good first impression in high school. I needed to save as much money from my paper route as possible during August to reach my goal. Unfortunately, my number of subscribers was small. I was pocketing about $8 per week. The newspaper distribution company took the majority of the money for themselves. I delivered papers daily, and on Friday would go door-to-door to collect $2.50 from each subscriber. Fifty cents would be my cut of the profits. Unlike Neville's neighborhood, some of the buildings I delivered in were unsafe. Unfortunately, I had no choice; they were part of my route.

On Friday, I went on my scheduled collection run as usual. I slipped into this particular building about three blocks from my apartment. I picked up the money from my subscriber with no problem. As I was walking through the hallway, approaching the exit, five guys appeared out of nowhere. They intercepted me and pinned me up against the wall. One of them said, "Yo, you collected $2.50 from my mother. Somebody else already came to our house saying they were the paperboy and took $2.50 from her. You have to give me my mother's money back!" I belted out, "That's impossible! I'm the only paper guy, and I've been delivering to your apartment for two weeks." He said, "I don't got nothing to do with that...You gotta give me that $2.50 back!" I'm pleading with this guy while still pinned against the wall, "Nah, man, you don't understand. I'm the paper guy; I don't have anything to do with that other guy." He said, "I'm gonna ask you one more time." All I remember saying was "Yooo but..." and POW!! This guy punched me right in my ear, hard. I was screaming in pain. I didn't even know your ear could swell, but my ear began increasing in size. I screamed, "Arrghh!! Here, take your money!" I gave him the $2.50. He could've robbed me of everything I had, but he only took the $2.50 and left with his boys. I exited the building teary-eyed. My ear was still ringing as I continued to make my other collections.

When I arrived home, I had enough. My neighborhood was too dangerous for a paperboy. I was fortunate that I hadn't gotten robbed before. High school was about to start soon, so; I was going to have to quit delivering newspapers anyway. This incident hastened my departure, so I came up with a plan. I went to the newspaper distribution office. I told them I'd gotten robbed in one of my buildings and I was quitting, which was true. I then added that the assailants took all the money I had collected. The supervisor at the newspaper office was skeptical of my story. He looked at my unmarked face and said, "Really? Where did they hit you?" I told him my ear. He glanced at my ear. The swelling had subsided a bit, but one of my ears was still larger than the other. He said, "All right, we'll assign your route to someone else." He had no choice but to cut his losses.

The money I collected ($50), which I owed to the Daily News, was now mine. Add my little commission to the pot, and I had about $60 to spend on school clothes. In 1980, you could do a lot with $60. I bought two pairs of Converse All-Stars. I bought a pair of denim Lee jeans, which were very popular in my neighborhood, along with some other pants and shirts. I was all set for the all-important first week of school. I was happy. I guess my ear paid the price for me to get some new school clothes. I didn't tell anyone about my assault and robbery. I told my mother I'd been saving money. She was happy about that. Now she only needed to focus on Larry's wardrobe. I don't remember if she bought him anything.

Larry didn't seem too concerned about attending high school anyway. He never mentioned it. His primary focus, as usual, was rapping. Across the street from Darrell's house lived a guy named "Pop." His nickname pertained to Breakdancing. "Breaking" had become a popular form of street dancing in New York City. "Breakers" would compete or "Battle" to see who was the best like Rappers did. By this time, Bronx community leader and DJ, Afrika Bambaataa, organized Rapping, Breakdancing, Graffiti Art, and Deejaying under one umbrella. They called it Hip-Hop. If a person claimed to be part of the Hip-Hop culture, it meant they participated in one or more of these four art forms. Hip-Hop wasn't considered an art form by the mainstream media in 1980.

This guy Pop specialized in the form of Breakdancing called "Popping." A dancer would move his arms and legs in a way that made him look like he was trying to dance with broken limbs. Sometimes, he would move his body in slow motion to make it look like his body consisted of rubber. Pop was a member of an organized Hip-Hop collective called 'The Galaxy Crew.' They performed at a local roller skating rink on Bedford Avenue. Larry wanted to join Pop's crew. He felt he was now good enough to be one of their featured rappers. The Galaxy Crew flat-out rejected him. I doubt they allowed him to audition. Larry was disappointed but not discouraged. He continued to work on his craft.

The brutal summer of 1980 came to an end. The arrival of September meant the arrival of my long-awaited event; The first day of high school. Although I was all set with my school clothes, I was still overwhelmed with nervousness. I knew nothing about a high school. Would I get lost on the train ride over there? Could I handle the work? Are the White Boys going to chase me home? Even the term "freshman" implies that one doesn't know what the hell is going on. I rode the D train for close to an hour. I arrived at the Ocean Parkway subway station in the Brighton Beach section of Brooklyn. I could see The Atlantic Ocean and the boardwalk from the subway platform. I was a long way from home.

I began walking towards the school, which was a few blocks away. As I got closer to my destination, I could see Abraham Lincoln High school. It was larger than my junior high school. There was a sea of students everywhere, all heading in the direction of the school. My anxiety began to rise. I tried to calm my nerves, "Everything is going to be ok," I said. Without warning, a random black guy, who appeared to be an upperclassman, approached me. He said, "What's up, man, you're a freshman?" I said, "Yeah." He says, "Let me ask you a question...Have you ever bust a nut before?" Huh? I never heard that phrase before. I asked him, "What do you mean?" He said, "You know, bust a nut. You don't know what that means?" I became confused. I said, "Nah, what is it?" He says, "You know, have you ever had sex with a girl before?"

Oh, now I get it. I didn't want to answer a question like that because the truth would've been most embarrassing. This guy, who I didn't know, was persistent. He said, "Come on, man, it's no big deal. I know you're young, don't worry, you can tell me. I won't say anything. I was a freshman before." Instead of dealing with this idiot properly, all I said was, "Nah." This guy then turned in the direction of about twenty other guys leaning on the school gate. He yelled, "Yoooo! Guess What? This nigga said he never bust a nut before!!" The whole crowd burst out laughing. I felt humiliated. I hadn't entered the school yet, and I was already having a hard time. Is this high school life? Somebody shoot me now!

After the first week of school, I managed to settle in. Classes didn't start for freshmen until 9:45 am, ending at 3:45 pm. Perfect! More time to sleep. Ironically, a school named after Abraham Lincoln was racially split right down the middle. The school was 50% White students and 50% Black students. No one chased anyone home, but all the Black students sat together on one side of the cafeteria. All the White students sat on the other. My new high school was segregated just like the rest of Brooklyn. The majority of the White students were from the Bensonhurst or Bay Ridge sections. I never heard of these parts of town. I hadn't experienced real segregation, either. The school wasn't straight racist; certain things were sort of "understood."

Most of the Black students were from either Coney Island or from my area. The Coney Island guys nicknamed my neighborhood, "Cross Town." Coney Island dudes and Cross Town dudes were rivals and didn't get along. Forget about the White boys; I needed to watch out for the Coney Islanders. Go figure.

After a couple of weeks of high school, I was anxious to resume playing basketball. I had grown into a 6'2" fourteen-year-old. I even caught up to Larry in height. Larry settled into Grady High School without any problems, or at least he didn't mention any of them. Anyway, there was a guy from the varsity basketball team in my Physical Education class. He was a junior named Derek. I would play him one on one in gym class and lose each time. He would talk trash to me afterward and say to my face that I wasn't any good. He was a confidence crusher.

My mother, who was forever looking to enroll me in an after-school program, approached me about joining The Boys Club Of America. I wasn't thrilled about it until she mentioned they offered a basketball league. Oh, where do I sign up? The first day I walked into The Boy's Club, I felt right at home. The overwhelming majority of the guys there were super cool, except for one troublemaker named Darren. He had a muscular, football build. Of course, it didn't take long for Darren to begin bullying me. What else was new? He wanted to fight me one night for no reason, but a guy named Kojo intervened and told Darren to leave me alone. Soon after, The Boy's Club suspended Darren because of his aggressive behavior. A few years later, I heard Darren wound up in prison. He was bad news. With him gone, The Boys Club became a paradise. I would race there after school.

Meanwhile, one month into my freshman year at Lincoln, I saw a sign on the school gymnasium door. The sign announced tryouts for the Abraham Lincoln High School basketball team. Lincoln was a perennial sports powerhouse. They also didn't have a junior varsity team. You either made the squad, or you didn't. I wanted to try out, but I wasn't confident I could play on that level. I saw Derek in gym class and told him I wanted to try out. He rolled his eyes and told me, "You can't make the team. You're not good enough. Look at me, I'm way better than you, and I don't get any playing time. I sit on the bench." Once again, Derek discouraged me. I took his advice and decided to stay in my comfort zone at The Boys Club and play there after school.

As luck would have it, I met a counselor at The Boys Club named Jack. He worked as a teacher, along with my high school basketball coach at another junior high school. What a small world! Jack told the coach there was a 6'2" freshman enrolled at Abraham Lincoln H.S. that was pretty good. The varsity coach told Jack to tell me that the basketball season was already about to start. He suggested I come down and work out with the team anyway. I guess the coach wanted to evaluate me in person. What a great stroke of luck! A second chance to try out for the team? I needed to take advantage of this opportunity. The following day, Lincoln played their first preseason exhibition basketball game. My schedule had Physical Education as the last class of the day. As I exited the gym, the other high school team, Alexander Hamilton High School, was entering the gym at the same time. They were the defending New York City PSAL champions. They all came walking into the gym wearing matching leather jackets. Bright colored lettering reading "Alexander Hamilton City Champs" draped across the back. I stood there, gazing at them like, "Wow, this is the team my school is playing today?"

All of a sudden, the final guy enters the gym. He stood at an incredible 6'8" tall. He had to duck to enter the gymnasium. I looked up at this giant, and he was the tallest person I'd ever seen before. I shook my head and thought, "This is high school basketball? Hell no, I'm not trying out!" I left the gym and hurried home. I didn't know at the time that this 6'8" colossus was Jerry "Ice" Reynolds. He was the number one high school basketball player in The State Of New York. He was a future NBA player. Everyone who played high school basketball wasn't as imposing as he was. This caliber of player was by no means a true reflection of high school basketball. It didn't matter; I was a coward. I blew a golden opportunity that year because I was afraid of Jerry "Ice" Reynolds.

Right around the time that I was hiding under the covers from Jerry Reynolds, my mother received a phone call from Larry's high school principal. Larry got suspended from school. Well, that was a new twist, Larry never got into this much trouble before. It appeared that Larry and another student had an altercation, and he beat up the other student. Larry told my mother that this kid was trying to steal his MTA train pass, and he fought back. My mother called the school and asked for an explanation. Why was Larry getting suspended from school when the other kid was trying to rob him? Once again, where was the school security guard? The principal explained that the school's zero-tolerance policy required suspension for both students. I didn't agree with the school's assessment, and neither did my mother. There was nothing she could do about it, so Larry had a week off from school. Later on, I quizzed Larry about the details of the fight. He told me the guy was trying to rob him of his train pass. They got into a tussle and fell to the ground. The guy attempted to punch Larry in the face. At the split second when he swung, Larry moved his head. The guy hit the ground, breaking his hand. After that, Larry kicked his ass. I was happy for Larry. If it were me, that guy would've taken my train pass with ease.

Following the suspension, Larry returned to school, or so we thought. The principal called a couple of weeks later, inquiring why Larry hadn't returned to school. What? He had been getting up and getting dressed for school every morning. Larry was leaving the house but going somewhere else. He was in big trouble this time. Larry later told me the truth. He confessed to me that he couldn't go back to school. The guy who Larry beat up, along with his boys, was out looking for him. Instead of alerting the authorities, he stopped attending altogether. Larry dropped out of high school. He never completed the first semester of 9th grade. This news was shocking, or was it? You could almost see it coming. Larry was fifteen years old now and never had any interest in school. My mother wasn't thrilled with his decision. She seemed unable or unwilling to deal with his academic problems anymore. Meanwhile, I received my first semester grades, and I scored a B average. Larry and I were heading in opposite directions now.

1980 transitioned into 1981. I used the welcome lull in our family drama to create some kind of daily routine. I would attend school and then go to my Boy's Club sanctuary. One day my former junior high school teammate "John-John" showed up at The Boys Club. Everyone knew him there. John was now the point guard for the number one ranked high school basketball team in America, Tolentine High School. He was only a freshman, impressive. The temporary lull in my family's never-ending drama came to an abrupt halt. I arrived home from school to find our apartment burglarized once again. It was reminiscent of the previous year when we lived on East 35th Street, and I came home to find our apartment ransacked. This time they took my mother's new stereo, her sewing machine (which she loved), and a few other items. These crooks even dared to go into the refrigerator, take out some dinner rolls, and try to heat them in our little toaster oven.

This violation was worse than before. We couldn't figure out how the thieves managed to gain entry to the apartment. The previous tenants installed a 'Police Lock' on the front door. This level of security should have raised concerns from the beginning. A Police Lock was a metal pole bolted from the floor of your apartment to the back of the front door, on a slant. The only way to open the door was to slide the Police Lock over first. Once you bolted the Police Lock shut, it wasn't possible to open the door. How did these crooks get in? Did they come through the window? We had no clue. When my mother came home, she was boiling mad. I was angry too. My anger caused me to become bold enough to utter, "Man, I wish I was here when they came!" My mother turned to me and yelled, "Shut up! You wouldn't have done nothing!" I put my head down in shame. It was a very hurtful thing to hear your mother acknowledge that she felt her son was a punk.

"Be careful what you wish for; it might come true."

A few days after the burglary, I had a half-day schedule at school, so I arrived home early. I was relaxing in my room when I became startled by a hard knock at the front door. I assumed it was Larry; he must've forgotten his key. I opened the door, and two guys rushed into the apartment! I recognized one of them as part of the group who robbed me of the pizza a few months earlier. The other one was a shorter guy who I'd never seen before. They bolted past me like I wasn't even there. They began walking through the apartment, looking around like they forgot something. I knew right away that these were the culprits who burglarized our residence earlier in the week. I mustered up the courage to say, "Y'all have to get out of here." The bigger one said, "Shut the fuck up!" He continued to stroll from room to room, looking around. He picked up different things and examined them like he was in a department store. I felt terrified. What was I going to do? I said in a meek voice, "You guys have to go, my mother's on her way home." The bigger one looked at me and didn't bother to respond.

Seconds later, he told the shorter one, "Wait here, I'll be right back" and left the apartment. His departure was my small window of opportunity. It might've been my only chance to do something about this mind-blowing situation I found myself in. I needed to think of something quick, who knows what the bigger guy had in store when he returned. I noticed that the shorter guy appeared nervous without his ringleader present. I towered over this guy. I had to roll the dice. I took one step towards him and said, "Get the fuck out!" He looked up at me, turned around, and left. I ran over and bolted the Police Lock. My heart was pounding.

All of a sudden, there was another hard knock on the door. I went to the door and looked through the peephole. Someone placed a hand over the peephole, so I couldn't see who was out there. I didn't say a word. The guy yelled, "Open the door!" I still didn't respond. The next thing I knew, one of the guys in the hallway slid a thin piece of a metal strip between the door. He was trying to nudge the Police Lock over. What the Hell?? I didn't know what to do. I decided to call my mother at work. When she answered, I told her what happened. I also told her they were still outside, trying to gain entry to the apartment. She told me to hang up the phone and dial 911. I immediately called the police. I told the 911 dispatcher that some guys were trying to break into my apartment. The operator asked, "When did this happen?" I yelled, "Right now! It's happening right now!" She said, "Ok, the police are on their way." I went back to the front door. I began holding on to the Police Lock so the metal strip wouldn't be able to slide the pole over.

In less than sixty seconds, there was another knock on the door. They yelled, "Open up, it's the police!" I could hear the sound of a walkie-talkie in the hallway. I opened the door, and there were police all over the hall. They pinned the bigger guy against the wall with his hands behind his back. He was yelling, "I didn't do nothing! I didn't do nothing! I'm friends with his brother!" I knew that was a lie; my brother doesn't have any friends, asshole! I told the police that he was the guy who broke into the house. They caught him red-handed in the act of trying to "jimmy" the lock. They handcuffed him and took him away. I called my mother back and told her what happened. She told me not to stay in the apartment alone and come to Manhattan to her job. I jumped on the subway and met her at work. When we returned home together, Larry was there. I filled him in on the details. I was the victim of a home invasion.

The very next day, I entered the building. The same guys were hanging in the hallway, including the thug who broke into the apartment. He looked at me and told one of his friends, "There he goes right there! That's the one!" I went inside our apartment, terrified once again. What are they going to do to me? I decided it was no longer safe to enter the building from the front anymore. The only other way into the building was through the back alley, where the tenants placed the trash. I started entering the building through piles of garbage.

I hated my living situation. I knew from the very beginning that moving there was a bad idea. I didn't tell my friends what happened; I dealt with it like I did everything else. By the way, someone burglarized our apartment a few days later.

I tried to carry on as best I could after that horrifying experience. Darrell and I talked on the phone often; he was now my closest friend. One day his brother Kevin told me about this girl who used to call him a lot, but he didn't have time to talk to her. He asked me if I wanted to talk to her. I said sure; I would never turn down the opportunity to speak to a girl, even if I never saw her. Kevin gave her my phone number. She immediately began calling our house to the point of excessiveness. I didn't have time to talk to her either; I had school work. The only person around with unlimited time to speak to her was Larry; he had no responsibilities. Larry would go to the public library and read all day or sit around the house, writing Rap lyrics. He would listen to the underground Rap mix shows that aired on public access radio, WHBI FM at night. These shows would broadcast at 2 or 3 a.m. No one our age would be awake at that time except Larry. There was nowhere he needed to be in the morning.

    One day, Larry and I were talking about our lives and how hard it was. We began daydreaming about what we would do if, by some miracle, we had access to $1,000 (equal to $3,000 today). I had it all planned out. I said, "Man, I would buy some brand new Adidas, a leather goose down bomber jacket, Lee jeans, everything. I would be so fresh!" Larry said, "You know what I would do? I would make a record." What? I said, "Are you crazy? We don't have nothing. No clothes, no shoes, nothing! We don't even have food! If you had $1,000, you would make a record?" He said without hesitation, "Yes! I would make a record." I lost my mind. I told him, "That is stupid! You're crazy! This conversation is over!" and I stormed off. I thought Larry had lost his mind, but his behavior was becoming more bizarre. Besides writing Rap lyrics, Larry would stay on the phone for hours talking to this obsessive girl. My mother would get annoyed with him, but he wouldn't stop. She installed a lock on the phone, but Larry broke it off.

    One day, without warning, Larry left the house and did not return that night. For the second time in his life, Larry ran away from home. It didn't appear as if anything significant happened. This time, I had no idea where he was. Once again, my mother seemed calm. She went about her daily life as if nothing happened.

    After a few days, she got a call at work explaining how security had spotted her son at Grady High School. The school official said Larry aroused suspicion because of his physical appearance. Larry wandered into the cafeteria, looking for food, and the security guard noticed him. Upon questioning, Larry claimed to be a student there. When they took him to the office to look up his name, they discovered that he hadn't attended school in six months. That prompted them to call the number they had on file for him. The school also mentioned Larry had an unknown female with him. It became clear that Larry and the obsessive girl made a pact to run away from home together. They became hungry and needed food. That's when he decided to visit Grady and try to get something to eat.

    This story my mother was telling me was unbelievable. Somehow, Larry agreed to come home and talk to my mother. I don't know all the details, but he did return home. Larry and I didn't talk about anything that transpired. It didn't matter, I thought he was crazy anyway. A couple of days later, Larry ran away again.

The summer of 1981 was close at hand. I completed my freshman year with a B average, not bad. I didn't have too many problems in high school other than the usual jokes about my physical appearance. Those school clothes I bought back in September were looking pretty worn by May. To make matters worse, our cat Pepper began peeing on everything in the apartment. People in school would say, "What is that smell? Somebody has a cat?" It wouldn't take them long to figure out who it was—more embarrassment. When school finally recessed for the summer, so did The Boys Club. I was going to miss The Boys Club, but I was ready for the summer to begin.

One day in early June, I arrived home. My mother tells me, "I was on my way to the grocery store. I happened to look down at the sidewalk and noticed a dirty, homeless man lying on the ground. I was about to walk past him when I looked closer and realized the homeless man was my son!" It was Larry. She told me he was almost unrecognizable. She picked him up, hugged him, and told him to come home. He agreed. When Larry came back, I was happy to see him. He was gone for almost a month. Nobody questioned Larry about why he ran away or what took place while he was out there, we only welcomed him back.

Over the past few months, my mother befriended a co-worker named Dee. She was a single mother with three teenage daughters. Dee was approximately my mother's age. Dee told my mother about a vacancy in her four-family building. Dee lived in the Crown Heights section of Brooklyn, which was about two miles away. With Dee's help, my mother was able to secure the third-floor apartment. I was beyond happy.

The moving day was a joyous one. We placed all of our things right in front of our apartment before loading the rental van. Some of the thugs who loitered in the hallway came around the bend. They appeared to be surveying our belongings to see what they could steal. My mother and Larry were outside with the van, so I was alone with our things for a brief moment. What if they try to take something? Was I going to have to fight to defend our stuff? They looked but didn't come any closer. We loaded the van and finally moved away from that Hellhole. Thank God!

I had endured another awful twelve-month period of time. I got slashed with a bottle and nearly shot. A group of guys jumped and robbed me of a pizza. Another group assaulted and robbed me while delivering newspapers. My little sister got kidnapped and was missing. A pedophile lured me away. Our house got burglarized twice, and I was the victim of a home invasion. My brother dropped out of high school and ran away from home twice. Could things get any worse?

CHAPTER 6
DOG DAYS OF SUMMER

Moving to the new apartment in Crown Heights was like a breath of fresh air for our family. My mother had her best friend, Dee, living right upstairs on the 4th floor. No hoodlums were hanging in the hallway or on the block or anywhere. It was perfect. Both Larry and I had become more dedicated to our perspective passions. Larry began frequenting Neville's house more often. Neville owned a stereo system with a built-in turntable and a microphone, which could record music and vocals simultaneously. Neville also collected all the latest Rap records. It was customary for record companies to add the song's instrumental on the B-side of the 12" single. Using the B-side instrumentals, Neville and Larry Gee began making homemade Rap recordings. Neville became Larry's DJ and engineer. However, Neville's set-up had one problem. His family owned a full-grown German Shepherd that would get excited whenever music played in the apartment and consistently bark. Neville was powerless to stop him.

One day Larry returned home excited and said, "Yo, I made a tape at Neville's house. Check out my tape." Okay, let's hear it. Larry pops in the cassette, and the music begins to play. Sounds good so far. Larry starts to rap but wait; I can hear the dog barking on the tape equally as loud as Larry's vocals; Woof!!! Woof!!! Woof!!! I'm like, "What the hell is this? The dog is barking on the tape!" Larry seemed oblivious to the fact that the dog is barking in the background. He was nodding his head along to the music. "This is terrible!" I said to him. Larry became annoyed. I said, "Let me ask you a question...If you owned a boombox, would you walk down the street blasting this tape?" Larry said in defiance, "Hell yeah!" I'm like, "How can you have a tape with a dog, barking?" Larry then said, "You're jealous." Now I'm angry. I say, "I'm not jealous, a dog is barking on your tape as loud as you are rapping!" We started arguing. I guess Larry felt like he was taking the next step in his rapping evolution by recording his first tape. Instead of encouraging him, I criticized him. I wasn't criticizing, but I wasn't going to stand there and tell him that his tape was "Fresh" when it wasn't. I don't even know how his rapping sounded; we never got that far. All I heard was a duet with a dog, and I wouldn't listen anymore. If he had come with a disclaimer, warning me about the dog barking, I could've listened with a different ear. Regardless, Larry wasn't discouraged by my opinion at all. He kept on rapping.

As for me, I was evolving as a basketball player as well. Several summer basketball leagues were about to begin. I became obsessed with being on a team. Rick, my friend from The Boys Club, told me about a tryout for a particular team he'd heard about that might interest me. I went down to the location. After a grueling, competitive workout, I made the squad. It was a cause for a celebration! Shortly after that, the games began.

I arrived at the basketball league's Brooklyn location on the first day. I discovered, to my surprise, that this league was part of the City-Wide tournament. The same league I wanted to participate in the previous year. They handed me a gold-colored league t-shirt. The same t-shirt my former teammate "John-John," used to wear to practice at Walt Whitman. I felt (prematurely) like I had arrived. As a New York City basketball player, you were nobody unless you played in this tournament. I felt like I was in the big leagues. I wore my City-Wide t-shirt every day for the entire summer, including days when there were no games scheduled. I would wash my shirt by hand and put it on wet. It was my prized possession.

Now that The Boys Club was on a summer hiatus, Darrell's house became the next best thing. I would hang out there all day. Larry hung out there, too; he knew all my friends. Still, most of the time, he would be on his own. His attitude began to change. He was becoming more distant. We didn't talk as much as we used to. We started arguing about petty things that we never disagreed about before. We were heading in two opposite directions. I ate, slept, and breathed basketball, nothing else. Larry was more interested in visiting the public library to research philosophy and subjects of that nature. He expanded into studying Buddhism, Hare Krishna's, and all kinds of religions. Larry spent his nights writing rhymes and poetry. My mother wasn't thrilled with his lifestyle; they would argue. She would say, "You are not going to sit in my house and not work or go to school. You're going to do something around here!" I could see the tension building between them.

My mother confided in me that she met with a teen boot camp organization called 'Job Core.' Parents could enroll troubled teens into this organization, and they would take them up into the mountains of Upstate New York where they couldn't run away. While under the supervision of Job Core, teens would have a rigorous schedule of academics, discipline, and long days of hard labor. My mother felt like this was the best place for Larry and her only option at this point. It sounded like a nightmare, reminiscent of "The Bad Boy School." I didn't want Larry to go there, but I understood her perspective. I knew if Larry found out, he would run away for sure. Job Core told her all she had to do was sign the paperwork. While she was mulling it over, I contemplated giving Larry a heads up, but I wasn't sure. Maybe it was for his own good? Ultimately, she decided against it. I was relieved. I didn't want Larry held captive in a place like that, but we weren't even functioning as a family by this point. We were three people living in one place, doing their own thing, like roommates.

As the summer progressed, so did my play in the City-Wide tournament. Right on cue, a familiar problem arose. The sole of my right Converse sneaker, where the glue held the rubber together, ripped. The tear wasn't noticeable if I stood still. But, when I jumped, you could see the sole separate from the shoe and flap in the air. My mother claimed there was no money in her budget for new sneakers. She offered a solution. She said, "Instead of playing basketball all the time, why don't you get a job packing bags at the grocery store or something?" Great. I didn't want to pack bags. I wanted to play ball. I decided to play in the tournament anyway. I suited up, in front of dozens of spectators, with a tear on the side of my Converse All-Stars. I became determined to play, no matter what. My coach saw my sneakers' condition and said, "I can't have you playing like this," and found me a pair of Converses. My mother didn't say anything.

As the summer moved along, and I spent more time around Darrell, I made an interesting observation. Whenever we would hang out or play ball, for some reason, guys would always hassle me. They would try to degrade or intimidate me almost immediately upon my arrival. Darrell was only about 5'5" and yet no one ever bullied him. I couldn't understand it. What was the problem? I needed to sit down and analyze the situation. After revisiting countless scenarios in my head, all of a sudden, I had an epiphany! I realized the problem was something no one ever taught me. The difference between Darrell and l was that he would stand his ground early while I failed to do so. If someone approached Darrell, punched him in the arm, and said, "Hey Darrell, what's up?" He would immediately strike them right back. Even though they were joking around, he would set a boundary right there. On the other hand, if someone punched me in the arm, I would think nothing of it and laugh it off.

The following day that same person was now emboldened enough to slap me in the back of the head. I would say, "Yo! stop playing!" and leave it at that. On the third day, that same dude would be choking me, and I would be wondering, "How the hell did we get here?" We got there because three days earlier when this prankster punched me in the arm; I didn't put a stop to it right then and there. A situation will escalate if you let it fester and become an absolute problem in no time. I needed to step outside of myself and look at my behavior in the third person. I finally understood what was happening. It was like a revelation. At long last, I figured out what my problem had been my entire life.

I looked back at every problem I had with anyone. It always started as a little joke or some slick comment I let slide. I rewound my life to the fourth grade to revisit my fight with the bully Marcus. Why did Marcus offer me a peace treaty after his friends jumped me in the park that day? There was no doubt in my mind I lost the fight. The reality was completely different. The reason why Marcus decided he wanted to be friends was that I stood up for myself. His friends felt compelled to come over and help him because I was winning the fight. From their vantage point, I looked like the bully beating up on Marcus. Marcus realized the next time we fought; his friends might not be around. He could lose the rematch. Marcus didn't know I was more afraid of him after the beatdown from his friends than before the fight. For all he knew, I was ready to fight him again the next time we met. He chose to be my friend rather than losing to a superior opponent in a fair fight.

In reality, Marcus was the punk. But, like every other bully who tormented me, Marcus tested me early, and I failed. Had I stood up to Marcus on the very first day I met him, he would've backed down or known he was in for a fight. No one taught me this valuable lesson. I had to learn the hard way by getting bullied my entire life and finally observing Darrell's behavior.

I should have learned this most crucial lesson when I was five years old, and those tenement boys from across Lenox Terrace chased me home. John Parker should have taught me right then not to back down but stand my ground. Instead, he showed me that running away was an acceptable alternative, the best option. Big, tough, Rastafarian Joe should have taught me that sometimes in life, you have to stand up and fight. You have to defend yourself even though you know you might lose. It's better to go down fighting than stand there and get "Punked" day after day. Everything started to make more sense to me now. At the age of fifteen, a switch turned on in my brain. I wasn't taking anyone's crap NO MORE!!.

"God Works In Mysterious Ways" - William Cowper

Right around the time of my life-altering epiphany, I also had a significant growth spurt. To my surprise, I woke up one August morning and had grown three inches over the summer. I was now standing at a towering 6'5" tall. I didn't realize how much taller I was until I banged my head on the top of the subway entrance. Wow! I have to duck to enter the train? According to the statistics, I was now taller than 99.8% of all adult men in The United States Of America, and I was only fifteen years old! I even surpassed Larry in height, who was no slouch either at about 6'3". I was a freak of nature. Almost overnight, I had morphed into this giant 6'5" kid with an attitude. I began overcompensating for any perceived slight aimed in my direction. If anyone said anything that was the least bit disrespectful, my whole demeanor would change.

People weren't prepared for the new Kenny at all. For some reason, no one realizes how tall you are until you get angry. All of a sudden, it became, "Why are you acting like that? It's because you're so big." Well, that was only half true. But still, wasn't I this big a minute ago when you made your slick comment? Now that you realize I won't stand for your verbal abuse, I'm too big? Too bad. My attitude changed completely. If someone committed a routine foul on the basketball court, I was ready to fight. I became annoying, but I didn't care. Adopting Darrell's "no-nonsense" attitude changed everything. All the bullying I dealt with my entire life disappeared overnight.

I discovered that once you let the right couple of guys know you're not a pushover, everyone will see your attitude and fall in line. Granted, I was no bully or tough guy, and I still got along with almost everyone. I only chose to present myself in a more masculine way. I learned that the way you walked down the street in Brooklyn would set the tone for whether people would mess with you. I used to look scared and unsure of myself. I was always walking with my head down, trying not to make eye contact with anyone. Now, I walked with my head up, feeling like I'm bigger than everybody else; why am I afraid? I wasn't stupid, though. I knew who the hard rocks were in the area. I steered clear of them as best I could. Even when I was in their presence, I still stood with my head held high, not trying to show any fear, and it worked! Sometimes, the wannabe comedians would crack jokes about my appearance. Even then, I attempted to keep those jokes to a minimum. No longer would I be the source of endless entertainment for those idiots, either.

Many people describe the last couple of weeks in August as the "Dog Days of Summer." I have never understood this sentiment. I loved summertime. On one of those hot "Dog Days", I was walking down the street, and I heard a guy's voice from behind say, "Hey man, you got a quarter?" I've heard that question many times in the past. Usually, right before, I got robbed of whatever change was in my pocket. Things were different now. As I prepared to turn around, my only thought was, "Let me make sure this guy knows I'm not afraid." I turned around with a stern facial expression and looked. Uh oh!! It was Eugene! The same organized criminal terror from my junior high school years. I guess my new "anti-bullying" campaign was about to get tested.

For some reason, Eugene looked different now. He was by himself and didn't have the same menacing look. He had no real swagger at all. A glimpse of desperation was on his face. My blood began to boil. I was looking at this guy, remembering him trying to hit me with his bicycle outside of school. I remembered his homeboy punching me in the face. I recalled him hanging in front of the school, robbing all the students. Now, I'm towering over him. The 11-year-old Kenny was telling the 15-year-old Kenny to seek revenge. There was no doubt in my mind that I could destroy Eugene right now.

Despite all my vengeful thoughts, in reality, all I did was a pause and looked into his face. I could tell he was in bad shape. I didn't need to exact any revenge on Eugene. I could tell his future was bleak. Instead, I looked him right in his eyes and said, "Nah." He looked crushed. He was in desperate need of that quarter. He said, "Damn, alright, man" and walked away. I felt great. A small victory for me. Fuck Eugene!

As the summer winded down, so did the City-Wide tournament. Our team made the playoffs and matched up against another quality team. Their big man was the same height as I was. People lined up all around the court to watch the game. I ended up dominating the other center, and scored 19 points. We lost the game, but everyone was patting me on the back, saying, "Yo, you can play man."

Back around my way, Mr. Screen announced tryouts for a Flatbush team to play against another team from Crown Heights. The year before, I couldn't try out because of being stabbed with a bottle. Now, I didn't have to try out; he asked me to be on the team. We beat the team from Crown Heights. I was the game's high scorer with 21 points and earned MVP honors. My basketball game improved by practicing every day and growing to 6'5". I felt like a real ballplayer. I felt like I belonged. I also received another tournament t-shirt. Yes!

CHAPTER 7
RICE & BUTTER

"*Music is the great uniter. An incredible force. Something that people who differ on everything and anything else could have in common.*" - Sarah Dessen

One day, towards the end of August, Larry and I discovered an advertisement for a giant block party a couple of blocks away from our apartment. They held this massive, free event at an outdoor field next to an elementary school. The party was to begin right around dusk to avoid the hot summer sun. By the time Larry and I arrived at the field, over a thousand people were already in attendance. As it turned out, there was a live DJ crew providing the music. They had a stack of speakers on each side of the turntables, a microphone, and stage lighting so everyone could see the deejays and their colorful banner. They called themselves, 'The Soundmasters Crew.'

Where we lived didn't offer many opportunities to see live deejays. It was a regular occurrence in The Bronx, but in Brooklyn, not so much. The most famous Hip-Hop DJ of the era was the future Rock & Roll Hall Of Fame inductee Grandmaster Flash. The problem with Flash was if you didn't live in The Bronx, you wouldn't get to see him spin. Most people didn't know what Flash looked like much less ever saw him or any other DJ spin before. For us to be at a party with a real live DJ was awesome. These deejays were throwing on all the latest R&B and Hip-Hop jams plus "cutting up" some classic breaks as well. The song that stole the show was 'Before I Let Go' by Maze featuring Frankie Beverly. People were singing and dancing and having a great time until the police came and shut the party down. These guys didn't have a proper permit. It was still a fantastic Hip-Hop event. Even getting shut down by the police was so Hip-Hop.

The fall of 1981 arrived. So did the start of my sophomore year at Abraham Lincoln High School. As usual, I had no new school clothes. On a brighter note, Lincoln announced basketball tryouts, but this year was different. I was now the tallest student in the entire school, and the coach was already familiar with me. I was a 6'5" sophomore, my chances of making the squad were pretty high. Still, making the varsity basketball team as a sophomore was an accomplishment. I met the coach; his name was Bob Hartstein. He was a White, Jewish man, around 30 years old.

Our basketball team was excellent, featuring two outstanding seniors. One was Don Marbury. He was from Coney Island and is the older brother of future NBA all-star Stephon Marbury. He possessed a sweet jump shot and phenomenal leaping ability. Now, I don't know if it was because I was from "Crosstown," but Don Marbury never spoke to me. We shared gym class and were teammates on the same basketball team. But, in one year, if I combined all the words Don Marbury ever said to me, they still wouldn't equal one complete sentence.

The other exceptional basketball player was a PSAL All-City performer named Ham. He was 6'3", from my neighborhood, and was like a rock star in high school. Coach Hartstein asked him to take me under his wing and mentor me. Those practices were hard. The seniors were much more physical and advanced than I was. Ham would yell at me, "GO UP STRONG! WE DON'T PLAY WEAK AROUND HERE! YOU FROM BROOKLYN! GO UP STRONG!" I had a lot to learn.

After the first month of practice, the most circulated newspaper in NYC, The New York Daily News (whom I once delivered for) published a preview of the upcoming 1981-82 PSAL High School basketball season.

They reviewed the best teams in Brooklyn. When they arrived at Abraham Lincoln High School, they wrote about Don Marbury, Ham, and a new star sophomore player named "Silk." Further down the article, it read, "One of the key reserves will be sophomore Kenny Parker." What? Did I get a mention in the newspaper? To put that into perspective, in 1981, getting mentioned in the paper for any reason was a significant accomplishment. There was no internet or social media. You had to either do something extraordinary, commit a crime or die to make it into the newspaper.

I was ecstatic. I ran home and showed my mother. She seemed excited for me. I figured now would be the best chance I would ever have to ask her for some new sneakers. Out of nowhere, she says, "Ok. here's $40." Wow! Is she serious? I ran to the store and bought my first pair of leather basketball sneakers. They were Converse "Dr. J" sneakers. Things were looking good. The following day, she came to me and said, "Ya know Kenny, I want you to know, I'm not coming to any of your games. I don't like basketball." Huh? Knowing her personality, I was a little surprised, but then again, I wasn't. Most parents would be supportive of their children finding something positive that they were passionate about pursuing. It would give them something to strive for in life. Not my mother, she was faithful to her word. She never came.

The basketball season began with me playing in a reserve role. I was receiving about 10 minutes per game. Our team was so good that earning any playing time was hard. Derek, the same guy from my freshman gym class who convinced me not to try out because I wasn't good enough, was still on the team. He was still sitting at the end of the bench. I was now ahead of him in the rotation. I should have told him, "I guess I'm better than you now," but I didn't.

Early in the season, a few starters, including Don Marbury, got suspended for violating a team rule. Coach Hartstein said, "Kenny, you're going to start today against Canarsie High School." What? Start? In a real high school varsity basketball game? When the other team arrived, a gigantic 6'9" guy walked through the gymnasium door...Oh, Lord! He happened to be John Salley, a future NBA player, and four-time World Champion. A teammate said, "Oh, he's hurt, he's not playing today"...YES! I ended up playing the entire game, scoring 13 points, and we won. I was floating on a cloud.

If you've been following this story closely, you can almost anticipate when the "other shoe" was about to drop. Murphy's Law was always present in our lives, like an invisible family member. After the first six games of the season, the report cards arrived. For the first time in my entire life, my grades were terrible! My mother saw my report card and freaked out, "What the hell is this? I know what it is. It's because you're on that damn basketball team. You're quitting the team." It was almost like she couldn't wait to blame something on basketball. This news was devastating. I had to go and tell Coach Hartstein I was quitting the team. He completely understood. He always stressed education first.

Despite my poor academic showing, I was still eligible to play under the rules of the PSAL. By my mother's standards, I wasn't. In some ways, I could understand her decision. I was an excellent student up until that point, and then my grades dropped. It must have been the basketball team. Well, not exactly. During my Freshman year, I spent more time at The Boys Club than I did practicing with my school team, and still managed to maintain my good grades. The problem was getting to school on time. My new sophomore schedule had classes starting at 8:30 am instead of 10:45 am. We also moved, which added an extra 15 minutes to my commute.

I failed my first and second-period classes for excessive lateness. The grade for "excessive lateness" or "excessive absence" was an automatic 41. A passing grade was 65. For the rest of my classes, I passed but with C's. Now THAT was my fault. I started slacking off. Who knows why? What I needed was a swift kick in the butt to "re-motivate" me. Still, I felt my punishment was severe. Basketball was all I had. After that, I didn't care anymore. I had nothing to look forward to in life. I couldn't talk to Larry; he was in his own metaphysical, Rap world. He checked out long ago. Everything for me was a blur now too. I had nothing.

Christmas of 1981 arrives with an unexpected announcement from my mother. She declared that, "I'm not getting you guys anything for Christmas this year, you know why? Because y'all didn't get me anything for Mother's Day. You two have not been good sons to me." Huh? What was she talking about now? I thought we didn't exchange gifts in our household. We hadn't enjoyed a proper Christmas since 1972. It was now 1981! We received $5 once about three years ago. That was it. We never had a Christmas tree in all that time. We never once celebrated any holiday whatsoever. We never ate a Thanksgiving dinner. We never did anything for Easter Sunday or Labor Day or Memorial Day or Halloween, nothing. We never even celebrated our birthdays. We would say "happy birthday" to each other in passing, and that's it. We NEVER received or exchanged any gifts amongst each other over the past nine years. Holidays meant nothing to us. Mother's Day? The fact that she brought it up was the only reason why it crossed my mind. I put my head down and went to my room. I couldn't care less to be honest.

"What is useless to one person is valuable to another"

One day I was walking home from school and spotted an old vintage radio sticking out of a garbage can. I picked it up and examined it. Despite looking about ten years old, it appeared to be functional. There was only one problem; a dead roach sat inside the window where the dial was. After some deliberation, I decided to take the radio home anyway to see if it worked. Now, I know what you're thinking. But, there was a legitimate reason why I decided to take this "roach radio" home. Ever since those burglars stole our record player, we didn't have any music. My mother appeared to have no intention of replacing the stereo set. She used to buy music all the time, but now she didn't even buy music anymore. Don't judge me; I was desperate for some sounds. Anyway, when I finally plugged in my disgusting discovery, it worked! Now I had access to AM and FM radio. I needed some sort of escape. Music came to my rescue. I kept that radio on 24/7.

Right at the top of 1982, my mother walks through the door with a new, brown cat. Her co-worker gave it to her. She named the cat "Infinite." I have no idea why she called the cat Infinite but, there he was. Now we owned two cats, which meant another added chore, beautiful! Of course, Pepper wasn't thrilled with Infinite, either. They immediately began fighting. Pepper was bigger and stronger and would attack Infinite with ferocity. My mother would get upset and start screaming, "I can't believe Pepper is doing this! Y'all need to keep that cat away from my new cat!" Huh? How did you think Pepper was going to react? Cats are territorial; even I knew that. We tried to build a makeshift barrier to keep them separated, but that didn't work either.

One day, Pepper jumped over the barrier and attacked Infinite, scratching him pretty bad. We had to break them up. By the way, trying to break up a catfight is difficult without proper gloves. Anyway, my mother was furious. She declared that Pepper needed to go. She was screaming at Larry, "Get that damn cat out of here!!" Larry loved Pepper. He used to hand wash

Pepper in the tub. Three years earlier, when we voted on the cat, I voted no. My feelings changed, and I grew to love Pepper too. He was a part of our family. None of that mattered. My mother wanted him out, so Larry picked up Pepper and went outside. It was January, in the dead of winter. Taking domesticated Pepper outside in that kind of weather could be a death sentence. My mother didn't care at all.

Larry returned home about twenty minutes later without Pepper. He looked upset. Larry rarely got upset about anything. I asked him, "What did you do with Pepper?" Larry said he took Pepper over near the Franklin Avenue Shuttle subway overpass. That area was disgusting. Junk and debris were everywhere. It was a place where bums would go to take a piss. Larry told me that he carried Pepper far enough away where he knew Pepper couldn't find his way back home. He put him down on the ground and left. That was a horrible ending for Pepper. We were both sad. Afterward, we never mentioned Pepper again. It was like he never existed.

I drifted through the winter of 1982, numb to my surroundings. Our household had been quiet for a couple of months. I considered any period of non-events to be one of those good streaks. However, one Saturday evening, March 13th, to be exact, all three of us were home. We were in different parts of the apartment doing our own thing, as usual. Larry and I were waiting for my mother to cook dinner so we could eat. She made a small pot of white rice and went upstairs to talk to her friend Dee. My mother said she would make something else to go with the rice when she came back downstairs. My mother had been gone for quite a while as both Larry and myself were sitting there starving. Larry says, "Yo, I'm gonna take me some rice while we wait." He takes a little rice, puts it on a plate with some butter, and begins eating.

I was apprehensive at first because she told us, "I'll be right back." That meant, waiting for her to return. Meanwhile, I was hungry. After Larry was bold enough to help himself to some rice, I decided to follow his lead. I took some rice as well. We both finished our rice meal but were still hungry. Larry decided to take a little more rice, so I took a bit more rice too.

After our rice & butter meal, I went back to my room and began listening to Marv Albert broadcast a New York Knicks game on my radio. After what seemed like an hour, my mother finally returned home. The Knick game was already at halftime, so it was approximately 8:15 - 8:30 pm. She goes into the kitchen, opens up the pot, and begins screaming, "Y'all ate all the rice! Y'all are so selfish! I'm sick and tired of this! GET OUT!!" She starts screaming at the top of her lungs, "GET OUT, GET OUT!!"

We've seen her get upset over food before. On occasion, my mother would buy a single quart of orange juice and put it in the refrigerator. She would expect the container to be full, three or four days later. If it weren't, she would start yelling. This time was different; she was beside herself with rage. She wanted us out of the apartment immediately. I grabbed my coat and met Larry at the door. We walked into the hallway, and she slammed the door behind us. It all happened so fast, in less than two minutes. The National Weather Service says the temperature was 35 degrees that night. Larry and I owned matching coats. The zipper on Larry's coat ripped so he couldn't fasten it. He used to cross his arms to keep his coat closed. That was it. We had no gloves, no hats, no boots, no keys, and NO MONEY.

I was fifteen years old, and Larry was sixteen, and we were both out on the street. At first, we wandered around Brooklyn, trying to make sense of it all. Larry was super calm, but I was freaking out, "I can't believe she did this! Over a pot of white rice? What are we gonna do?" Larry said, "Yo, we're gonna sleep on the train tonight. We gotta get to Manhattan because we are gonna sleep on the E train tonight." I asked him, "Why the E train?" He said, "The E train is the only train in the New York City subway system that travels underground the entire time. It doesn't go outside. The ride is short, only two hours, but it's warm. You can get two hours of sleep before they tell you to get off at the last stop." Wait, how does he know that? I asked Larry, "How are we gonna get to Manhattan?" He said, "Well, we gotta sneak on the train, if the police are there then we gotta walk over The Brooklyn Bridge." I asked, "You can walk over The Brooklyn Bridge?" I didn't know that was possible. I then asked, "How do you know that? You've walked over The Brooklyn Bridge before?" Larry said, "Yeah, a bunch of times." I wondered, "What the hell does Larry be doing out here when he's by himself?"

Luckily for us, there were no police at the subway station, so we jumped the turnstile. We rode to The World Trade Center station and boarded the E train. I sat there for a minute in disbelief. I had only been on the subway as a passenger, but now I was going to have to sleep here? It was no easy task. First, trying to sleep on a hard bench-style seat, while leaning your body to one side is very difficult. You can never get comfortable. Second, the light is always on in the train car. Trying to sleep with that super bright light is not easy. Then, there is the noise. You can deal with the sound of the train moving. Even the stopping and starting of the train as it enters and exits a station is doable. It's the sound of the alert that goes off every time the train door closes that's most annoying when you're trying to sleep. Every few minutes, "Ding Dong!" Each time the door closes at a different station, "Ding Dong!" It is hard to get used to it.

Sometimes the conductor would make an announcement. Even worse, The conductor might announce each stop. That's guaranteed to keep you awake. Then, there are other passengers getting on the train who might want to sit next to you. You have to either be mindful not to lean on them or get up and find another spot. That's easier said than done because late at night, there were other homeless people on the train. You didn't want to get too close to one of them. Sometimes by the time you've found the right spot and got ready to doze off, you've reached the end of the ride. You would have to get off and wait to catch the train traveling in the other direction. The process would start all over again. We only got a little bit of sleep, in two-hour intervals, on the E train for the entire night.

I woke up starving. All we had to eat was that rice from the previous night. It was morning, so we decided we would return home, apologize to our mother, and hope she takes us back. We arrived at 7 am and knocked on the door. She opens the door, and we greet her with, "We're sorry, Ma, we didn't mean to eat the rice." She yelled, "Get away from the door and get out of here!" We turned and left. What are we going to do now? It was Sunday, so there was no school that day. Larry said, "Let's go to the library at Grand Army Plaza. We can chill there for a while and read some books too." That sounded like a good idea. As soon as we got there, I opened up a book and fell right asleep. I was so tired. The library workers would walk by and see us, but they didn't say anything.

We slept there for a few hours and then walked around some more to pass the time. It was now around 7 pm. We planned to intercept my mother before she went to bed and again beg her to take us back. We knocked on the door and pleaded, "Can we please come back?".... "NO, GET AWAY FROM THE DOOR!" That meant another night outside with no food. We slept on the E train another night. The next day we hung out at the library once again, starving! We returned to the house on the second night. Once again, we plead, "We're sorry, can you please take us back….. "NO!" (slams door). We sleep on the train yet again.

The 4th night was a Tuesday night. We hadn't eaten in three days, and I hadn't been to school in two days. I was cold, hungry, and exhausted. We knocked on the door once again. My mother opens up the door and says, "Here, take this." She hands us a bowl of spaghetti wrapped in aluminum foil. It was enough to feed two people. She then gave us $2 and said, "Take this and don't come around here anymore." She closes the door, and that was it. Larry and I agreed that I would eat the spaghetti, and he would take the $2 and get something to eat from the store. We went back to the E train and spent our 4th night sleeping on the train.

The next day, we were sitting in the library, and Larry began talking to me. He says, "You know...there's this place I heard about called Covenant House. It's for teenage runaways. We should go there." I became angry. I said, "Fuck Covenant House! I'm not a teenage runaway. I don't want to be out here. I wanna go home." Larry was looking at me and said, "Yo, we gotta start preparing to be out here now." I said, "I'm not preparing to be out here; I'm going home!" We got into a little argument over his suggestion. This runaway life was his world, not mine. I wasn't trying to hear any of that Covenant House nonsense. I told him I was going back tonight to beg once more, we are not giving up!

It was now Wednesday night, our fifth straight night out on the street. We went back home again and begged, "Can we please come back in, Please!!" My mother says, "You know, I was thinking about letting you guys in, but this girl keeps calling here for Larry, and she won't stop. Why won't you make her stop calling here?" It was the same obsessive girl from the year before who ran away with Larry. His tone changes. Larry says, "How am I gonna make her stop calling here? I'm not even in the house to answer the phone. You're so stupid!" I couldn't believe my ears. Larry stunned me with that response. I looked at him like, "What the Hell are you doing?" She finally showed a small sign of giving in, and he calls her stupid? My heart was racing. I looked right at him with a facial expression like, "I don't even know you."

Before I had a chance to say anything rational, Larry adds, "As a matter of fact, I don't wanna come back. I have a bag in there with my writings and poetry. Give me my bag, and I'm outta here!" My mother responded with, "Fine!" She went and got his bag, handed it to him, and slammed the door! The noise echoed through the hallway. It was over for us.

We left, and I was furious with Larry. He didn't care about anything. I now realized Larry kept coming back only because of me. He didn't want to return home at all. He yearned for the street life. For the 4th time in his life, Larry had run away. Now that I experienced a taste of the streets, I couldn't understand him. As bad as our mother was treating us at home, how could he choose this life? Larry's attitude appeared to be that the E train was better than dealing with her. The subway was better than our home. Larry had changed. He was always rebellious, but he never talked to my mother like that, ever. I spent the entire night mad at him but also dejected. By the time Thursday, our 6th straight night on the street arrived, I was desperate. I was so dirty I could feel the dirt in my hair. If I squeezed my scalp, it would stick together for a second before the skin would separate. I smelled horrible. I had only eaten one time in 5 days, and I hadn't been to school all week. School was the last thing on my mind by this point.

I decided to do the only thing I knew how to do; go back home and beg my mother once again and hope she changes her mind. This time I was going by myself. I didn't have any choice. Larry was NOT coming with me. I knocked on the door, and my mother opened it. I said, "Can you please let me back in?" She said, "You know Kenny, I talked with Dee upstairs, and she was telling me how much she didn't like Larry." As it turned out, Larry called Dee stupid once before. I never knew this. My mother then told me Dee was trying to convince her that Larry and I were two different types of people. Larry was ready for the streets, but I wasn't. She said, "You know, after talking to Dee, I've decided to let you back in the house." THANK GOD!!!

My heart was beating so fast, and I felt this overwhelming feeling of relief. I walked right into the house. There was a little leftover food in the refrigerator, so I ate it and took a long shower. I was so dirty. Dirtier than I ever been in my entire life. After the shower, I got into my warm bed and slept all night and the following day, which was Friday.

As the weekend arrived, the whole experience finally began to sink in. The events of the past week rattled me. I had already been through so many unimaginable things in my life, but this was the most devastating. For that entire week, I had no idea what was going to happen next. It was frightening. Then, there was Larry; although I was still angry with him, I didn't want Larry living out there on the street like that. In the past, I didn't understand what homeless life was like, but now I knew first hand. It was worse than I could've imagined. I became depressed. I was happy to be back home, but it was bitter/sweet. I wished I could have given Larry some help, but I couldn't. I would have tried to sneak him some food, but there was hardly anything to eat at home. I wanted to give him some clothes, but I didn't have any clothes myself. There was nothing I could do for him. I now realized what little possessions Larry and I had. Larry took everything he owned with him in a small bag. I felt the only difference between living outside and living at home was a bed and some walls. My mother and I never talked about what happened afterward. We never talked about how I was feeling, and we NEVER mentioned Larry. It was like he never existed. My depression deepened. Was I suffering from some sort of post-traumatic stress disorder?

Monday morning arrived, and it was time to return to school. I felt like, "Man, I'm not feeling school today; I'll go tomorrow." Tomorrow turned into the entire week. My mother would wake me up for school in the morning and then leave to go to work. I would pretend like I was getting up and then lay right back down after she left. I would sit around the house all day watching television and listening to the radio. I could hear songs that will transport me back to those difficult times even to this day. Songs like 'I Specialize In Love' by Sharon Brown, 'Murphy's Law' by Cheri, or 'Inside Out' by Odyssey.

Two weeks turned into three weeks that I hadn't gone back to school. I would go to The Boys Club at 3 pm and then return home by 10 pm. That became my daily routine. Although my mother agreed to let me back into the house, our relationship hadn't improved. There was one baffling aspect I could never understand. All she ever did was complain about how difficult it was to raise children. Now that it was only the two of us, my life didn't improve at all. She still didn't buy any new clothes for me to wear. I found myself hungry most of the time. She bought less food now than she had before. Her fits of rage were still present as well. Not at first, but she began to revert to her old yelling self once again.

A month turned into six weeks since I attended school. I had no desire to do anything. I still hadn't gotten over my removal from the basketball team a few months earlier. The last time I was present in school, the other students were laughing at me. I tried to respond as best I could, but what could I say? What they were saying was true. My clothes looked tattered and torn. My sneakers smelled terrible. At night, I would have to leave them outside on the window ledge because Dee began complaining about the stench traveling upstairs. I felt like no one in school was going to miss me anyway. No one would even notice I was gone. Who cares? Two months passed, and I still hadn't returned to school. I had enough. I quit. I went from being a lifelong honor roll student to a high school dropout in six months. My life was going down the toilet. If ever something good was going to happen, now would be a great time.

Enter Coach Hartstein. The high school basketball season ended in March. In May, he began monitoring the academic performance of the players who could be returning the following season. While investigating my grades, he learned of my extended absence. He immediately contacted my mother. He said, "Are you aware that Kenny hasn't been to school in two months?" Coach Hartstein had never called my house or spoken to my mother at any time before. When I returned home from The Boys Club at 10 pm, my mother called me over and asked in a calm manner, "How was school today?" I said, "Fine." She said, "Oh really? Your basketball coach called here and said you haven't been to school in two months." Damn! I got busted. She continued with, "You know Kenny, if you don't want to go to school that's on you. I'm going to get my education, and no matter what happens, when you turn eighteen, you're getting out of here."

That's all she said. Her same old "when you turn eighteen" speech, but in a calmer manner. She surprised me with her lack of reaction. Usually, she would go ballistic if I left a mustard stain on the kitchen cabinet, but now she wasn't yelling at all? Why not? Could it be that she didn't want to make a big deal about it? Then she would have to discuss the origin of my delinquency? Would she take responsibility for her role in my current situation? Perhaps she didn't want The Board Of Education to know I was sleeping on the E train for a week out of those two months. My mother didn't tell Coach Hartstein the whole story. She left out the part about how she threw two minors out on the street during the wintertime, and one of them remained at large.

There was no other reason I could think of to explain why she wasn't making a big deal out of this. She didn't care about what could have happened to us out there on the street. The one thing she did care about was her image. No one else knew what was going on in our home except Dee, who felt Larry should've been out there anyway. Coach Hartstein left a message for me through my mother. He said I must return to school the next day and come to his office afterward.

I went back to school, embarrassed, and still looking as awful as I did two months earlier. To my utter surprise, everyone I saw was saying the same thing, "Yo, where you been? We thought you moved away." Their comments shocked me. I didn't think anyone would notice I was gone. I didn't realize I had that many friends in school. I got the impression they generally liked me despite their non-stop ridiculing of my clothes and appearance. Who knew?

Coach Hartstein didn't wait until the end of the day to find me. He hunted me down during lunchtime and began his interrogation, "What's wrong with you? What were you thinking?" I had no answers. I didn't understand myself. I answered him with, "I don't know, Coach." I guess he chalked it up to either immaturity or plain stupidity. I didn't tell him what really happened. We moved on.

Coach Hartstein told me he had spoken to some of my teachers. A couple of them would allow me to take some make-up exams, but the semester was all but over. I was going to fail most of my classes (grade 41) for excessive absences. That sucked, but there was a silver lining. Coach Hartstein spoke to my guidance counselor. Thanks to my good marks during my freshman year, my cumulative two-year grade point average would allow me to play basketball next season. Great news! When I returned to my classes for the first time, some of the students were looking at me, confused. It felt like I had come home from prison or something. Still, I felt relieved to be back in school. I knew in my heart that dropping out wasn't the answer. I needed something to give me hope because I had lost my way. I needed something to show me that I shouldn't give up on my life. That something came in the unexpected form of Coach Hartstein. Sometimes a person will never know how much they affected someone else's life by showing that they cared.

My sophomore year of high school ends, and I start hanging around Darrell's house once again. Larry resurfaces out of the blue. It had been three months since I'd seen him. When Larry first showed up at Darrell's house, I didn't need to wonder. He was so dirty that I already knew what was going on in his life. We talked, and he said, "Yo, what's up, you made it back in the house, right?" He didn't even know for sure. I guess he assumed that was the case when he didn't see me anymore.

One thing I observed about Darrell was; despite his daily smart-ass remarks, he never said anything disrespectful about our appearance. No matter how we showed up, he and his family always accepted us into their home. No questions asked. Even this time, when it was clear by Larry's appearance that something was wrong. Everyone could tell Larry was homeless. He was wearing some dingy pants and ragged sneakers. You could see his ankles, and there was a layer of dirt covering them. It looked like he was wearing black socks, but it was his skin. Regardless of his circumstances, Larry was in good spirits. He told me he was staying at a church. They would allow him to stay there in return for him cleaning up and doing odd jobs. I knew that wasn't true. Judging by his appearance, no church in America would allow a person to live there in that condition. Darrell's older cousin Gerard took Larry over to the side. After a short, private conversation, they both left together. When they returned, Larry was wearing a brand new pair of sneakers. Gerard saw the condition Larry was in and took matters into his own hands. It was an incredible gesture from a man who didn't have to do that for my brother. It was heartwarming.

Meanwhile, back at home, my mother hit me with a new ultimatum. She said, "I've decided that since you refuse to get a job, I'm not buying any more food for you around here. I'll provide you with dinner, but THAT'S IT!!" She didn't buy much food anyway, but now she made it official. I guess she chose dinner because that's the time when she cooked food for herself. I couldn't help but compare my life to the other teenagers that I knew. None of my friends or classmates had jobs. No one mentioned looking for a job, and yet they had everything. I had nothing, and now I wouldn't have breakfast or lunch either. Why was I put under all this pressure to support myself at age fifteen? Even the cat ate more than I did. I couldn't understand why my life was so hard. What did I do to deserve this?

Despite the difficulties at home, I still found time to make a lot of new friends. One of my friends, "Money Mike," used to play ball with us every day in Walt Whitman Park. As it turned out, he was also a DJ who owned real DJ equipment. Of course, all my friends knew my brother Larry was a rapper. Somehow, Mike invited Larry, homeless and all, to come down to his basement and make a tape. Larry went by himself to Mike's house and recorded some vocals. Larry wasn't around when Mike played me the tape they made. This new recording was about eight or nine months after the "Dog Whisperer" tape Larry made at Neville's house. This new tape featured Larry rapping on a microphone and Money Mike deejaying on turntables. Mike "cut-up" the classic funk song 'Sing Sing' by the group Gaz.

It was a DJ staple.

I was now hearing a clear copy of Larry Gee rapping over 'Sing Sing,' and he sounded way better. I don't know if he was actually better or the quality of the recording was better. Larry may have already been the greatest rapper in the world when he was recording with Neville. Once I heard the dog on the tape acting as his "hype man," I wouldn't give it a chance. Now I hear Larry with a real DJ, and he sounded pretty good. For the first time, in my eyes, Larry seemed like a serious rapper. He might have real potential.

During the middle of June, Larry once again disappears for about a week. I didn't get a chance to talk to him about Money Mike's tape. I was home one late afternoon and the phone rang. My mother answers the phone, and it's the police! They say, "Hello, is your name___? Do you have a son named Lawrence Parker? "Yes," she replies. The police officer says, "We have your son here at the precinct. Someone spotted him leaving the scene of a burglary." It appeared that Larry was in the vicinity of Kings County Hospital near Wingate Park, and an alarm went off. When the police arrived, they saw him running by and arrested him. Larry was like, "I didn't do anything, I jog around here sometimes, trying to keep myself together." I believed him 100%. Larry was not a thief. He never stole anything in his life, not even when we were out on the streets together, starving. The police said, "We brought him here to the precinct, and he's acting very wild and belligerent." My mother said you could hear Larry in the background cursing at the police, "GET THE FUCK OUTTA HERE! I DIDN'T DO SHIT! FUCK Y'ALL!!!" The officer said in an aggravated tone, "Ma'am, how your son is acting right now, we wanna fuck him up. But, because he's a minor, we decided to call you first. If you don't come and get him right now, we're going to fuck him up!" The officer then said, "He wouldn't give us your name or anything until we threatened to lock his ass up. He then gave us your number."

So that was the situation. My mother needed to get Larry immediately. She agreed, and we both walked over to the precinct. I waited outside until they both exited the station. Larry looked as filthy and homeless as ever. My mother hadn't seen him since he called her stupid when we were in front of the door, begging to come back home. That was three months ago. We began walking home, and you could already feel the tension between the two of them. I was silent.

When we reached a few blocks away from the precinct, my mother starts going right after him. She said, "So what are you doing with yourself?" Larry says, "I work at a church, and they give me a little money to clean up the place, and I sleep in the basement." My mother says, "How much do they pay you?" Larry said something like $100 a week. My mother says, "Ok, you're going to pay me $200 a month for rent 'cause you're not gonna stay in my house for free. You're not going to school; you're not doing nothing!" Her voice is getting louder as we're walking home. I'm looking at her like, "Well, damn, you're already starting with your attitude." I'm looking at Larry's face, and he's getting mad. He says, "I didn't wanna come home anyway." My mother says, "If you don't wanna come home, then you can go!!" Larry says, "I can't go 'cause the police said if I run away again, they're gonna lock me up this time." My mother says, "You really wanna leave? Then leave now! I won't call the police!" Without saying another word, Larry turned left and began walking in the other direction. I watched him walk off into the distance, and he never looked back. Larry was gone again.

For the 5th time in his life, Larry had run away. He didn't even make it back home this time. Now I'm standing there like "Holy shit!! This dude is freakin' nuts, man!" I didn't have the guts to say or do something like that. We started walking home. Now, my mother starts crying, "Ohh, I can't believe he did that, I can't believe it" in a sobbing voice. I tried to comfort her. I said, "You can't make somebody stay in the house that doesn't wanna stay. He wants to be outside; there's nothing you can do. You have to forget him." She's crying, "But that's my son! That's my son!" Now I'm confused.

Larry has told you twice he doesn't want to be here. What does he have to do to make you believe him? She was still crying and sobbing. The craziest part to me was; I had never seen my mother cry before. I was more shocked by her response to his behavior than I was to Larry leaving again. I couldn't understand her. You made him go, so why are you crying? Neither one of them wanted to be around each other. I thought Larry was crazy, but I also thought my mother should have embraced her son and brought him home. She could have worried about the details later. I also felt like Larry should've pacified her by agreeing to whatever she said at the moment. That way, he could have come home and cleaned himself up. He was so stubborn; he wouldn't budge. After that, Larry disappeared. He all but vanished.

A few months prior, my mother had set a 10 pm curfew for me. During the winter months, that rule was easy to follow. I would be at The Boy's

Club until they closed at 9 pm. That gave me plenty of time to get home. The summertime was different. I didn't own a watch, so I never knew what time it was. All I knew was when it got dark; it was time to leave. Sometimes I took off right in the middle of a basketball game. I lived 45 minutes away, so I needed to leave by no later than 9:15 pm. Sometimes I would have to run home. One night I came back from a long exhausting day, stuck the key in the lock, and unlocked the door. When I turned the knob, BOOM!! The chain was on the door. Why was the chain on the door? My mother yelled from the other side, "I told you to be home by 10 o'clock. When I say 10 o'clock that means 10 o'clock!! You can go back to wherever you were that caused you not to be here on time!"

Ah man, what am I going to do now? I can't go back to Darrell's house. I was so tired that I had no choice but to sleep on the floor in the hallway. I laid there in and out of sleep from 10 pm until 7 am the next morning when she left for work. We didn't say anything when we passed each other. I entered the apartment and went to bed. I never received my one meal of the day either.

Getting locked out became a recurring theme. Anytime I returned home late, even at 10:03 pm, the chain would be on the door. Of course, I felt my mother's punishment for my lateness was excessive. It wasn't like she didn't know where I was. I was never more than a few minutes late. Sometimes, all she needed to do was look out of the window, and she would see me rushing down the block. It was another hardship added to my list of things I couldn't quite understand. Several nights that summer, I slept in the hallway. Dee from upstairs would see me lying in the hallway and say, "Damn, you were late again?" She would have to step over me to go upstairs. One night, Dee stopped and said, "You know Kenny, I don't like seeing you sleeping in the hallway like this. But, you are not my child so there's nothing I can say or do. I want you to know that I disagree with this." I told her "Thank you" and laid back down on the floor.

One night, I was running late. In a panic, I decided to take the subway home despite having no money. I arrived at the subway station, checked for the police, and then jumped the turnstile. The token booth clerk yelled on the intercom, "Pay your fare!" but I kept going. I didn't know the police were hiding in a backroom trying to catch people "Fare Beating," a substantial problem in New York City. The MTA was losing millions of dollars per year. The cops grabbed me, handcuffed me, and led me to a waiting city bus converted into a makeshift holding area. There were about thirty guys on that bus who the police busted for various crimes. I was scared. My mother had warned us, "If you ever get in trouble with the police, I'm not bailing you out. I'm not one of those parents who would sell everything they owned to get their kids out of jail. If you get locked up, YOU ARE ON YOUR OWN!" I knew she wasn't playing either. I was in a bad situation.

I heard one of the officers say they were taking us to 'Central Booking.' Ah, man!! The police took a young guy off the bus and around to the back of the bus. The next thing I knew, the police were beating him up. He was screaming, "Ahhhhh!!" He got back on the bus and sat down right next to me. He told his boys, "I didn't say nothing, I didn't say nothing!" I don't know what he did, but the police wanted a confession. Now I was terrified. Are they going to beat me up too? Shortly after, one of the officers approached me and said, "What's your name and how old are you?" I told him my name and said I was fifteen years old. He said, "Fifteen? Are you really fifteen?" I said, "Yeah." He shook his head and said, "Get off this fuckin' bus! You're not worth the paperwork!" THANK GOD! I jumped off that bus and hustled home. I was considerably late by this point. I turned the key slowly, and the front door opened. Yes! I guess my mother went to bed early. I dodged two bullets that night.

July of 1982 arrived. My sixteenth birthday came and went as usual. The most memorable event of the early summer was the release of a brand new Rap song. It was different than any rap song released before. At that time, Rap artists created songs to play at parties. They used backing music that was usually a remake of the latest R&B crowd pleaser. This new Rap song had a slow, funky mid-tempo beat that wasn't recognizable at all. The subject matter was unique, as well. They weren't bragging about money or girls. They weren't encouraging the audience to scream, and no one asked about your zodiac sign, either. Instead, they described the condition of the ghettos of New York City and the difficulties of growing up under such circumstances. The mood of the song was somber. The group behind the music were the hottest rappers to date, Grandmaster Flash and The Furious Five. They called the song, 'The Message.' This tune contained a haunting chorus that captured the entire experience of living in NYC.

'The Message,' elevated Rap music. It showed the world that Rap lyrics could represent something more than getting the party started or battling another emcee. This thought-provoking song, not meant for parties, became the biggest song on the radio and in the streets. When 'The Message' blew up, the first person I thought about was Larry. I knew he would've loved this song. Sadly, he was nowhere around.

One bright summer day, I completed all my chores and ventured out on my daily two-plus mile trek to Darrell's house. When I arrived, I rang the bell and waited for someone to respond; routine stuff. When the door opened, Darrell was standing at the door, laughing his ass off. He was trying to tell me something, but he was struggling to gather his composure. What could be so funny? He finally looked at me with a grin and said, "Your mother called. She said when you arrive, I should tell you to go back home and close the kitchen cabinet door. You left it open." He burst out laughing again. What? Is she serious? If this were happening to someone else, I would've been laughing too, but since it was happening to me, I was not amused.

Darrell knew it was a 45-minute walk between our two locations. Having to turn around and do it all over again in the sweltering summer heat was going to be brutal. My mother knew it too. She could've waited until I returned home in the evening to express her displeasure. Instead, she wanted to inflict maximum pain by making me walk back home and embarrass myself in front of my friends. My relationship with my mother was deteriorating at a rapid pace. I couldn't understand why. I turned around, walked back home, and closed the kitchen cabinet door that I left open by accident. I then turned around and walked back to Darrell's house for the second time.

After the kitchen cabinet incident, I was walking on thin ice. It was only a matter of time before I did something so "terrible" that we would reach the breaking point. It didn't take long for the inevitable to happen. I don't recall what the infraction was, but it had to be minor because I rarely did anything outside of my routine. Regardless, my mother was furious. She began screaming at the top of her lungs. Before I knew it, I heard a familiar phrase I thought I would never hear again, "GET OUT!!"

In the summer of 1982, my mother threw me out for the second time in four months. My worst nightmare came to pass once again. This time I was all alone. I did the only thing I knew how to do, find my way back to the E train. I slept on the subway that first day, with no food. I slept on the subway the following day, with no food. I didn't even bother to return home and beg this time. I sat there on the train in shock, contemplating my life. How did I get here again? What am I going to do with my life? Why me? Then it hit me, another epiphany, "You know what? Larry was right!" We should've gone to Covenant House the first time this happened.

My anger turned to sadness because I finally realized Larry was right, and I couldn't even tell him. As I sat there on the train feeling sorry for myself, I noticed a man sitting across from me. I wasn't paying him any attention, but I happen to look up at him, and he winked his eye at me, very slow and seductive. What the Hell? This creep was all I needed right now. What was I going to do? Was I going to have to fight this dude? I was angry but also confused, why is he winking at ME? Do I look gay to him? I was a young, baby-faced teenager on the train late at night by myself. I wasn't getting off at any stops, so I guess I must've looked vulnerable. He took his shot. I thought to myself, "I gotta get off this train, this guy looks crazy."

When the train pulled into the station, I stood up to get off the train. This weirdo stands up too. I turned right, and he turned left. Now, he's at one door, and I'm at the other door. The train doors opened, and we both exited the train. We were in Queens around 4 am at a deserted train station. Now I'm thinking, "Ok, I'm going to have to fight this man." I get off the train, and he gets off the train. We're both standing on the platform, looking at each other. I turned to walk towards an empty stairwell, and he turns too. He's mirroring my every move. Right when the train door was about to close and made the "Ding Dong" sound...I jumped back on the train in one motion. He tried to jump back on the train too, but the door closed in the nick of time. I was looking right at him as the train pulled off, and he says, "Fuck!" I'm standing there thinking, "This dude was gonna try to attack me."

That's when I really felt like, "What am I doing out here?" It was a real eye-opener on how dangerous it was for a sixteen-year-old to be roaming NYC alone at 4 am. Even at my size, anything could've happened. Anything still could've happened. How was I going to fall asleep after that? What if I ran into that pervert again? I stayed up all night, but I realized I needed to do something. I thought about going to Covenant House and trying to live the life of a teenage runaway, but I didn't have the courage. I wasn't like Larry.

After three days of no food, I decided to return home. My mother relented and allowed me back in. I have no idea why she changed her mind, but I had a whole new perspective this time. Before, I thought the main reason my mother kicked me out was that I got caught up in the mix with Larry. I thought things would never reach that level between my mother and me again now that he was gone. I even convinced myself that the nights she made me sleep in the hallway were my fault for disobeying her rules. This time, she kicked me out over an incident so petty that there had to be something else going on here. I couldn't figure it out, but I knew it was getting worse.

Once again, I had endured another awful twelve-month period of time. Because of my low grades, my mother forced me to quit the basketball team. Our beloved cat Pepper got tossed out like trash, in the dead of winter, to almost certain death. My mother kicked me out of the house, and I spent nearly a week homeless with no food. Larry returned home only to run away two more times (a total of 5), and now my brother had vanished. I missed two months of high school and eventually dropped out. I got kicked out of the house again and spent three more days homeless with no food. I narrowly escaped another encounter with a sexual predator. I slept in the hallway several nights, and my mother decided she was only feeding me once a day. Could things get any worse?

CHAPTER 8
BASELINE

After a summer filled with confusion, hunger, and homelessness, the fall of 1982 arrived. I was entering my junior year of high school. As usual, there wasn't much preparation required. My mother refused to buy any new school clothes. I had no choice but to recycle the same clothes I'd worn the previous semester, consisting of two pairs of pants and two shirts. My mother also decided that she was only required to do laundry once every two or three weeks because she had enough clothes to last her that long. I only had enough outfits for two or three days at the most. Therefore, the majority of the time, my clothes were dirty and smelled musty. I was already a teenage boy who didn't shower as often as I should have. Now, my clothes, which had always been dingy, were downright gross.

After the first week of school, I came to another humbling realization. I had no proper shirts to wear. The only shirts I owned were t-shirts given to me at basketball tournaments. I went to school every day wearing a tournament t-shirt with a number printed on the back. No one ever commented. But, if some smart-ass would've challenged me to show up to school without a number on my back, I couldn't have done it.

The only thing I could look forward to was the start of the new high school basketball season. Coach Hartstein sat me down right before our first practice. He said, "Look, Kenny, you have a great opportunity right now. Most of the top players from last year are gone. You have a chance to start as a junior. Even Don Marbury didn't start as a junior, and you see how good he was. You're going to have to work hard to earn it, though." That was the first piece of good news I'd heard in a long time. I had a pretty good preseason and indeed earned a starting position on the team. It was a great accomplishment for me. Despite everything, I still managed to improve my game over the summer.

The 1982-83 PSAL Basketball Season was now in full swing. After the first six games, our record was 4-2. We looked like a team that could make some noise in Brooklyn. Then, the unthinkable happened. Our best player, nicknamed "Silk," got shot at a party in Coney Island. This act of violence shocked the team. Everybody liked Silk. He had the perfect nickname because he was smooth and laid back both on and off the court. Who would want to shoot Silk? He wasn't the type of guy who would get into any altercations. It was another reminder of how dangerous Brooklyn was at any given time. Luckily, Silk's injury wasn't life-threatening, but he would have to miss the entire basketball season. That sucked. We all went as a team to visit him at Coney Island Hospital. Seeing him lying there was surreal. We had to take it all in stride. Life goes on, I guess.

Not long after the Silk shooting, Lincoln matched up against arch-rival Alexander Hamilton. The same high school that scared the hell out of me as a freshman because of Jerry "Ice" Reynolds. He was long gone, replaced by new guys with colorful nicknames like "Devil Dog" and their best player, "Bug Eye." This game was one of the biggest of the season, a complete sellout. To everyone's surprise, despite losing our best player, we beat Hamilton! I had an excellent game, 13 points and 11 rebounds, a double-double. Everyone was jumping up and down with excitement. As I exited the gym, who did I see? Ham! My friend and mentor from the previous year who used to yell at me to "GO UP STRONG"! He graduated but came back to watch this big game. Ham stopped when he sees me and gazed at me without saying a word. He had no facial expression at all. He was a tough customer. I looked down at my feet and confessed, "I know what you're gonna say, I was playing weak." Ham said, "Nah, I wasn't gonna say that" and smiled. That's all he said and walked off. I was ecstatic! Ham didn't even compliment me but for him not to say "I was weak" meant everything to me because I looked up to him so much. He was so hood and cool at the same time that all he could muster was a smile, which was good enough for me.

Not long after the big Alexander Hamilton game, Lincoln had an even bigger game on our schedule. The talk of NYC high school basketball was Dwayne "Pearl" Washington of Boys and Girls High School. He was the number one ranked high school basketball player in America. "The Pearl" was spectacular. His ball-handling skills were already legendary. He pioneered the modern-day crossover move used by every NBA player today. He was embarrassing defenders on the basketball court. Every single game he played in was standing room only. Boys and Girls were in our division, so we had to play them twice. I'd gone to see The Pearl play earlier in the season. I wanted to get a good look at this playground legend before we played against him. Pearl had recently signed a letter of intent to play for Syracuse University.

The first thing I noticed about him was his brand new pair of Nike 'Air Force Ones.' This revolutionary sneaker had an astronomical retail price of $80. That was double the cost of Adidas or Puma. It was rare to see anyone wearing Air Force Ones. I had only seen two colors before; white with a black swoosh and white with a blue swoosh. The Pearl was wearing white Air Force Ones with an orange swoosh and orange strap to match the Syracuse University colors. They were bananas! They weren't even available in stores. As for the game, he was electrifying and had the entire crowd chanting his name.

Now, it was Lincoln's turn to play against Boys & Girls High. Our gym was so crowded that the school hired extra security and police to deal with all the spectators. I felt confident going into the game because I had been playing well. I even scored the first 5 points of the game. Unfortunately, that's all the points I had for the entire game. We got crushed. Pearl Washington scored 45 points in a 32-minute high school basketball game. Keep in mind; there was no three-point line AND no shot clock! He was on a different level than everyone else. After the match, Coach Hartstein told us not to get discouraged. He said, "That guy will be in the NBA one day."

Two weeks later, we played them again at Boys & Girls High. Channel 7

ABC News was doing a feature on The Pearl. Television film crews set up along the sideline. Highlights of our game would air on the evening news. Coach Hartstein gave us a new scouting report on The Pearl based on our previous defeat. He stressed to us how Pearl Washington liked to dribble the ball along the baseline. We were going to try and force him in the other direction, allowing another teammate to help guard him.

Fast forward to the day of the rematch, and the game was underway. Pearl Washington gets a steal, and he's dribbling the ball along the baseline (of course). Unfortunately, I was the only defender left between him and the basket. Everyone in the gym was standing and watching. The Pearl was coming right at me. Everything seemed to be moving in slow motion. I was thinking, "Do not let him drive baseline!" I put my right foot on the baseline so he couldn't go that way. The Pearl dribbled right at me and noticed my foot on the baseline. He goes into his famous crossover move. I've seen his crossover before, so I anticipated his move. Right when he crossed the ball over, I jumped to the left and got right in front of him. I was confident I had beat him to the spot where he wanted to go. But, instead of crossing the ball over, he kept the ball in his left hand. He only faked like he was going to crossover. That move is what we now call an "inside out dribble." In 1982, no one, on any level, could do that fake crossover move like Pearl could. He brought the ball back with his left hand and went right around me along the dreaded baseline like I wasn't even there. It was a classic "Ankle Breaker." He blew past me so fast that he dared to slow down, look back at me and shake his head in disappointment as he laid the ball into the basket. Everyone was screaming in amazement at his funny theatrics. I was so embarrassed.

The Pearl's display of ball handling was so devastating that the nightly news chose to use that play as one of the featured highlights. Coach Hartstein called me at home around 8 p.m. and said, "Hey Kenny, guess what? You made the news for playing bad defense! Pearl Washington went right around you, and it was on Channel 7 news!" We both started laughing. My first time ever on television was as a victim of a Pearl Washington ankle breaker. At least I had my "15 minutes of fame," sort of...(R.I.P.) Dwayne "Pearl" Washington.

The high school basketball competition in New York City was among the best in the nation, and I held my own most of the time. I had come a long way since shooting at the wrong basket in 8th grade. Coach Hartstein began calling our house regularly. He would give my mother updates on my academic performance and general behavior, considering my two-month absence from school the previous semester. He would say things like, "Kenny's doing this or Kenny's doing that... Kenny cut class; I made him run 20 laps today." Coach Hartstein and my mother would talk quite often, not only about me but life in general. I found their new dynamic, both cool and odd at the same time. My mother didn't have many friends. The phone didn't ring that often.

Coach Hartstein had no idea what was going on in my household. My mother left out crucial details about our daily life. Regardless, I had a tremendous amount of admiration for Coach Hartstein. He was the only adult male in my entire life besides Darrell's cousin Gerard who ever showed that they cared about my well-being. Please make no mistake about it; Coach Hartstein was tough. He would often yell at me about basketball-related things, but I knew he was doing it to make me a better player and person. He wasn't like Joe, who would yell at me and beat me with no purpose. Coach Hartstein would talk "to me" not "at me." Joe would ask me unanswerable questions like, "Why are you so stupid?" Coach Hartstein would show me what I did wrong and help me correct it. He stressed the importance of education and how it was the only way to break the poverty cycle. He, along with the entire coaching staff, was terrific. I needed their guidance during that difficult period of my life.

CHAPTER 9
MEAL TICKET

The new year of 1983 arrived in a rather dramatic fashion. One winter evening I was relaxing in my room when my mother summoned me to the kitchen. I could tell by her aggravated tone that I once again had done something wrong. I think I failed to wash a dish. After her usual temper tantrum, she returned to her bedroom. I was standing over the kitchen sink washing dishes, annoyed with her attitude. My mother returned to add some more of her two cents. She began screaming once again, and finally, I couldn't take it anymore. I turned my body halfway in her direction and glanced at her with a slight frown. I voiced one word in defiance, ALRIGHT! She yelled, "What did you say to me?" and went berserk! My mother punched me right in my mouth, busting my lip wide open.

She began to throw a series of punches in my direction. Another punch landed on my face before I could block her barrage of blows with my arms. The entire time she was assaulting me, she was screaming at the top of her lungs, "Don't you ever talk back to me again! Who the hell do you think you are?" I finally broke free from her attack and ran into my room. She retreated to her room, still yelling as her voice faded into the distance. I sat down on my bed, my mouth filled with blood, and cried. My tears weren't from the pain of my busted lip but from the utter shock that my mother tried to fight me like I was some man in the street. It took me quite a while to regain my composure.

As I sat there on my bed, feeling the lowest I'd ever felt in my life, I had another epiphany. For the very first time, I finally realized two things. One was the hard, cold fact that my mother didn't love me. After replaying in my mind, all the cruel and unusual decisions she made over the past few years, I could only come to one conclusion. She hadn't loved me for quite some time now. Still, the second revelation was even more significant. I realized I didn't love her either. After our altercation in the kitchen, something inside of me changed. Up until that point, despite every questionable decision she made, I still loved my mother. Now, those feelings were gone. It was like a piece of my soul had flown away. My heart turned to stone.

After the kitchen incident, we didn't speak at all. I would only say "good morning" if I happened to see my mother in passing. I didn't even make eye contact with her anymore. The feeling appeared to be mutual. The only time she ever addressed me was to send me to the grocery store. That was it; our relationship was ice cold. Even our occasional mumbles became routine. Two weeks later, I was home relaxing, and I left my room to use the bathroom. As I exited my room, my mother was entering the apartment, accompanied by a man I'd never seen before. She introduced us, "Kenny, this is Gerard." I said, "Hello." He responded in a West Indian accent. It sounded like Haitian. After that, I went back to my room and closed the door. About a week later, my mother knocks on my room door and says, "Hey, you remember Gerard, right?" I said, yes. She said, "Well, he's downstairs in his car. I want you to go with him and help him with some boxes; he's moving in with us." I rode with this guy Gerard to some location to gather up his belongings. We returned to our apartment, and I helped carry his stuff upstairs. I went back into my room, closed the door, and that was that. Now there were three of us living in the apartment. I couldn't care less. I decided to have as little contact with Gerard as possible.

February arrived, with Gerard having lived there less than a month and me not speaking to either of them. One day, my mother intercepts me in the hallway. She declares out of the blue, "Gerard and I are thinking about moving to Florida in June, do you wanna come?" Huh? Florida? I paused for a second to absorb her announcement. She added, "The reason I asked you was because I wasn't sure if you wanted to come with us." No kidding, I didn't want any parts of Florida. I then thought about the alternative, which was me fending for myself alone in New York City. I realized I didn't have a choice. I agreed to move with them to Florida. Somewhere in the back of my mind, I felt like she would change her mind anyway, so I didn't think about it after that.

Meanwhile, Gerard's addition to our household still didn't encourage my mother to funnel any more money in my direction. My clothes were still dingy and smelly, and I was still hungry most of the time. My first meal of the day would be free lunch at school. Sometimes, after basketball practice, the guys would buy 50 cent buttered bagels from the nearby deli. I would be so envious. Sometimes I would ask for a piece, but they would get annoyed and yell, "Damn! Stop begging!"

One day, Coach Hartstein asked the players if we wanted to order new team jackets. They would have our names embroidered on them. Everyone said yes. Coach Hartstein said it would cost $20 per person, and the money was due by Friday. Of course, I wouldn't dare ask my mother for $20, so I figured I would do without one. When Friday arrived, every team member, including the managers, produced their $20 for the jackets. It was embarrassing to be the only one not to have the money. To my surprise, an honorary assistant coach named Tony (R.I.P.) donated $20 to the total cost. He wanted to make sure I wouldn't be the only one without a team jacket. It was a nice gesture. I wore that jacket with pride for the rest of the school year.

The basketball season ended in late February. I had a solid junior season, averaging about 10 points and seven rebounds per game. I set the school record for field goal percentage by shooting 62%, earning the team's "Most Improved Player" award. Not bad considering everything that was going on at home.

By March of 1983, things appeared to simmer down at home. What a perfect time for "the other shoe" to drop. I returned home one evening around 10 pm to find an envelope on the kitchen table addressed to me. That was odd. Inside was a typed letter from my mother. The letter stated that she and Gerard decided to move to Florida, but they chose not to invite me to go with them. She claimed I had been walking around the apartment for months without saying anything to her, and I never "warmed up" to Gerard either. It was apparent that I didn't want to go with them to Florida, so they were leaving me here in New York. She would help me as best she could, but in June she was leaving.

After reading the letter, I didn't know what to think. I became confused as to why my mother felt I should have "warmed up" to Gerard. I don't think I comprehended what the letter was saying. Right on cue, as I finished reading the letter, my mother and Gerard walked into the kitchen. She looked at me and said, "Did you read the letter?" I said, yes. She asked me if I had any questions. I didn't know where to begin. My mother initiated the conversation by saying, "Here's what I think you should do. You need to start looking for a job and then an apartment. I'll help you look for the apartment and give you the first month's rent." What? Job? Apartment? I was a clueless sixteen-year-old. I asked her, "Well, what about school?" She said, "Oh, now you want to worry about school? Did you know I spoke to your principal? Do you know what he told me? He said at the rate you're going; you're probably not going to graduate until you're nineteen years old (huh?). You might as well drop out now and get a job."

This grim picture my mother painted of my immediate future felt like someone poured a bucket of ice down my back. Gerard, who had been silent the entire time, finally spoke. He said, "Kenny, I want you to know that I don't agree with any of this. Leaving you here was not my idea. I don't ever want you to think that I took your mother away from you." I turned to him, nodded my head, and said, "Ok." I knew it wasn't his fault. This plan had my mother's fingerprints all over it. After our brief conversation, she said goodnight, and we went to our respective rooms. For some reason, I wasn't worried at all. It was a classic case of denial. I was too immature to grasp the gravity of the situation. I didn't think about a plan. The only thing I knew for sure was, I wasn't dropping out of high school again. Since it was "only" March, I figured I had time to come up with something. I didn't mention my plight to anyone. I continued my daily routine.

April 3rd, 1983, was Easter Sunday. I reached out to a person I hadn't seen in quite a while, my old friend Neville. I decided to stop by his apartment and hang out for a bit. I was there for about an hour when there was a ring on the intercom. Someone was at the entrance of his building, trying to get in. Neville asked, "Who is it?" The caller said, "It's Larry." What? Did he say, Larry? It couldn't be. Neville buzzed him in, and we ran to the front door. To our astonishment, it was Larry! When we saw him, we could not contain ourselves; we jumped all over him. I was ecstatic! Not only was it Larry, but he looked fantastic! He sported a fresh haircut cut, straight from the barbershop. He was wearing a brand new pair of white Converse All-Stars and some grey-colored, Lee Jeans. He was also wearing an off-white windbreaker jacket. Larry was spotless, the cleanest I had seen him in his entire life.

Larry entered Neville's apartment with us still draped around his neck and sat down. I hadn't seen Larry in eight long months; I had so many questions for him. First of all, what was he doing there? Larry said he had gone to our apartment in Crown Heights first. My mother told him I was at Neville's house. How did he get those new clothes? Larry explained that he was now living in something called a "Group Home." It was like a boarding house for troubled teens located in The Bronx. I said, "Really? You live in The Bronx now?" Larry told me he didn't want to come around, looking dirty and homeless anymore. He waited until he was in a better situation before returning.

Larry then stated the primary purpose of his trip. He needed to get parental permission to live in the group home permanently. They enrolled him in a G.E.D. prep program in The Bronx. To continue living there, he needed my mother to relinquish all her parental rights. Her signature would allow Larry to become a ward of The State Of New York. She agreed to sign the paperwork severing all ties with her son.

I was so happy for him. It was the most responsible thing I ever saw him do. Of course, I still had one more question. What happened when he first came to the door of the apartment and greeted our mother? Larry told me he knocked on the door. When my mother opened it, he said hello and told her that he was sorry and that she was right and he was wrong. I then asked, "What did she say?" He said she started to cry. Well, that took the cake! I wouldn't have expected that exchange from either one of them. Larry then said he had to return to The Bronx because there was a curfew, but he would stay in touch. Larry was back!

Definition: "Game-Changing" - Completely altering how something is done, thought about, or made.

The frigid winter of 1983 finally broke. New York City began to thaw out right in time for the release of a new innovative Rap song. Most hit songs explode on the radio first. However, this song was under the mainstream radar, so it took me some time to hear it. I overheard some guys talking on the basketball court saying, "Yo, did you hear the new song?" What new song? No one had much information about this elusive song. The next day, I was in the park playing ball when someone walked past us from across the street, blasting music from his "Boombox." Between the distance of the radio and some nasty echo, it was difficult to make out what he was playing. Someone on the court yelled, "That's the new song!" Everyone stopped to get a good listen, but the guy was too far out of range to hear it. Damn!

The following day, Larry finally had an opportunity to travel from The Bronx to Darrell's house in Brooklyn to visit me. When Larry arrived, he had two recently purchased 12" vinyl records tucked under his arm. He asked me, "Did you hear the new song?" No, I hadn't. Darrell didn't have a record player, but my mother did. Gerard brought it with him when he moved in. Larry suggested we walk back home so we could listen to the new song. We left Darrell's house and embarked on our 45-minute journey to Crown Heights. While we were walking, I asked Larry to let me see the record. He passed me one of the 12" records for examination. The official title of the new song was 'Sucker MC's' by a group with a weird name... Run-DMC. What kind of name was that for a Rap group? All the popular Rap groups had names with colorful adjectives, describing the number of members in the group. There were The Treacherous Three, The Fearless Four, The Furious Five, The Fantastic Five, and The Cold Crush Four, to name a few. The name Run-DMC gave us little to no information about the group.

When we arrived home, my mother was there. She said hello to Larry, but the dynamic was different. It felt like I brought one of my friends over like Darrell or Neville instead of her firstborn son. It had been over a year since Larry lived there so I could've been imagining things. Anyway, we went into the living room where the record player was. Larry cued up 'Sucker MC's' on the turntable and turned the volume up to about level 8. My mother never listened to music louder than level 3. The song begins. The very first thing that stood out was the earth-shattering drum sound that began pounding the speakers. It was the hardest drums I'd ever heard in my life. Harder than any Rap song ever released. My mother immediately started screaming, "TURN THAT MESS DOWN!" I knew at that precise moment that 'Sucker MC's' was a game-changer. We turned the volume down and continued listening. The first voice you heard was from a super aggressive emcee named "Run Love." He introduced himself with a flow that was more intricate and "fresher" than the emcees we were accustomed to hearing. His style of Rap seemed to "run" rings around the "Party Rap" style that was popular at the time. He proclaimed in no uncertain terms that the absolute worst thing a rapper could be was copycat or "Biter." That was his definition of a sucker emcee.

Another element that stood out was the lack of musical instruments featured on the song. There were only drums. This stripped-down approach made the track appear more aggressive than the other Rap songs and more authentic to an actual breakbeat played at an outside park jam. I was in Hip-Hop Heaven! If we thought the song couldn't get any better, there was a big finale, with some never before heard on record, but authentic to a park jam, scratching by a real DJ. Along with the scratching, the song introduced a new emcee. He called himself DMC. It was incredible! At the song's conclusion, Larry lifted the needle off the record and placed it back at the beginning of the song. We listened to the song again in its entirety before my mother couldn't take anymore and began complaining. It was like old times for Larry and me, sitting in the living room listening to a new Rap release on the stereo.

When the Hip-Hop world finally got a full dose of 'Sucker MC's,' there was a seismic shift, a changing of the guard. The 70's style of Rap became outdated and no longer acceptable. Those syrupy R&B-sounding backing tracks were no longer hard enough. Run-DMC brought a new, 80's style of Rap to the Hip-Hop game. As it turned out, Sucker MC's' wasn't intended to be the lead single. It was the B-side of the song, 'It's Like That' which received a ton of radio airplay and was a hit record in its own right. Still, it was 'Sucker MC's' that changed the game forever.

After reuniting with my brother, it became clear that his demeanor had changed. Larry's new environment seemed to have raised his spirits and brightened his general outlook on life. Larry began traveling from The Bronx to Brooklyn more often to visit me. I would ask him many questions about his new life in the group home. Larry told me that he would attend his

G.E.D. classes during the morning hours and then have the rest of the day to himself. Larry was always interested in artwork dating back to his days of drawing comic books. That love of illustrating had somehow morphed into an insatiable passion for Graffiti writing. Larry would travel all over The Bronx, "tagging" his name everywhere. He even confessed how he and his friends would take risky excursions into the MTA subway yards to "bomb" the train cars. Larry also revealed his other favorite past time which was battling rival emcees throughout The Bronx. Huh? Larry wasn't a battle rapper when I'd last heard him rhyme a year ago. He explained that in The Bronx, you HAD to battle; that was the only way you could earn respect. Every day was a competition for him. Battling didn't seem like his personality at all. Larry was low-key and laid back. Many aspects of his life appeared to have changed since he moved to The Bronx. Larry seemed happier than I'd seen him in years.

After listening to Larry's fantastic stories, I began to think this "glorified orphanage" called a group home didn't sound that bad compared to my living situation. I also thought about the extreme conditions Larry endured to wind up in that group home. I realized his journey wasn't for me. I wasn't strong enough to go through what he went through. A week on the street was enough to break my spirit. Larry lived out there off and on for almost three years now. The group home life sounded pretty good for a hot minute, but it was back to reality.

As time progressed, I continued my daily routine as if everything was wonderful, and before I knew it, two months passed. It was now the last week of June, 1983. Because of our schedules, I hadn't spoken to Larry in a few weeks. I was hanging around Darrell's house, drifting through life. I arrived home one evening at my usual 10 pm curfew. My angry mother confronted me at the door. What else was new? She said, "You know, Kenny, I took the day off from work today. Gerard and I drove all over Brooklyn, looking for an apartment for you. We happened to drive past the basketball courts, and there you were, playing basketball." She then said, "At that point, I realized that you either don't care or don't believe that I'm leaving, but it doesn't matter now. I don't care what you do, but Gerard and I are leaving here in two days, and you have to get out!" I went to my room and sat there with my head down. I had forgotten all about this moving stuff.; the whole situation was too overwhelming. I hadn't mentioned any of this to anyone; my mother hadn't mentioned it either, until right then. The countdown was almost at zero.; this was for real.

"You never realize how strong you are until being strong is the only choice you have."

I came home the following evening, and there were several boxes in the living room. My mother was all packed up and ready to go. We didn't say much to each other that night. I don't remember feeling much of anything. That was odd for an emotional person like me. Somehow, I managed to fall asleep. What else was I going to do? The next morning, a loud banging on my bedroom door startled me out of my sleep. I opened the door to find my mother standing there. "Wake up, Kenny; today is the day! Get your stuff together; you have to go now!" I hadn't packed anything. She gave me a small box, and I put my belongings inside. It didn't take long; I hardly had anything to pack. Most of her belongings were already gone. I remember her rushing me, "Hurry Up! Hurry Up!" After packing my box, I then realized I had nowhere to take it. Where was I going? I said to her, "I will leave now, but can I keep this box here? I have nowhere to put it." My mother, who was becoming agitated, said, "No! Gerard found someone to take over this apartment tonight. Everything has to be out of here today."

I had no choice but to leave my stuff in the hallway. Anyone could've walked off with what little I owned or threw it away. Luckily, only Dee lived above us. I knew she wouldn't mess with the box, but I had no idea what the new tenants would do. My mother said, "Here, take this," and handed me $100. She was basically saying, "Have a nice life." My heart was pounding. As I put my stuff in the hallway, she confiscated my key. I was in a bad situation. All of a sudden, I had another epiphany! There was one person who could help me—a person I trusted who specialized in cases like this, my brother Larry. The only problem was, I didn't know how to reach him. I had no phone number, no address, nothing. I went back into the apartment and asked my mother for Larry's number. She got angry and started yelling, "Why didn't you ask me that earlier? It's all packed away now; you get on my nerves!" Her negative tone made my blood boil. My despair turned into feelings of intense anger as she grabbed a pen and paper and jotted down some information. With an attitude, she handed me the piece of paper with Larry's address. She said, "Here, it's called Christian Academy Home For Boys or something like that."

I took the piece of paper and headed back into the hallway to organize my stuff a little neater. My mother followed behind me, slammed and locked the door. By the time I stood up, all I could see was the back of her head going down the stairs. She never looked back. I remember watching her go down the stairs and thinking, "You know what? Fuck you!" I knew this was finally the end. I didn't know what was going to become of my life, but one thing was for sure, I NEVER wanted to see her again. By the time I got downstairs, I could see her and Gerard driving down the block, off into the distance. On June 27th, 1983, at the age of 16, my worst fear came to pass; I was homeless. I had only one mission, find Larry.

Locating Larry would not be easy. Despite having the address, how would I find it in a borough with a population of 1.4 million? I mentally replayed everything Larry told me about his group home life. I recalled him mentioning that the group home's location was in the Soundview section of The Bronx. Ok, I'll start there. But how do I get to Soundview? I went to the subway station and looked at the map. It showed that the number 6 train ran through Soundview. Great! I rode "The 6" out to the Parkchester Station in The Bronx. I asked someone to direct me to the street I was searching for, Lacombe Avenue. They told me it was about a mile up the road (1.4 actually). I was used to walking, so that wasn't too bad. It was a beautiful summer day, which made the commute easier. After about 30 minutes, I arrived at Lacombe Avenue and felt a sigh of relief. All I needed to do now was find the address. However, when I reached the street address, it wasn't there. The street numbers didn't go that high. Ah, man! How can this be?

I remembered passing a taxi dispatch office, so I decided to walk over there and get directions. I wandered in and asked the dispatcher if I could catch a cab to the address given to me by my mother. The dispatcher pulled out a gigantic address book, thumbed through the directory, and said, "No such address exists." I asked him, "Are you sure?" He said, "Positive." I now realized that my mother didn't know the exact street address. She wrote down anything on the paper to get rid of me. I expected nothing less from her.

What was I going to do now? I needed to figure this out. It occurred to me that the street name might've been correct, but the address was wrong. I decided to walk the entire length of Lacombe Avenue until I saw something resembling a boy's group home. I proceeded to stroll up and down that street for almost two hours. I didn't see any structure that looked like a boy's home at all. I was quite exhausted and out of ideas by this point. I needed to stop and regroup. A lady was watering her lawn right next to me; I said, "Excuse me, miss, I'm looking for The Christian Academy Boys Home." She said, "Oh, it's right there" and pointed directly across the street. I stopped to rest right in front of the building I was searching for all along. What were the odds of that happening? A little divine intervention never hurt anybody.

The group home was a residential house in a quiet neighborhood. There were no identifying markings at all; I would've never found it. I dragged my tired legs into the building and ran right into the counselor on duty. He looked at me and said, "You must be Larry's brother, you look like him." He then said, "Larry's not here, all the residents went to the beach. They should be back in about two hours." He explained that the other counselor who was supervising the trip was going to call soon to check-in. He would inform Larry that I was there waiting for him. Great! All of a sudden, he blurted out, "Did you know your brother is crazy?" We both burst out laughing. Where have I heard that one before? He then said, "Everyone here loves him, but he's nuts! Let me show you his room." We went upstairs to the sleeping quarters, and when we entered Larry's room, it looked like the inside of a subway car. Everywhere you looked, there was graffiti. Every inch of the walls, the ceiling, and even the floor had graffiti. The counselor said, "Can you believe we've already made him paint the entire room over himself? What you see here is the second time he's done this." I had no words. What stuck out the most amongst the madness in Larry's room was that every tag in the entire room read the same thing, "KRS!" Was Larry going by the moniker KRS now? One of the stranger tags on the wall read, "KRSNAPHOBIA." I recalled seeing him at the library on a few occasions studying Hare Krishna books in the past. The name KRS must have originated from there. Of course, I was going to ask him later on when I saw him.

After two hours, a van pulled up and out jumped the residents of the group home. As soon as Larry saw me, he said, "She threw you out, didn't she?" I lowered my head in shame and said, "Yeah." Larry said, "I knew this was gonna happen. I had a dream about this. Don't worry, I have it all planned out," and with that, all my fears disappeared. There wasn't any doubt in my mind that I wasn't going to be ok. This time, I was going to follow his instructions without question. Larry revealed his plan. He said, "Tomorrow, we're gonna go to The Bureau Of Child Welfare (BCW) in Manhattan to see my social worker. She'll take care of you." I asked him,

"What about tonight?" Larry said, "Tonight, I'm going to take you to the men's shelter. We're going to stay there until the morning and then go to BCW." Fine, whatever you say.

We relaxed at the group home until sundown, and then we ventured out to Manhattan. It was already approaching 10 pm when we left. The group home enforced a strict curfew. Each resident had to be home and accounted for by 11 pm or face disciplinary actions. Larry chose to violate his curfew, knowing the consequences, to take me to the men's shelter. Where would I have been without him?

We arrived at the shelter, which was an armory located off Bowery Street in lower Manhattan. When I watched the old black & white movies on television, The Bowery was where all the bums congregated. When I saw the Bowery Street sign, I realized I had hit rock bottom. We entered the shelter and filled out a brief questionnaire asking who, what and why? I received a meal ticket for breakfast in the morning, a white sheet, and a blanket. The shelter was massive, with hundreds of beds inside. The shelter staff instructed us to pick a bed, put the layer on the bed, and sleep until the morning. I was nervous because I still had about $90 of the $100 my mother gave me. I didn't want anyone to steal my money while I slept, so I hid the cash in my sock. I didn't sleep much that night anyway. I kept waking up and checking my money. At some point during the night, I glanced over at Larry. He could have been lying in his bed but choose to sleep in a shelter for the homeless to make sure I was ok. How could I ever thank him?

The next morning we were up bright and early. Larry and I headed to Manhattan's Financial District, the location of the BCW. When we arrived,

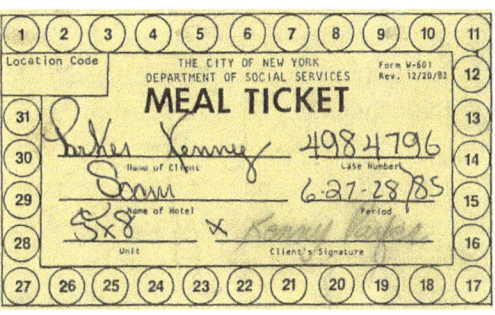

Meal Ticket

Larry's social worker agreed to see us without an appointment. She was an African-American lady who was quite pleasant. She appeared to know Larry very well. He introduced me as his younger brother and informed her that my mother kicked me out of the house. She immediately replied, "I don't believe that. There's no way a mother would throw both of her children in the street. I don't believe this story." I told her it was true. She said, "Do you have a contact number for her? What is her job number?" I gave her the information, and she called my mother's job right on the spot. My mother's employer told the social worker that my mother quit on Friday and no longer worked there. The social worker called my home phone number. No answer. She was shaking her head in disbelief. She turned to Larry and said, "Ok, you can go home now; I got it from here." I told Larry I would call him as soon as my situation got sorted out and gave him some of the money I had leftover from the $100. He left.

The social worker said, "Your case requires immediate attention. I'm going to place you in a group home for now while we investigate your story." Fantastic! I liked Larry's group home and asked her if I could go there. She said, "No, two brothers aren't allowed to live in the same group home." Well, that sucked. As I waited for my new social worker to fill out the paperwork, I spotted my summer league AAU coach "Doc" Nicelli (R.I.P.). He appeared to be a supervisor at the BCW as well. What a coincidence! When he heard my story, he directed my social worker to "Make sure you put him in a group home in Brooklyn so he can still attend Lincoln. They're going to have a good team this year." Of all the things to be thinking of in a moment like this. My social worker informed me that she indeed found housing for me in Brooklyn. Excellent! The good news was, the location was only eight blocks from my former home in Crown Heights. The bad news? That location was in the Bedford-Stuyvesant section of Brooklyn. This area was another rough part of town nicknamed "Bed-Stuy, Do Or Die."

In the hierarchy of crime, Bed-Stuy would've ranked third, right behind Brownsville and East New York. The social worker gave me a subway token for transportation and sent me on my way. I arrived at The Pyramid Group Home, a four-story, unmarked brownstone located on Franklin Avenue. The counselor on duty greeted me at the front door and showed me around the facility. He introduced me to the other residents and showed me where I would be sleeping. That was it. I was now an official member of a group home. In less than 24 hours, Larry's plan had worked to perfection.

That evening, I laid my head down in my new room, next to my new roommate. I finally had a chance to exhale and absorb everything that transpired over the past 36 hours. I've always believed in a higher power. I interpreted how everything fell into place as a sign that I was there for a reason. I was about to embark on a whole new chapter of my life. One thing was for sure, I had a lot of growing up to do in a hurry. I had no choice.

"New beginnings are often disguised as painful endings." - Lao Tzu

The very first thing I did after I settled in was called Larry from a payphone set-up in the hallway of Pyramid. I thanked him for everything he had done for me at the spur of the moment. The next thing I did was walk over to Darrell's house, which was now an hour away. We had a long, serious conversation. I finally confessed to him everything that had been going on in my life. He was furious. He couldn't comprehend my mother's behavior and asked me why I didn't come to his house instead of going to a group home. I explained that I felt it wouldn't have been right to burden his (now separated) mother with another mouth to feed. The group home was where I needed to be. That was my path. I told him I didn't want anyone to know that I lived in a group home. It wasn't anybody's business anyway. He agreed.

I left Darrell's house and went back to my old apartment building to retrieve the box I left in the hallway. I sorted through my belongings, only keeping a few personal items. Everything else I threw in the garbage. I even tossed my "roach radio," which had given me two years of reliable service, in the trash. I wanted a fresh new start. With the leftover money, I bought new clothes, sneakers and prepared myself for the summer.

Days passed since my arrival at Pyramid, and the reality of my new environment began to sink in. My goal was to keep a low profile and observe everything. The first thing I noticed was; this group home was very different from Larry's group home in The Bronx. His group home was on a quiet block surrounded by houses with fences and trees. My group home was on a busy two-lane street with dozens of people walking past at any given time. The Franklin Avenue Shuttle and the A train subway station were on the corner. When Larry introduced me to the residents of his group home, they all seemed like cool guys. Larry and his homeboy "Ace" appeared to be the ring leaders. At Pyramid, most of these guys had hardened faces. They looked like they either suffered a lot of trauma or committed lots of crimes in their young lives. It felt more like a juvenile detention halfway house. I never spent any extended time around guys of this caliber before. It didn't take me long to figure out the pecking order amongst the residents. Out of the twelve guys living there, about four of them were tough guys. The others were cool. Each of them had their reasons for ending up at Pyramid.

At the corner of my block was Fulton Street, which you could consider the "Main Street" of Bed-Stuy. That's where all the action was and not in the right way either. The interior of Pyramid was decent. Despite being an older building, it was clean and functional. Pyramid housed twelve residents ranging from ages 16 to 19, who bunked two to a room. The bedrooms were on the first and second floors. The living room was on the first floor, right by the front door. There was a huge television in the living room, along with a couple of couches. The kitchen and dining room area were on a lower level, along with a ping pong table. In the basement was the laundry room, equipped with two washers and one dryer available 24 hours a day. Pyramid featured two full bathrooms, one on the second floor and one on the lower level. Thick metal bars covered the first and second-floor windows. That was common for brownstones in the area. The backyard area is where you could go and relax if you wanted to. The counselor's office was on the 4th floor. My bedroom was simple, with only two beds, a desk, and two huge lockers. Pyramid gave every resident a padlock for their locker to make sure their stuff was secure. They supplied me with soap, shampoo, towels, deodorant, lotion, and hair tonic.

Now the kitchen, that was the highlight. There were all sorts of food a hungry teenager like myself would enjoy. Breakfast was from 6 am to 9 am. You had your choice of boiled or scrambled eggs, bacon, sausages, toast, waffles, oatmeal, or cold cereal. There was coffee, tea, milk, orange juice, soda, anything you wanted to drink. I tried Kool-Aid for the first time that week. At 9 am, they closed the kitchen. The counselor on duty would padlock the refrigerator shut and then lock the kitchen door. At 11 am, it was snack time. They would reopen the kitchen for 15 minutes, enough time for you to choose between an assortment of cookies or donuts. At 1 pm, it was lunchtime. From 1 to 3 pm, you could go into the kitchen and make yourself a sandwich. There were at least five different types of cold cuts in the refrigerator. At 5 pm, it was dinner time. From 5 to 7 pm, residents were only allowed to eat dinner at the dining room table. Every day of the week, the counselors would prepare something different for dinner. They cooked baked chicken, fried chicken, pot roast, steak, pork chops; I even had my first taste of lamb chops there. To top it off, at 9 pm, the kitchen opened for one final snack before bedtime. Of course, I took full advantage. I went from eating once a day to eating six times a day!

Pyramid's curfew was set at 11 pm, a full hour past my mother's old limit of 10 pm. Now, I didn't have to be the first to leave the rest of my friends and rush home. Each resident got a weekly allowance of $5. That number could increase to as much as $15, depending on the completion of your assigned daily chore. When I first arrived, they assigned me to the downstairs bathroom. I scrubbed the bathroom to the best of my ability, and collected my "points" for the evening. The following day, the head supervisor named Mr. Horton visited Pyramid. He was in charge of three other group homes in the city as well. After using the downstairs bathroom, he asked, "Which resident cleaned this bathroom?" One of the counselors replied, "The new kid." Mr. Horton declared, "That's the cleanest I've ever seen the bathroom! Make sure he stays on bathroom detail." I received a compliment for something I might have gotten yelled at for being unsatisfactory the week before. All this encouragement would be something I'd have to get used to now.

After a few days, the Pyramid administration had to decide what to do with me for the summer. As per policy, every resident had to either attend classes or have a job. Since I arrived at the end of June, it was too late to assign me an official, sanctioned, New York City summer job. The only alternative was to enroll me in a summer school remedial program. I wasn't happy with their decision at all. I didn't want to spend the entire summer in a hot classroom, but I had no choice.

When I arrived at the small annex, one of the instructors asked me what level of high school I completed? I told him I finished my junior year of high school. He suggested I take a placement exam to see what level of instruction I would need. He led me to a private room, where I took an extended reading and writing test. Afterward, I joined the other students and awaited my results. The teachers were already working with some of the students. One teacher was trying to help a female student with a math problem. The teacher asked her, "If you have two apples, and I give you three more apples, how many do you have?" The girl was utterly lost. The teacher repeated the question to her very slow, trying to give her a chance to visualize the answer. The girl began using her fingers to try and count it out. She was still struggling. The teacher finally gave her the answer, five. I found this shocking! This girl appeared to be around my age and couldn't do basic arithmetic. I shook my head and thought to myself, "What am I doing here?"

Finally, the results of my placement exam were ready. According to this test, the instructor told me, "Kenneth, you are already reading on a college level. This place is not for you." He sent me back to Pyramid and forwarded my test results. After some deliberation, the counselors at Pyramid agreed that it was too late to enroll me in another program. They decided to wait until school resumed in September. What a lucky break! My timing was perfect. I had the whole summer off as I'd wanted.

About two weeks had passed since my arrival at Pyramid, including my 17th birthday. The counselors decided to assign a new resident to my room. In walked this flamboyant character named Stanley Carter. He was dark-skinned, about 5'9", with short wavy hair. He was very charismatic with an incredible gift of gab. In no time, Stanley became very popular with both the residents and the counselors. He was very unpredictable and would do all sorts of wild things. One day his girlfriend came to visit him. Female visitors were only allowed in the living room area. When the time came for her to leave, Stanley offered to walk her home. First, he needed to take a shower. After his bath, Stanley decided to walk her home wearing only his robe and some slippers! He walked her hand and hand through Bed-Stuy in a bathrobe. It was hilarious! He told me that guys were cheering him as he walked down the street. Another time, Stanley emerged from the shower completely naked. Without warning, he jumped up on a chair and began gyrating his genitals in front of everybody. He was yelling, "Y'all didn't know I was a swinger in New York, did ya?" What the hell? I thought he was nuts, but he was always good for a laugh.

Stanley had a dark side, though. His neighborhood reputation was that of a kleptomaniac, and he had a criminal record for "Jostling." Stanley would go to Times Square, known as "The Deuce," and either pickpocket or flat out rob people. The police caught and arrested Stanley, which was one of the reasons he got placed in Pyramid.

On July 22nd, 1983, mega R&B icon Diana Ross performed a free concert in Central Park attended by over 250,000 people. There were reports of chaos at the show due to the overwhelming amount of people who attended. Stanley, who had gone to the concert with his "friends", returned to Pyramid later that evening. He told me that he and his friends made it to the front of the stage. What? How did they navigate through 250,000 people? Stanley said, "Yeah, we were wildin'!" I knew what that meant...they were part of the chaos in Central Park and robbed a lot of people there. I had never been around an individual like this before, and now he was my roommate. Despite it all, Stanley and I got along very well. I kept my locker padlocked shut, though.

One evening I arrived at Pyramid right at curfew time, 11 pm. I saw Stanley talking to a random girl outside. About half an hour later, I was preparing for bed. Stanley enters the room and asks me for a favor, "Yo, Kenny, help me sneak this girl into the room." What? I told him no! I'd only been there for three weeks; I wasn't going to do anything that could get me kicked out. He pleaded with me, "C'mon man! I would do it for you. We're roommates, we're supposed to stick together." After going on for what seemed like forever, Stanley finally revealed his plan. He said, "All you have to do is ask the counselor for a glass of water; that's it." After 11 pm, there was only one counselor on duty for the overnight shift. I agreed to do that one thing, nothing more.

I went to the living room where the counselor watched television and asked him to get me a glass of water. He agreed and left his post to go downstairs and open the kitchen to get me some water. It only took two minutes for the counselor to return to the living room. That's all the time Stanley needed to open the front door and usher the girl into our bedroom. She said hello to me and then sat on Stanley's bed. He cut off the lights, and they immediately began kissing. It was evident that they were going to have sex right there in the room with me only five feet away. I had no interest in watching Stanley have sex, so I rolled over, faced the wall, and went to sleep.

The next morning Stanley was able to sneak the girl out while the counselor cooked breakfast. Stanley immediately bombarded me, "Yoooo, did you see me last night?" He was looking for some sort of accolades. I told him, "No! I went to sleep." He was so disappointed. He asked, "How could you go to sleep?" I brushed him off and went on about my day. The following night, I arrived home at 11 pm. Somehow, Stanley managed to sneak the same young lady past the counselor once again and into our room. Unbelievable! The same routine happened all over again. She said hello to me, sat on Stanley's bed, turned off the lights, and began kissing. As clothes came off, I rolled over and faced the wall. As soon as I started to doze off, I felt a kick on my leg. What the hell? Then I felt another kick. I rolled over and looked. Stanley somehow stretched his leg over while the girl wasn't looking and began kicking me! He wanted to make sure I saw him this time. I knew if I didn't face his direction, he would find some way to keep disturbing me. Ok Stanley, now I see you. He proceeds to climb on top of this girl and start having sex. After watching him for about a minute, I rolled back over. That's all Stanley needed, a brief audience. The next morning at breakfast, he said,

"I know you saw me last night." "Yeah, Stanley, I saw you," I replied. He was so happy.

I later learned that this young lady was only 13 years old! Stanley was about 18 years old. To make matters worse, Stanley knew her age the entire time. I felt disgusted. I didn't rat him out, but I knew one thing for sure, I wasn't getting involved in any more of Stanley's schemes.

During my third week at Pyramid, they informed me that New York State law required all new residents of a group home to have a complete physical and psychological evaluation. I hadn't received a physical since I was a baby. After completing the physical, they sent me to a psychiatrist for a one on one examination. He had me look at inkblots and tell him what I saw. I had to match various shapes into their corresponding holes. I did memory and word association tests. He asked me a series of questions about past and present world events. We then had a detailed conversation about my family life and my general outlook on life. After that, I went home.

Shortly after my examination, I received a phone call on the main office line at Pyramid. That was odd. When I got to the 4th floor and answered the phone, there was a familiar voice on the other line, Coach Hartstein. The tone of his voice sounded very concerned. It turned out; he bumped into my AAU basketball coach, Doc, who worked at the Bureau Of Child Welfare. He informed Coach Hartstein of my situation. Coach Hartstein asked me what happened in disbelief like he needed to hear it straight from my mouth. I told him the truth; my mother moved away and left me in the street. He used to talk to her all the time and had no idea she was capable of something like that. I should have told him what was going on earlier, but I was too embarrassed. Coach Hartstein assured me that everything was going to be alright. He promised to do everything in his power to make sure I got into college next year, one with a dormitory so I wouldn't have to live in a group home. I thanked him. He told me if I needed anything to call him and we would speak more in-depth in September when school resumed. It was a great phone call. He always seemed to go above and beyond for me.

A few days later, I once again got summoned to the 4th-floor office. They informed me that I had been residing at Pyramid Group Home for thirty days, and it was time for my evaluation. I was only assigned to live at Pyramid for a one-month trial basis. I had been under observation the entire time to see if that group home was a good fit for both myself and the staff. The report stated that I was well-liked by both the counselors and the residents. Based on their assessment, they decided to make me a permanent resident of Pyramid Group Home. Great news! My new permanent status also meant I was now considered a Ward of the State Of New York. My birth parents were no longer my legal guardians. Governor Mario Cuomo was now my father.

One of the counselors, who had access to my files, gave me some information I wasn't supposed to be privy to, my psychological evaluation. The results showed I had the highest IQ test scores in their entire group home system. For me, this information wasn't that big of a deal considering the cast of characters I had come across. He also mentioned that the psychiatrist diagnosed me with a form of depression stemming from my mother's abandonment of me. I disagreed with that assessment. I felt relieved to be away from her. After living at Pyramid for only one month, I hadn't thought about my mother at all. The psychiatrist must have assumed that depression would be a natural reaction to my mother's abandonment. That couldn't be further from the truth. After thirty days, I already knew that Pyramid was a far better environment for me. For no other reason than I had access to necessities like food, laundry, and medical attention. I didn't miss my old life at all. The "expert" was wrong.

My 17th birthday arrived in July, and I finally felt free of my mother's constant physical and mental constraints. I decided to venture out and experience more of what life had to offer. Larry invited me up to The Bronx to chill out with him for the day. I rode out to Soundview and met him at the train station. He suggested I ride with him on one of his train "bombing'" runs. Larry had a small backpack with multiple homemade markers created from cut up strips of erasers soaked in bottles of ink. This technique caused big fat strokes when you tagged on a wall. Larry's fingertips were stained blue from handling so much ink. I found that funny. We jumped from train to train. Larry tagged KRS, on the walls, the ceilings, the windows, the seats, everywhere. I had an absolute blast being his lookout. On our way home, I made an interesting observation. July of 1983 was the first time since we were little children that we were both wearing new sneakers at the same time. We had a good laugh at that one. I enjoyed my experience so much that I started traveling to The Bronx a couple of times a week to visit him. Larry took me everywhere. We even stopped by an all-girls group home affiliated with his group home. I loved that! We would visit there quite often to mess around with the girls. I was late to the game, but at least I was a player now.

CHAPTER 10
HOE STROLL

One of the favorite summer pastimes for the residents of Pyramid Group Home was sitting outside on our brownstone's front steps. We called these steps a "Stoop." Our block was always busy, with hundreds of people walking by on a hot summer day. All the residents would be sitting on the stoop together. Most of them would be yelling and hollering at the girls strolling by. One hot July day, during one of those "stoop" moments, a girl approached our group home. She began talking to a resident whom she knew there. Her name was Teisha. She was about 5'7", dark-skinned, with a lovely smile. After chatting with the other resident, she then struck up a conversation with me. As it turned out, she was my age and only lived a block away. We hit it off immediately. I found Teisha attractive and considered trying to pursue her, but I found out she dated some street hustler from Coney Island. Damn! I figured we could be cool then. It was my first venture into the dreaded "Friend Zone." To my knowledge, that term didn't exist in 1983, but I found myself trapped in it.

Teisha would visit Pyramid first thing in the morning and ring the bell. She would greet me with, "What's up, Kenny, come outside." Teisha would already be smoking weed at 9 am! She used to warn me, "Listen, Kenny, don't ever do this..it ain't for you" as she exhaled the marijuana smoke. Like myself, Teisha was about to be a senior in high school. She came from what appeared to be a beautiful family and seemed to be on the right path despite her chronic weed habit. Teisha began hanging around Pyramid so much that soon, she could enter the building unannounced. All the counselors knew her. Unfortunately, Teisha had a friend named Red. She acquired that nickname because she was a mixed, light-skinned black girl with freckles and red hair. Red was a little older than Teisha and dabbled in a lot of "street activities." Even I could tell she was bad news. Red was the type of person who made friends fast, but in a slick way, like a used car salesman. I used to wonder why Teisha would hang out with a character like Red. Teisha wasn't like her at all. Because I was friends with Teisha, I became friends with Red, to an extent.

One day, Teisha took me to Red's apartment about a block away. I found out Red had a baby, approximately six months old, who cried a lot. Red complained, "The baby is making too much noise." Suddenly, Red inhaled a puff of weed and exhaled it right into the baby's mouth. I saw the weed smoke come out of the baby's nose! Red thought nothing of it. Like she had done that before. She said, "That'll calm him down." I knew this was wrong in my heart and soul, but sadly, I didn't say anything.

Speaking of characters, one morning, I woke up to find that Stanley hadn't returned home from the previous night. One of the most significant infractions a resident could commit was missing our curfew. If you didn't call or have a legitimate excuse within 24 hours, you were "AWOL," which was grounds for discharge. It was very unusual for Stanley to miss curfew. Everyone knew that Stanley always had his hand in something street-related, but he'd still find his way back to Pyramid on time. The following day, there was still no sign of Stanley. Everyone, including the police, was looking for him.

On the third day of Stanley's disappearance, we got the sobering news, Stanley was dead. Someone murdered him in the most gruesome fashion imaginable. It appeared that there were signs of torture. Afterward, Stanley was set on fire and burned to death. This news was shocking. Who would do this to Stanley? One of the residents heard on the street that Stanley had stolen something from the wrong people. They caught him and made an example out of him. I didn't know how to feel about this terrible news.

I never dealt with someone so close, who had his life taken before. I'd only known Stanley for about five weeks, but he was my roommate. I slept five feet away from him every night. We talked, ate, hung out, and even played basketball together. I was sad, but I also knew what type of person he was and only a fraction of what he did in the streets. His behavior finally caught up with him. R.I.P. Stanley Carter.

Pyramid Group Home's location was only eight blocks away from my old apartment building. I would walk past my former "crib" several times per week. One day, I was on my way home, and I ran into one of the Pyramid residents along the way. Since we were both heading to the same place, we decided to walk back together. Along the way, I ran into an old familiar face. It was my friend and basketball mentor from high school, Ham. I hadn't seen him in quite a while, and we were both excited to see each other. While we were shaking hands, I noticed a strange look on the face of the Pyramid resident. His entire mood had changed in less than thirty seconds. After I finished talking to Ham, we continued home. The resident immediately began interrogating me, "Yo, how do you know him?" I told him Ham was a high school teammate of mine. He said, "How well do you know him?" I became confused. I said, "I know him pretty well; he's cool." The resident then asked me, "Did you know he was a Stick Up Kid?" What? No way!

A "Stick Up Kid" was a term used to describe a guy who used a gun to rob people. A Stick Up Kid was right at the top of the most feared individuals in the neighborhood. I told him there was no way my boy Ham was the same guy who he described. I had seen Ham in the area a few times before, even at night, and there was never a problem. This guy would not change his stance. He claimed that he was born and raised in the neighborhood and was 100% positive that the guy I was talking to was a very dangerous individual. For the record, I will never believe that my friend and mentor, Ham, was a Stick Up Kid.

In 1983, the crime rate in New York City continued to soar to record levels. No matter what type of kid you were, an A student, a thug, or anywhere between, the danger was lurking. Even on the basketball court, where I felt the most secure, I was not immune to drama. During that summer, various ballplayers from the Flatbush area converged on our park every day. I knew almost everyone there. One of the older guys, named China, used to play ball with us. He wasn't that old, but to a 17-year-old, a 21-22-year-old man was an older guy. He happened to be Puerto Rican, so I don't know why his name was China. Anyway, he would sometimes show up with his friends, but we didn't care, he was cool. We would talk trash to each other while competing on the court. It was all in fun. During one heated exchange, I called traveling on China. I said, "Yo, China, you walked!" He barked back, "No, I didn't." We started arguing. Suddenly, this random stranger from the sideline who nobody knew said, "Yo, man, you might have traveled." China's whole demeanor changed. He said, "What? Nobody ain't fuckin' asked you nothing. Who the fuck are you?" The next thing I knew, China and his boys started beating him up right there on the court. The stranger had to dash out of the park, barely escaping China and his boys.

I watched all this feeling awful like, "Damn, I should've never called traveling on China." I didn't know it would've resulted in a beatdown. That's how quickly things can escalate in the hood. A simple chain of events turned a traveling call in a meaningless basketball game into a life and death situation in mere seconds. The streets have strange Karma, though. I heard the stranger returned the next day with a gun and shot China in the leg! We never saw the stranger or China ever again.

Another day, we were all out there playing ball. For some reason, the park was extra crowded with dozens of guys hanging around watching the games. Meanwhile, guess who comes strolling onto the court? My old nemesis DJ. The same guy from the 6th grade who extorted me for $1.50 on the very first day of school. He was a frequent visitor to the park, but our dynamic had changed. I was way bigger and taller than he was. DJ couldn't intimidate me, but for some reason, he still didn't like me. Sometimes, I would notice him looking at me with total disgust. He might have resented my growing popularity on the court. We never spoke to each other.

On this day, we had organized two teams with Darrell on my squad and DJ on the opposing team. During the game, Darrell steals the ball from another player and passes me the ball. I decided to dribble in for a routine lay-up, but out of the corner of my eye, I saw DJ running towards me at top speed. I could tell that he was going to try and block my shot. A blocked shot was always a big crowd-pleaser. I could see from the angle that DJ was coming towards me that he would attempt to pin my lay-up against the backboard. In my hood, this was considered very disrespectful. My adrenaline was pumping. We both jumped in the air at the same time. For some reason, when I jumped, I kept going higher and higher. The next thing I knew, I dunked the ball right in DJ's face... BANG!! When I landed on the ground, I could hear the whole park yell in unison, "OOOOH SHIT!!"

After that, the entire park exploded! Guys were running all over the court, hugging me while laughing and pointing at DJ. I looked at him, and he was utterly humiliated. Getting your lay-up pinned against the backboard was terrible, but getting dunked on is THE most disrespectful thing that could happen to anyone on a basketball court. Most of the guys in the park couldn't dunk at all. I could dunk with ease, but I never tried to dunk on an opposing player before. The aggressive way that DJ was coming towards me made my basketball instincts take over. It felt like everything was moving in slow motion. I was looking at him while everyone was laughing, and I thought, "You took my money in 6th grade...Look at you now!" I tried to keep a straight face and play it cool, but I couldn't. Everyone else was screaming so loud that I began laughing myself. The park was in an uproar. So much so that Darrell's brother Kevin, who was a block away, came running over to the park to find out what happened. It was the ultimate revenge. Whatever DJ had done to me in the 6th grade was nothing compared to what I had done to him now. To this day, it ranks among my top 2 or 3 greatest basketball moments of my life; Posterizing DJ!

Right around the time of my "Michael Jordan" moment, a new flamboyant resident moved into Pyramid Group Home. He was cool with all the residents, a very likable guy. He stayed dressed in his stylish 80's street clothes, even to run simple errands. He always wore a "Du-rag" on his head to make sure his hair stayed wavy. His favorite clothing accessory were these popular designer glasses called 'Cazal's,' featuring gold-plated frames. They cost about $110, a hefty price for eyeglass frames in 1983. Most guys wore them as a fashion statement. They would pop out the lenses and sport only the frame. Of course, Cazal's became an irresistible target for thieves and robbers.

One evening, the new resident was riding home on the subway wearing his Cazal's. Out of nowhere, some guys attacked him for his glasses. The robbers beat him so severely that he spent over two weeks in the hospital. A few of us residents went to the hospital to visit him. When we entered his room, what we saw was shocking. His head was three times its regular size, and his face was completely black and blue. He looked unrecognizable, like

"The Elephant Man." All this over some stupid glasses?

As he laid there, in the Intensive Care Unit, he said to me, "Yo Kenny, man, they still ain't get my glasses. I held them tight in my hand, even when I was unconscious. I never let them go." I didn't know what to say. Those thugs nearly beat him to death, but he was still talking about those glasses. I don't know what he did to acquire those Cazal frames, but he sure wasn't letting those Brooklyn dudes have them. The saddest part was, he wasn't the type of guy whose behavior would attract trouble, but once he put on those Cazal's, he became a target. Amazingly, the minute they released him from the hospital, he put those glasses right back on.

The summer of 1983 came to a close. What a wild ride it turned out to be. Despite experiencing some unusual and frightening things, I still felt like my life was better than it had been living with my mother. No one was ridiculing me for every little thing. Pyramid discouraged the staff from raising their voices, except in extreme circumstances. I managed to eat so much food that, despite playing basketball every day, I gained five pounds! I also had a chance to interact with girls that I would've never met or had the confidence to speak to had I still been living my previous life. I had come a long way in a short time.

Now, my senior year at Abraham Lincoln High School awaited. To my surprise, I discovered that Pyramid would grant a clothing allowance to any resident attending school in the fall. Excellent! They allotted me $125, which was more money than I ever had to spend in my entire life. By 1983 standards, that was plenty. I bought some grey Lee Jeans that were popular and the new pinstripe Lee jeans too, dope! I also picked-up some Calvin Klein Jeans, a pair of leather Nike shoes, and a few other things that I needed. For the first time, in quite a while, I was ready for the first day of school.

I arrived at Lincoln on the first day, unaware of my previous semester's grades. My mother kicked me out on the day I was to pick them up. The good news was, I passed all my classes. The bad news? I was a whole semester behind where I should have been. That sophomore semester where I missed two months, had come back to haunt me. Based on my grades, I was still a junior in high school. I had to take a moment to let that sink in. I thought about all the residents at Pyramid. Out of the twelve of us, only one other guy besides myself was attending high school. He was nineteen years old in the 10th grade! That harsh reality hit me like a Mack truck. At that moment,

I decided I wasn't going to be nineteen years old still in high school. I can fix this. I am going to graduate this year!

I asked my guidance counselor what I could do to make up for an entire high school semester. She said, "It's possible. We have to create an academic plan for you to follow." There were seven classes that I failed, which I needed to make up. Also, I had to complete my senior curriculum, as well. First, I had to drop Physical Education and replace it with a tenth-grade English class that I failed. Now I had two English classes; 12th grade English with the seniors and 10th grade English with the sophomores. My counselor also stated that after the basketball season was over, I would have to attend night school to make up some more classes. I was like, "Ok, I can do this." She then followed up with, "Oh, you're going to have to go to summer school." Damn! To add to the drama, she warned me that I COULD NOT FAIL ONE CLASS!.

Coach Hartstein caught up with me and began talking to me about my future. He said, "You know Kenny, you have a shot at earning an athletic scholarship, but you're going to have to work hard on and off the court." He then reassured me once again by promising to help me get into a college with a dormitory. He was looking directly into my eyes while he was talking to me. It made me believe he had my best interest at heart. I still struggled to understand one thing. Why would this White Jewish man, from a completely different world than I was, take time out of his own life to care about what happened to me? He was a full-time teacher and a full-time basketball coach. He must've interacted with hundreds of teens. Why would he care about one dirty kid from Brooklyn? I didn't know the answer, but I was grateful that he did.

After a couple of weeks, I became reacquainted with life as a high school student. My homegirl Teisha would pass by Pyramid on the way to her high school and pick me up every morning. We would ride the D-train together. I didn't get to see Larry as much. I was too busy with school work and basketball practice, but we talked on the phone often. He was continuing his preparation for the High School Equivalency Exam (G.E.D).

Meanwhile, a new, talented basketball player from Coney Island named Damari transferred to our school. He stood at 6'7", I was no longer the tallest student in the school. Not only was Damari added to the team, but our best player from the previous year, "Silk" was back and recovered from his gunshot wound. We were going to be unstoppable! The USA Today newspaper ranked Abraham Lincoln High School as the preseason #1 public high school basketball team in New York City. It was a fascinating time in my life. I was going to be a starter on one of the elite teams in NYC.

Coach Hartstein enrolled me in a prestigious basketball camp featuring many of the top high school seniors in the New York area. College basketball scouts were in attendance to evaluate and rank every player. After the scrimmages, the scouts gauged me as having mid-major Division 1 talent. I was ok with their assessment of my basketball ability. Unfortunately, my cumulative grade point average (GPA) was no longer up to par. Failing that full semester during my sophomore year continued to hurt me. It wasn't the fact that I failed. It was that I failed with all grades of 41 for excessive absences. That destroyed my GPA. Had I failed with a 55 or 60 average, I still would've had a shot to recover. But, those 41's were too devastating to overcome by that point. Since my GPA would fall below a 70 average, NCAA rules would not allow me to play my freshman year. Because of this, Division 1 college coaches backed away from any interest in me. I expected the news, but it was still disappointing. All was not lost, though. I could enroll in a junior college for two years to increase my GPA. Then, I could transfer to a four-year university and play two years of Division 1 college basketball. That looked like my best option. After the camp, recruiting letters began arriving at the coach's office. They were from junior colleges around the country, expressing interest in me coming there to play. Great news!

One Saturday night in October, I was heading home and running late. I had missed my 11 pm curfew. While hustling through the streets of Brooklyn, I heard a guy with a boom box playing a familiar song. It was "Sucker Mc's" by Run-DMC. As I walked a little further, I heard someone else playing the same song from their box. I then realized the song was actually ON the radio, R&B station 98.7 KISS FM. That wasn't unusual until I heard the song transition into another song. Wait a minute! Was someone mixing live on the air? I arrived home and rushed to the radio. My suspicions were correct; there was a new Rap mix show on KISS FM. Hip-Hop mix shows weren't new to New York City radio. But, they had only been available on public access radio in the wee hours of the morning. This mix show was different. It was broadcasting on a top-rated R&B station. It was one of those pivotal moments when you could tell Rap music was turning a corner.

The DJ who was mixing on KISS-FM was Kool DJ Red Alert. He was playing all the latest Rap hits plus some new, unheard-of songs. In 1983, it was challenging to discover new Rap music. You had to know a DJ, which wasn't easy because there weren't many of them. Otherwise, you would have to spend hours in the record store listening to the demo music they displayed for customers to preview. Also, the music was expensive. Most people in my neighborhood didn't have the disposable income to spend keeping up with the latest music. With the addition of a mainstream mix show, you could hear all the latest Hip-Hop jams at one time for free. This new development was essential in the evolution of Rap Music. DJ Red Alert was cutting and scratching Rap music live on the radio like the deejays I'd seen in the park. It was the beginning of something fresh and new. The possibilities were endless.

The 1983-84 PSAL basketball season started with a bang. We won our first six games by lopsided margins. I was playing the best basketball of my life, averaging 14 points and 12 rebounds per game. Everything was going great (Insert "Other Shoe" here). I was chilling out in Pyramid's living room one Saturday afternoon watching an NBA game on television when another resident walked into the living room. He said, "Yo, I wanna watch this Karate flick." I was like, "No! I'm watching this game; I was here first, man." With blatant disregard for the rules, this jerk turned the channel to his Karate movie. What the Hell? I said, "Yo, what are you doing!" I went over to the television to change the channel back to my game. As soon as I put my hand on the knob, he kicks my hand off the tv. I was furious! We squared off. I was about to have my first fight in the group home. Somebody yelled, "Take it outside!" I said, "Yeah, let's take it outside!"

As I headed towards the front door, I went to make a fist and realized that I couldn't close my hand. This idiot broke my middle finger when he kicked my hand off of the television. Ah man, this was bad. I went to the doctor, and I received some disappointing news. He said, "You are not going to be able to play basketball for several weeks." Noooooo!!! I called Coach Hartstein and explained what happened. He was not happy at all but was sympathetic to my situation. Unfortunately, everything isn't always rosy living in a group home.

I missed the next two games before traveling with the team to a basketball tournament in Upstate New York. Despite my injury, I still wanted to enjoy the experience of going to another city. Before the championship game was about to tip-off, Coach Hartstein asked, "Do you think you can play tonight?" The doctor hadn't cleared me to play any basketball because I still had a splinter on my finger. My idol Bernard King of The New York Knicks had recently broken his middle finger. He taped his middle finger to his ring finger and continued playing. I thought if Bernard King could do it, so could I. I taped my fingers together and suited up for the tournament. I scored 11 points with ten rebounds, and we won the championship. From that point on, I was back to playing basketball; weeks before my doctor cleared me to play.

Meanwhile, the wins kept piling up. Since our team featured some outstanding players, several college coaches would attend our games. After one game, Coach Hartstein said to me, "You know Kenny, a few college coaches have approached me about your availability. Most of them are here to see ("Silk"), but after seeing you play, a few have asked about you. I would have to tell them you wouldn't be eligible next year because of your grades. It's a shame." That bit of news sunk my spirits a little.

Landing an athletic scholarship to a Division 1 college, the highest level of intercollegiate athletics sanctioned by the NCAA, was the crowning achievement for a high school athlete. It was essential to your academic future and was also a benchmark that established you as a good player. The odds of winning an NCAA sports scholarship were small. Only about 2% of high school athletes win athletic scholarships every year at NCAA colleges and universities. For the sport of basketball, the numbers are even smaller. Only 1% of high school basketball players move on to the Division 1 level. Yeah, the odds are that dismal. Despite those staggering numbers, I still wanted and frankly, needed a scholarship. My G.P.A. was killing my dream. I began feeling sorry for myself. What if I never missed half of my sophomore year? What if I received real parental support? What if I had proper sneakers, shorts, and socks? I could've had a legitimate shot. Earlier that year, I ran into my former junior high school teammate, "John-John." He was now a high school All-American at Tolentine High School. John had signed a letter of intent to play for The University of Virginia. If someone were to ask me, "What school are you going to next year?" I wanted to have a definitive answer too.

As fate would have it, a college recruiting coach began showing significant interest in my abilities. Coach Hartstein called me into his office. He said,

"Kenny, I had a conversation with a recruiter who wants you to attend his school. They are willing to enroll you as a student and have you sit out a year of basketball (redshirt) to focus on raising your grades. After that, they would offer you a full athletic scholarship." That was fantastic news! I asked Coach Hartstein, "What school is it?" He replied, "Saint Peter's College" (now University). I never heard of that school. Coach Hartstein said, "It's a Division 1 school, meaning they play top-level basketball and you can live on campus. It's an excellent academic school, and it's right across the water in New Jersey, you gotta take this!" He was right. It was my best offer. Outside of junior college, it was my only offer. Still, it was gratifying to know that somebody thought enough of my basketball skills to feel I was worth the risk. Coach Hartstein told me I had time to think about my decision. I wouldn't be making an official visit to the college until after our high school basketball season ended. Meanwhile, our basketball team continued to steamroll through Brooklyn at a near-record pace.

Despite the occasional drama caused by certain guys within the facility, Pyramid's goal remained the same. They were there to assist the residents in any way possible. I soon discovered that the mere mention of academics would produce immediate results. When classes first resumed in the fall, my free monthly MTA subway pass hadn't arrived yet. I told the counselor I needed money for transportation in the meantime. Pyramid allotted two subway tokens every morning for my roundtrip travel to school. When I finally received my train pass, I um, neglected to mention that bit of information to the staff. As a result, I continued to receive two tokens every morning. The NYC subway fare increased to around $1 during this time. Everyone was furious with the MTA but, I was happy. Subway tokens were almost equal to real money. You could cash them in at any subway station. For me, it was like an extra allowance every day. The previous year, I had to beg my teammates for a small piece of their buttered bagel. Now, I could buy a bagel in the morning AND after practice. Sometimes I would buy bagels for my friends too. I didn't care. I remembered how it felt to be hungry.

The arrival of Christmas marked a personal milestone in my life. It had been six months since I arrived at Pyramid Group Home. The counselors decorated the facility with Christmas ornaments. Still, I didn't expect much. It was a group home for goodness sake. I was wrong. Pyramid presented every resident with a gift of $50! Wow! That exceeded the total amount of every gift I had received in the past ten years combined. I purchased a pair of brand new leather shell-toe Adidas. The very same sneakers I was afraid to wear as a freshman. When I returned to school after the holiday break, I was fresh!

The good news kept coming. I did a little more investigating into what else Pyramid offered its residents. I discovered that Pyramid negotiated a deal with the barbershop on the corner. Any resident who wanted a haircut could bring a voucher and receive a cut. I mustered up the courage to stroll down to the barbershop and into the barber's chair. I finally received my first official haircut since the year 1972, a span of eleven years! Slowly but surely, my life completely transformed for the better. But wait, there's more.

Pyramid dedicated itself to creating as healthy an environment as possible under the circumstances. They wanted to expose the residents to new experiences that would assist in their growth. On occasion, some of the most prominent artists and entertainers in New York City would donate tickets to organizations caring for underprivileged youth. Because of their generosity, Pyramid had access to all sorts of live events. I saw, in person, my beloved New York Knicks. I witnessed the iconic Stevie Wonder perform at Radio City Music Hall, and I saw R&B stars Ashford & Simpson perform. I even experienced WWF Wrestling at a sold-out Madison Square Garden. When wrestling superstar Hulk Hogan entered the ring, the entire arena went nuts! Pyramid purchased everyone's tailor-made dress clothes, shoes, and ties and took us out to dinner regularly. They were teaching us the proper way to eat and act when dining at a restaurant.

As the days progressed, my confidence and self-esteem began to grow. I finally had proper clothing to wear. I was a senior in high school and a starter on the best basketball team in school history. In no time, I became one of the most popular boys in the entire school. I can recall during my freshman year, at the end of the day, my friends and I would sprint to the subway station. We wanted to avoid riding the train with all the other students. Now, as a senior, I would wait outside after school until everyone exited the building. We would all ride the train home together. Several dozen of us would be hanging out in the back of the D train riding "Cross Town." I loved it! In the cafeteria, I sat at the table with all the athletes and cheerleaders who walked around the school like they owned the place. I got to see what life was like from the other side. I was different, though. I was cool with the "in" crowd, but, sometimes I sat at the table with the nerds. I knew them, too; I was one of them. I was a nerd trapped in a jock's body. I was also cool with the guys from Coney Island. I was cool with the White boys. I was even cool with the underclassmen since some of the classes I had to make up contained sophomores. None of the other seniors interacted with the younger students.

I remembered how in awe I was of Don Marbury and how he never spoke to me. I was going to be different. I talked to everybody. It reached a point where I would arrive late to my classes because I spent too much time talking to my fellow students in the hallway. Everywhere I went, people were saying, "Yo, what's up, KP!" I would have to say, "Yo, I gotta go." It was easy to forget that a year earlier, I was wearing the same clothes to school every day. That seemed like a long time ago. I had no intention of looking back either. I loved being popular. It was like a dream. If this is what the other side looks like, don't wake me up.

When classes resumed after the Christmas break, I noticed that I hadn't seen Teisha going to school in the morning like she used to. I became concerned. When I finally tracked her down, she told me that she wasn't going back to school anymore. Teisha had dropped out of high school. What a shame. She only had one more semester left. I was very disappointed with her decision, but what could I say? One thing was for sure; she was hanging out with Red even more.

Sometime during January, our basketball team traveled to a scheduled road game. I rode to the game with Coach Hartstein. As soon as we departed, he immediately cuts on the car radio. To my surprise, he listened to the same radio station that we all listened to, 98.7 KISS FM. I was like, "Yooo! Coach Hartstein listen to KISS! Who knew?" As we were riding along, one of the year's hottest R&B ballads comes on the radio, 'If Only You Knew' by the legendary Patti Labelle. That was my jam! Coach Hartstein turned up the volume and said, "Hey, I like this song." What? I'm watching in amazement at a White Jewish man nodding his head to this smooth soul music.

The way I perceived Coach Hartstein, I couldn't believe he listened to music at all. I turned to him and said with sarcasm, "What do you know about Patti Labelle?" Coach Hartstein turned to me with a look of disbelief and said, "What? I've liked her ever since she was with The Bluebelles." I said, "Who?" Coach said, "Exactly," and turned the volume up louder. It was hysterical. When I got older, I discovered how ridiculous I must've sounded to him. I didn't know Patti Labelle was in a group called The Bluebelles in the 1960s. That would be comparable to a youngster claiming to like Beyonce and not knowing she was in a group called Destiny's Child. The way Coach Hartstein dismissed me was priceless. We shared a good laugh. I felt like in a small way, it elevated our relationship.

February arrived. Abraham Lincoln High School had rolled through Brooklyn undefeated for the first time since the 1940s. It was playoff time, and Lincoln was favored to win the Brooklyn public school title. We advanced to the Brooklyn PSAL championship against Boys & Girls High School. This squad featured several future Division 1 basketball players. They also added "Bug Eye," who was now a high school All-American headed to The University of Kentucky. Lincoln was still favored to win the game. Unfortunately, we lost at the buzzer! It was a crushing defeat, the worst loss of my life. Even some of the freshmen were crying. It wasn't only because we lost the Brooklyn championship but because our team was so tight-knit. I had become close with Coach Hartstein, and just like that, it was over. He wasn't my coach anymore. It was the end of my basketball career at Lincoln.

I ended up averaging 12 points and a team-leading eleven rebounds per game. Averaging a double-double on one of the best teams in the city was a great accomplishment for me. Now, I had to prepare for life after high school. I needed to figure out where I was going to college. Two of my teammates had already earned athletic scholarships to a Division 1 program. "Silk" was off to Rhode Island University, where he would become the school's all-time leader in both scoring and assists. My other teammate, Damari, was attending Fairleigh Dickinson University. He would later graduate second all-time in scoring and blocked shots. I could be the third member of our basketball team to receive an athletic scholarship. That would've put me in an elite company, but I first needed to graduate from high school.

Following the completion of the basketball season, my official visit to St. Peter's College was up next. The recruiting coach, Ron Ganulin, picked me up at Pyramid. We drove through the Holland Tunnel to Jersey City, NJ, the location of the school. Coach Ganulin gave me a tour of the school grounds. He walked me through the athletic facility and, most importantly, showed me the dormitory. Afterward, we went to dinner. He reiterated their interest in having me join the basketball program. Although it was my best move, I was still unsure for some reason. Coach Ganulin could sense my apprehension. He said, "Let me show you something." We took a quick five-minute drive from the campus to the Jersey City Waterfront. I could see the entire New York City skyline from there. He said, "Do you see how close we are to the city? You won't get homesick here. You could go home anytime you wanted to." That put my mind at ease. I was so accustomed to living in Brooklyn. The mere thought of changing environments made me feel uneasy despite living in a group home in Bed-Stuy. It was time to grow up. I chose to accept the offer to attend St. Peter's College. When we returned to the campus, I met with the head coach Bob Dukiet and signed a letter of intent that same day.

I was on my way to a Division 1 program like the other top basketball players in the city. As I was leaving, the coach handed me a brand new pair of Nike Air Force 1's. The same $80 sneakers that few in my neighborhood could afford. They were blue and white with a blue strap. The best sneakers money could buy. The next day I returned to Lincoln H.S. wearing Air Force 1's on my feet like WHAT! It wasn't that long ago that I walked around with a tear on the side of my Converse All-Stars. Now I owned several pairs of leather sneakers. I wasn't even thinking about the past. I was only looking towards the future and not trying to do anything to make the "Other Shoe" drop.

With the college recruitment process out of the way, my next step was enrolling in night school. I needed to make up two credits that I needed to graduate. The location of the night classes was New Utrecht High School in Bay Ridge, Brooklyn. Attending night school meant three more train rides per week. For me, that meant three more subway tokens. When I arrived at night school on the first day, there was another basketball player in my class. His situation was similar to mine. He had an athletic scholarship awaiting him but needed night school to graduate. My thought process was, "Ok, I need to pass these classes; there's no fooling around here." The other ballplayer walked in, put his head down on the desk, and slept for the entire class! I couldn't believe it.

After a couple of weeks, things were going well. I passed my first few exams with no problem. Meanwhile, this other dude was asleep the entire time without a care in the world. One day, I arrived at night school, and for some reason, I felt tired. I decided that today was the day I was going to get some rest too. The minute I put my head down, the teacher barked at me, "Kenneth, don't you sleep in my class! What are you doing?" I apologized and went back to my classwork, confused. Why hasn't she said anything to this other guy who's been asleep for two weeks? Later on, I realized what happened. The teacher had given up on the other ballplayer after the first day of classes. She saw potential in me and wasn't going to let me slack off for a second. Once again, my immaturity tried to get the best of me, but a nice kick in my ass set me straight. Night school ended with me passing both of my classes. That other guy, he failed everything. What the hell was I thinking? I had an athletic scholarship waiting for me, and I wanted to sleep?

After completing my night school requirements, I moved on to the next stage of my academic plan. I needed to pass my remaining high school classes and prepare for summer school. I could see the light at the end of the tunnel. As expected, that "other shoe" drop was never too far away. After conferring with my guidance counselor, she mentioned to me, "Have you taken the SAT yet?" Huh? What's an SAT? I soon discovered that it was an entrance exam used by most colleges and universities to make admissions decisions. All high school seniors who wanted to attend a four-year college had to pass the SAT or not get accepted. A perfect score would be 1600. A score of 1400 plus would be an Ivy League-level score. A score of 700 was the minimum required for college admission.

How come no one mentioned this to me before May of my senior year? No one brought it to my attention because college wasn't an option at the beginning of the school year based on my GPA. I became more concerned when I learned that a large percentage of the test would be math-related. I had missed several key math classes during my sophomore year that I needed to pass the test. To make matters worse, I already missed the first opportunity to take the SAT. Now, I would only have one chance to pass the test. My academic advisor gave me a piece of advice. She told me that you are only graded based on the questions you answer. She said, "If you don't know the answer to a question, don't try to guess, leave it blank. It's better than answering the question wrong and losing points."

The day arrived for the most important exam of my life. I had to travel to a different high school, sign in, and show ID to ensure no one else took the test in my place. If they caught you talking, you would automatically fail. The SAT was the hardest test I had ever taken in my life. When I reached the math portion of the test, I left the entire Geometry and Trigonometry section blank. After completing the SAT, the instructor told us to expect the results in a few weeks. I wasn't holding my breath.

The summer of 1984 had arrived. I passed all my exams and completed my senior classes. Yes! However, I was still three credits short of my graduation requirements. It was time for summer school, which happened to be at Erasmus Hall High School. It was also time to catch up with Larry. Summer classes were underway when I received a frantic call from St. Peter's College coach Ganulin. His voice sounded excited. He said, "We got your SAT results; you scored 910 on the SAT!" What? How could that be? I barely answered any of the math questions on the test. Coach Ganulin said, "It looks like you scored well on the English part of the test." He sounded more surprised than as I was. He never relayed his concerns, but I'm not sure how confident he was in me passing the SAT. He had only known me as a poor student. Although my GPA didn't reflect it, I proved I was more than some dumb athlete from the slums of New York City. Anyway, after receiving that fantastic news, I was now in the home stretch. All I needed to do was pass my summer school classes, and I was on my way to college. Coach Ganulin still had doubts about my academic abilities. He said, "You can't take any chances with summer school now. You should take the GED because if you fail summer school, you're going to lose the scholarship." I told him, "No! I am graduating from high school. I am going to pass these last few classes." He asked me, "Are you sure?" I told him yes! I was super confident now.

In my spare time, I started traveling to The Bronx more often to hang out with Larry. He had been taking GED prep classes for a year now and was about to take the test. Although Larry was still an avid graffiti writer, rapping appeared to become his top priority once again. We picked up right where we left off. I began hanging out at Larry's group home so much that sometimes I would sit at the table and have dinner like I was one of the residents. If I left the facility late, Their counselor on duty would call my counselor in Brooklyn and tell them I was on my way home. On occasion, the Bronx counselors would invite me to activities they planned for their residents. One evening, I attended a party thrown at the Bronx group home. The guest performer was none other than resident rapper KRS. He was dazzling! Larry had improved from the tape my boy Money Mike played for me two years earlier. Rapper KRS had call and response routines that I never heard anyone else recite before. I remember leaving the party feeling like Larry sounded as good as the guys who made real Rap songs. I was no expert, so I wasn't sure if he was that good, or I was happy to see my brother rapping. All I knew was, everyone else seemed to agree with my assessment.

On one of my excursions up to The Bronx, I got hit with some fantastic news. Larry passed the GED, by one freakin' point! It was a tremendous accomplishment. I always knew he could do it. Larry didn't have a learning disability. He finally buckled down and put his mind to it. For some reason, in that particular group home environment, he was able to find himself and focus. It was similar to my situation. Larry might have excelled in a visual and performing arts type of school like Fiorello H. LaGuardia High School in New York City. Who knows? I do know that the summer of 1984 was a great time academically for the Parker Brothers.

Although I visited The Bronx often, I still spent the majority of my time hanging around Darrell's house. By the time my 18th birthday rolled around, our backyard crew had expanded quite a bit. The regulars included me, Darrell, KoJo, Rick, Keith, Kurt, Anthony, King, Shawn, Jack, Aaron, and "E," to name a few. The most popular and respected member of the crew was still Darrell's older brother Chilly Kev. There were also two newcomers to the group who immediately fit right in—a likable guy named "Sid Love" and his older brother Steve. Most of our friends were of a similar mindset. They were either freshmen in college or were planning to attend college in the fall. Steve was the only crew member whose lifestyle and whereabouts were a question mark.

One day, Darrell and I were sitting on his front steps talking when Steve came over and struck up a casual conversation. Steve mentioned that he had recently begun selling drugs. At first, I didn't know what to make of Steve's confession. In 1984, hearing someone our age talk about selling drugs was rare. Even the guys at Pyramid, who spoke about crime all the time, never mentioned selling drugs. Steve continued the conversation by boasting about how much fun he was having and how much money he was making. He then took the conversation to a different level. He claimed a new drug on the market was so addictive that even young girls would do anything to get their hands on it. Now Steve had our full attention. He bragged about how these girls would have sex with him in an abandoned building for drugs. I flat out told Steve that was bullshit! I asked him what do these so-called girls look like who would have sex with an ordinary guy like Steve in exchange for drugs? He said, "I'm telling you, these girls are fly!" Both Darrell and I were skeptical. Steve then invited us to join him in his new occupation. We both declined his offer. I felt like Steve was full of shit and didn't give his story much consideration after that.

In hindsight, why did Steve bring up drug dealing around guys who he knew for a fact didn't use drugs, much less have any inclination to sell them? Knowing our personalities, he risked being shunned by everyone in our group instead of simply being brushed off. Was Steve trying to feel us out? Was he on some sort of recruiting mission for new workers? Or users? Who else in our crew did Steve try to lure? Did they brush him off too?

About a week later, I went to Darrell's house after summer school. I bumped into his brother Chilly Kev upstairs near his bedroom. I said, "What's up, Kev?" and smiled. Kevin looked at me with a serious face and said, "Shut up!" He then pulled out a sawed-off double-barreled shotgun and pointed at my chest. I yelled out, "Yoooo Kevin, stop playing!" He burst out laughing and said, "Stop acting like a little bitch! It's not even loaded!" I was like, "Are you crazy! Do you know how many people are dead because they thought a gun wasn't loaded?" Kevin said, "Chill out, man, I know what I'm doing." I was surprised by his behavior. Kevin was a good kid; this wasn't like him at all. The next obvious question was, "Where did you get a sawed-off shotgun from?" Kevin smiled and shrugged his shoulders without answering me. I didn't know what to say. I caught up with Darrell and never mentioned it.

A few nights later, Darrell and I were sitting on his steps chilling once again. Out of nowhere, we saw Kevin, Steve, and two other guys running through the alley at top speed. They were heading towards the house. Kevin was holding that same sawed-off shotgun in his hand as they ran through the door. About sixty seconds later, the block was swarming with police cars driving around looking for someone. It was obvious who they were looking for; Kevin, Steve, and the rest of them. We found out they robbed a taxicab driver of $100. Kevin, the oldest of the four, had incomprehensibly pointed the loaded sawed-off shotgun at the driver's head during the robbery. What the hell? The Kevin I knew had graduated from high school. He was working at a job paying him more than double what they stole from the cab driver.

What if the cab driver had refused to surrender his money or fought back in some way? Would "Chilly Kev" had blown his head off?

About five minutes later, all four left the house together on their way to commit yet another robbery! I kid you not. We were still sitting on the front steps. Darrell said to his brother, "Yo, man, don't go out there; the police are all around here." Kevin answered Darrell while using a Jamaican accent, "Me no worry dat!" Translation: I don't care! Darrell turned to me and said, "Why is he talking like that? He's not even Jamaican." The entire episode was surreal. Those fools didn't get one block before the police arrested all four of them. To add to the lunacy, each one of them had $25 worth of one dollar bills in their pockets. The police also recovered the shotgun Kevin tried to throw into the bushes. Kevin was the oldest of the four and considered the ring leader. He got sent to the notorious Rikers Island Jail Complex to await trial while his mother attempted to raise bail money. All this for $25 apiece?

I would have bet everything I owned in the world that Kevin would've been the last person in our crew capable of such an awful deed. I knew Kevin's parents. He was not raised in an environment that would breed that caliber of criminal, and yet, there he was. Kevin wasn't the only person in our crew to fall victim to the allure of the streets. A few of the guys from that earlier list of names decided to chose what was behind door number three and lost. Our boy Aaron, who was also a friendly kid, began selling drugs like Steve. Shortly after, we learned that someone had killed Aaron (R.I.P.). One of our closest friends, "King", from that same list, also decided to dip his hand in the drug game. He later chose to commit murder and got sentenced to 25 years in prison. King and I go back to The Boy's Club when we were fourteen years old. He hung out with us every single day during the summer months for four straight years. It turns out he was a killer. Another guy from that same list of names committed a bank robbery. This fool didn't have a getaway car, so he chose to catch a "Dollar Van" home instead. The police captured him, and he served ten years in prison. Unbelievable.

On the other hand, three of the names on that list graduated from college, with one becoming a lawyer. Most of the guys from that list are now homeowners with families and careers. The moral of the story is, you can never predict what path an individual will choose. Even if you know how their parents raised them, what advantages they had, or what hardships they had to overcome? Sometimes, all it takes is a casual conversation to lead a person astray or lead them back on the right path.

About three blocks from Pyramid Group Home is Herkimer Street. Prostitutes used to solicit there at night. Around my way, they didn't use the term prostitute. If a certain girl were a streetwalker, they would say she was on the "Hoe Stroll." One day, a resident of Pyramid asked me, "Yo, what's up with your girl Teisha?" I told him I hadn't seen her since she dropped out of high school months earlier. This guy was like, "Yo, I heard Teisha be on Herkimer Street." What? I told him I didn't believe that bullshit. He said, "Yo, that girl's on the hoe stroll." I was furious. I wanted to fight him for spreading lies about my friend. Asshole!

Shortly after that conversation, I was walking near Herkimer Street, and I saw Teisha. What a coincidence! She sees me and yells, "Yo, Kenny, what's up? I haven't seen you in so long, how are you doing?" As she walked over to hug me, I saw two cars slow down and stop across the street. I looked over, and who do I see getting into one of the vehicles? Red! I hadn't seen Red in months either. Red yells to Teisha from across the street "Yo...You ain't got no time for that; we gotta make this money! Get in that car!" Without hesitation, Teisha turns around and gets into this random car, and they sped off. As much as I wanted to, there was no denying it now. Teisha was on the Hoe Stroll! How could her life make such a drastic and destructive turn in a matter of months? It was heartbreaking to see her out there like that, but what could I do? I was still trying to figure out my own life. All I could do was pray for her and move on.

Every so often, a person receives an eye-opener that puts their entire life into perspective. You can choose to be in denial, but "The Truth" will reveal itself whether you like it or not. When I first arrived at Pyramid in 1983, it was too late to assign me a sanctioned New York City summer youth job. At the beginning of the summer of 1984, youth jobs were once again assigned. An official NYC summer youth job wasn't easy to secure. There were thousands of jobs, but at least five times as many teenagers applying for those jobs. NYC decided to assign each applicant a number in a sort of ranking/lottery system. The most "in need of assistance" teenagers in the city would get offered jobs first, and then everyone else would get to pick afterward. The first 100 or so teens ranked would be the worst by far. That number must have risen into the tens of thousands. One would assume that foster homes, group homes, and halfway houses would get assigned numbers first.

Although I was attending summer school, Pyramid still enrolled me in the program. I received my reply in the mail. The letter read, "Dear Kenneth Parker, thank you for applying. Your number is 36." Wow! If I hadn't already come to grips with how dire my situation was, according to The City Of New York, I was among the most troubled youths in the entire city. I could've had my pick of any cushy summer job that I wanted. Hey, at least I ranked in the top 40 in something.

After a month in Rikers Island, Darrell's mother raised the bail money to secure Kevin's release. Welcome home! The next day, we all went to an open gym and played basketball. During the game, Kevin got into an argument with some random guy. Kevin yelled, "What, boy! You don't want none of this! I just got out of Rikers Island!" The other guy heard Riker's Island and immediately backed down. Darrell whispered in my ear, "He didn't mention how he was calling my mother every night, begging her to get him out of there." We burst out laughing! Darrell was forever the asshole.

At long last, the summer of 1984 ended. I received my final summer school grades, and I passed all three of my classes. I graduated from high school and was college-bound. What an incredible journey! One year earlier, I couldn't have imagined I would've had the determination to overcome the obstacles in front of me and reach this milestone. I was grateful to be in the position that I found myself in. Things could have gone in another direction. Case in point, that other basketball player from my night school class who slept the entire time also failed summer school. I know for an absolute fact that this guy had enrolled in college and already moved his stuff into the dormitory when they released the summer school grades. Not only did he lose his athletic scholarship, but he also had to pack up his stuff, leave college, and enroll right back into high school to finish his senior year! That could've been me had I strayed from the path. Thanks to hard work, some quality people helping me along the way, and some divine intervention, I was able to complete that hurdle and move on.

In celebration of my college acceptance, Pyramid threw an impressive banquet in my honor at a dining hall in Manhattan. Several directors from various agencies around the city were in attendance. They treated me like a superstar. I was the poster child for what was achievable through social work. It was rare for a resident of a group home to attend college. None of the other eleven residents at Pyramid graduated from high school. They were so proud of me. There were about 100 people in attendance, giving me accolades, I couldn't believe it. I mean, I was still that same number 36 summer youth job kid. They presented me with an award that read, "This is a certificate of merit representing personal achievement through extraordinary circumstances." For a social worker, this was the most satisfying outcome. If you can help one kid, then you've made a difference in this world. There are honest, hardworking, unsung counselors all over the world. I was proof that the system works.

Finally, the summer of 1984 concluded. There were only a few days left to hang out. Instead of going to Darrell's house, I decided to make a detour and found myself on my old block, where I used to live. As I strolled down that old familiar street, I decided to visit the lady upstairs, Dee. I liked Dee and hadn't seen her since my mother kicked me out over a year ago. I went upstairs and knocked on her door. She opened the door and was like, "Oh my Gawd, I haven't seen you in so long. You look good. How are you doing?" Dee and I talked for a couple of minutes, and then she said, "Hold on one second, I'll be right back." She went into the kitchen and returned about thirty seconds later, smiling. Dee said, "Guess who I have on the phone. It's your mother!" What? It appeared that they remained friends and talked on the phone often. I was utterly shocked and blindsided by her actions. I had placed all the anger and resentment that I had for my mother far into my mind's background. I chose to focus only on the present. Now, without warning, here she was on the phone. I didn't want to be disrespectful to Dee in her home. What was I going to do?

Before I could say anything, Dee hands me the phone. I took the phone, put it to my ear, and said, "Hello." My mother responds with, "Hello Kenneth, how are you?" I said, "I'm fine" in a monotone voice. I could feel a lump in my throat. I didn't know what to say. I took a deep breath and realized there was only one thing I wanted to know. I asked her, "What did you think happened to me?" She responded without hesitation in a sarcastic voice, "I thought you went to go live at Darrell's house, you were always over there anyway." What? That was her plan? To dump her child off on another woman? I became furious all over again. She said it so matter-of-fact like it was nothing. I knew she didn't believe that. She wanted to have something smart to say. I responded with, "Nah, I live in a group home now, that's where I'm at." She didn't say anything. I added, "I'm about to start college now, so I'm doing good." She started saying something, but I handed the phone back to Dee and headed for the door. After her ambush, I'm pretty sure Dee noticed the change in my attitude. All I wanted to do was drop by and say hello, I didn't ask her to put my mother on the phone. I said goodbye and never saw Dee again. I found myself leaving that same building, one year later, with my blood boiling all over again.

My mother's distorted logic was beyond belief. Even if she assumed I would "go to Darrell's house" (which was a lie). Her decision to dump her responsibility onto Darrell's mother was still immoral. How dare she assume that another woman should have taken in HER son. She doesn't get to make that decision. The State Of New York determined that parents are responsible for their child until the age of eighteen, not sixteen or seventeen. A parent can't decide when their kid is mature enough or big enough or whatever other excuses a parent could conjure up to skirt their responsibilities. My mother stated on several occasions how she "couldn't wait until I turned eighteen." She knew the law.

On top of that, not only didn't she have a prearranged agreement with Darrell's mother to allow me to live there, but she never called Darrell's house to see if I arrived safely. Darrell lived in the same house with the same phone number. Not once did she call to check on my well-being in over a year. If Dee hadn't decided to put her on the phone, I never would have heard from her again. There was only one, indisputable truth. She didn't care.

Despite my initial anger, I realized how that short two-minute exchange was a positive experience. It was like a certification, a stamp from God that He had placed me right where I needed to be. If I had any doubt about who my mother was, hearing her talk that same old twisted rhetoric one year later made me a believer. I decided to leave her right where she belonged, in the past. She didn't matter to me now. I was only focusing on what possibilities the future might hold.

CHAPTER 11
SHO NUFF

Labor Day of 1984 was a little over a year since my mother abandoned me. During that time, The Bureau Of Child Welfare assigned me to a group home for boys. I became a Ward Of The State Of New York. I witnessed the statutory rape of an underage girl. Someone gruesomely murdered my roommate, Stanley, and another resident got beaten to within an inch of his life. My boy Aaron got killed, and my boy China got shot. My close friend Chilly Kev committed an armed robbery and was out on bail awaiting trial. I saw a baby given a controlled substance. My closest female friend, Teisha, was on the Hoe Stroll, and I broke my finger in a fight.

On the other hand, I finally buckled down and graduated from high school. I earned an athletic scholarship to attend a Division 1 college. I discovered what I was capable of if I put my mind to it. I even got a much-needed haircut. For the first time in my life, I could envision my future in a positive light.

A few days before I was to move into the Saint Peter's College dormitory, I stopped by Darrell's house for my final visit of the summer. Larry decided to travel from The Bronx to Brooklyn to see me off as well. Larry happened to have recently moved. Since he was now nineteen years old, The City Of New York provided him with individual housing. Larry was planning to attend art school after passing the GED exam. Larry arrived at Darrell's house, along with his close friend, "ICU." Meeting ICU marked the first time Larry ever introduced anyone to me as his friend who didn't live in his immediate vicinity (i.e., Group Home, Apt. Building). I was the one who always introduced my friends to him. We all agreed to meet back at Darrell's house the following week after I settled into college. We said our goodbyes and Larry was off.

A couple of days before I moved away to school, Pyramid surprised me with an unusual gift. In the past, any resident attending school received a clothing stipend of $125. This time, they presented me with an envelope containing $250. Wow! I guess they wanted their first-ever college student to represent Pyramid Group Home in style. I bought a bunch of new clothing and kept a little money for myself. I was all set.

I moved into the dorms over a weekend, which wasn't hard because all I brought was a duffle bag full of clothes. I bought a mattress and box spring from a nearby furniture store and had it delivered. After I settled in, I met my two new roommates and the rest of the coaching staff. I was an official college student.

I then encountered my first case of culture shock. All the stores in the surrounding area closed by 11 pm. In the nearby vicinity of the college, there were only houses, trees, and the campus. I began to think Jersey City was some rural, suburban area. If a cow had walked down the street, I would have been like, "Yeah, that makes sense." I had grown accustomed to Bed-Stuy, where 2 am looked like 2 pm. All kinds of people would be walking the streets late at night, most of them up to no good. New York is "The City That Never Sleeps." Everyone around here was asleep by 11 pm.

I met all the players on the basketball team for the first time. That was another eye-opener. For the majority of my life, I was the tallest person in my entire school. In college, there were seven guys on the basketball team taller than me. I went from being a very tall basketball player to being in the middle of the pack. Also, everyone on this team had been the star of their respective high school basketball teams. Each player earned either all-county, all-region, all-state, or "all-something" recognition in their hometown. The competition level was far beyond what I experienced in high school. Saint

Peter's College is a Jesuit institution which at the time, was about 95% White. I was coming from a home environment that was at least 98% Black. That would be something else I had to adjust to. My first order of business was to go to the registrar's office and fill out all the financial aid papers. My scholarship wouldn't take effect until the following year when I was eligible to play collegiate basketball.

On the first day of classes, I felt compelled to stop in the middle of the campus quadrangle to take it all in. I stood there, observing hundreds of students heading to class, and became very emotional. Everything hit me all at once. I couldn't believe I was there. I was a freshman, right along with the rest of my freshman class, right on schedule. I was pretty sure no other first-year student in the entire school endured what I had. I decided I wasn't going to tell anybody about my past or current situation. Nobody knew I was currently a member of a group home except the coaching staff. I was going to do my best to blend into this new environment; I belong here.

My academic advisor completed my schedule, and boy were the classes tough. Biology 101, Business Management 101, Finite Math, and Political Science 101. To top it off, my advisor enrolled me in level 3, advanced English, because of my high SAT score in English. How could he hit me with this crazy workload? Aren't I supposed to be here trying to raise my GPA?

Meanwhile, head coach Bob Dukiet summoned all six incoming freshmen to his office. He sat us down, looked into our eyes, and flat out said, "Not all of you will graduate from this school. A couple of you won't even be here next year." He then warned us, "Don't let it be you." I began to realize how different the coaching staff spoke to you during the recruiting process compared to after you arrived on campus. No more "sweet talk," it was a whole different ball game now (no pun intended).

After the coach's "pep talk," we went to an athletic orientation. A spokesperson from the NCAA came and spoke to us about gambling and point shaving. Betting on collegiate sports is a multi-million dollar a year business. In the past, athletes had taken money from organized crime to influence the outcomes of basketball games. The Spokesperson warned us of the severe legal ramifications associated with cheating. I got the impression that you were better off committing a murder than point shaving.

In one hour, my head coach warned me that I most likely wouldn't graduate from school, and a representative from the NCAA convinced me that point shaving was a capital offense. Throw in the fact that there would be random drug testing and severe gift restrictions. Sheesh, what did I sign up for after all?

As I digested the college lifestyle, I began to overhear other students engaged in various conversations. The general topics were far different than the ones I heard in my neighborhood. No one talked about how much money they had. No one wore any major jewelry. Almost everyone there was dressed in sweatpants and sweatshirts. No one talked about how tough they were or who came home from prison. There was no talk of any criminal activity at all. Most of the conversations I heard pertained to, "What's your major? What did you score on the test? What does your family do? Where are you going on spring break? What are your plans after graduation?" Everything I thought was cool my entire life was now unimportant. All the fly guys who hung out in the hallway, smoking, and drinking in high school, were now considered losers in college. Nobody laughed at you for going to the library. All that was over. People were paying large sums of money in tuition fees. They took their education and future seriously.

After a couple of weeks on campus, I came to a realization. I had more in common with these students than I did with most of the people I grew up around. This environment was more suitable to my personality than Bed-Stuy or Flatbush or The South Bronx or Harlem. To my surprise, it was a small college campus surrounded by students from all over the country that I felt most at home. I never would've predicted that in a million years.

Every weekend, I would return to Pyramid to do my laundry and say hello to everybody. So, Pyramid decided to bestow upon me another special privilege. Every resident was assigned at least one, sometimes two roommates per room. However, one small single room on the 2nd floor remained locked most of the time. Pyramid reserved this space for the most senior member of the group home, "The Top Dog." The head supervisor designated this room as my private bedroom whenever I chose to return home from school. However, the commute between New Jersey and Brooklyn became too costly. I also discovered that my financial aid check would be arriving two weeks later than I expected. One weekend, I had no choice but to travel back to Pyramid with my last few coins just to get a meal. I asked the counselor on duty if I could take some food back with me to the dorms. He told me I could not take food from the group home, but I could eat all I wanted as long as I was in the facility. Damn, that wouldn't work for me.

I began telling my plight to another counselor who was also on duty at the time. He was a muscular African-American man who stood about 6'3" tall. He happened to be a part-time competitive Karate champion who auditioned for a role in the classic action movie, 'The Last Dragon,' as the character "Sho Nuff." Let's call this particular counselor, Sho Nuff. He said to me, "You know what Kenny, I'll lend you $40 until you get your financial aid check, but you gotta do me a favor." I was like, "Ok, what favor?" He said, "Come upstairs, and I'll show you." We went upstairs to the 4th-floor office, and he closed the door. He then pulled out a journal with some hand-drawn sketches in it. Sho Nuff explained to me that he was trying to write an instructional Karate book. He was attempting to draw by hand all of the poses he wanted to teach in the book. He showed me detailed sketches of various poses and said, "I'm having a problem drawing the poses that I want to teach. I need someone to model them for me."

The deal was, if I agreed to pose for some polaroids of the Karate poses he needed for his book, Sho Nuff would lend me the $40 that I needed. I was apprehensive about doing these poses because I didn't know anything about Karate. I would look like a fool. Sho Nuff said, "Look, here are the drawings right here in my journal. All you have to do is copy these poses. I'll help you. It won't take long." Sho Nuff's request seemed odd to me, but I needed the money, so I agreed. How bad could it be? Sho Nuff said, "Ok, here's what I need you to do. In order for me to draw it properly, you have to take off your clothes." Huh? That caught me off guard. I said, "Nah, man, I can't do that." Sho Nuff said, "No, it's gonna be ok. I have a jockstrap that you can wear; you won't be completely naked. It's no big deal."

My instincts were telling me something was very wrong here. But, I figured, "Hey, Sho Nuff is an athlete, I'm an athlete, it would be like being in a locker room." I had known this counselor for a year and a half, and he was cool, I guessed it would be ok. I also took into account that he was also going out on a limb to lend me the money. Counselors were not allowed to give any resident unauthorized money. I needed the $40 so, I went into the bathroom, took off my clothes, and put on the jockstrap. I emerged from the restroom, wearing only a jockstrap, about as naked as a guy could be without being nude.

Sho Nuff showed no facial expression. He was all business. He pulled out a polaroid instant camera and showed me the first pose in his book that he wanted me to simulate. The pose was pretty simple. I did the pose, click, he takes the picture. I do the next pose, click, he takes another shot. After about five or six poses, they started becoming more detailed. He turns the page in the journal and says, "Ok, kneel, one knee up and one knee down"...click. At this point, I'm thinking, "This is taking longer than I thought." Seven or eight minutes elapsed by this point, but it seemed longer. I was starting to feel more uncomfortable, but Sho Nuff kept taking pictures. We were moving pretty fast now. He then shows me this one drawing of a guy with his hands down like he was doing pushups. His legs were far apart, "Spread Eagle," with his ass pointing to the ceiling. Sho Nuff said, "Do this pose so I can take the picture."

I was about to get down on my hands when something came over me. I began thinking, "There is no way on earth I'm doing a spread eagle in a jockstrap on the floor." I turned to Sho Nuff and said, "Nah, man, I'm not doing this one." He said, "Ok, ok, it's over, that was the last one. Go into the bathroom and put your clothes back on." I went back to the bathroom, feeling weird. I came out of the bathroom dressed, and Sho Nuff hands me $40. He said, "When you get your money in a couple of weeks, you can pay me back. Thank you, you've helped me out so much." I took the money and headed back to New Jersey.

I was sitting on the train, replaying the entire scenario in my mind. What struck me as odd was; Sho Nuff already sketched in the journal all the poses he claimed to have trouble drawing. That's how he communicated what poses he wanted me to do. How was he having trouble with his illustrations? Even the spread eagle pose was already there, drawn in detail. Was this about the poses, or did he trick me into taking pictures in a jockstrap? I was so embarrassed. I vowed to never, ever, mention this episode to anyone. After two weeks, my financial aid check arrived. I returned to Pyramid and repaid Sho Nuff his $40. We never spoke about it again. Somewhere, out there, are pictures of me in a jockstrap, doing karate poses. I'm glad I finally drew the line at spread eagle. To make matters worse, I still had to pay Sho Nuff his money back. I should've been a smarter negotiator. Lesson learned.

After two months, I adapted to my new life as a full-time college student. One thing was still bugging me; I hadn't heard from Larry. We agreed to meet a week after school started, but he never showed up. He hadn't called Darrell's house either. I decided to investigate. I traveled to The Bronx to look for him. I went to his former group home to see if anyone had any information on his whereabouts. No luck. I checked the girl's group home, and no one had seen him. I went to a couple of other hangout spots, and no one had seen him there either. Larry disappeared. I was very concerned, but I convinced myself that he'd resurface sooner or later. After that, I didn't leave the campus. I distanced myself from "all things, Brooklyn." I was still required to check in with Pyramid monthly to keep them updated.

Meanwhile, the Hip-Hop mix show seen in NYC expanded in 1984. Not only was my favorite DJ, Red Alert, mixing on the weekends, but 98.7 KISS FM added another DJ to the lineup as well. His name was DJ Chuck Chillout. Not to be outdone, rival station 107.5 WBLS began airing "The Rap Attack" mix show featuring Mr. Magic and his DJ/producer extraordinaire Marley Marl. The late-night DJ competition made for some great radio. Of course, I was wide awake with my tape recorder ready. No one else in my dormitory seemed to want to stay inside on a Saturday night and record Rap songs off the radio. I guess they had a life. But, when Monday rolled around, and everyone recovered from their weekend festivities, I was the only one who had all the latest songs. Everyone would be knocking on my door, begging for a copy of my mix show cassette. Meanwhile, still no sign of Larry, four months, and counting.

Christmas of 1984 was a quiet one. Most of the students went home for the holidays, but I stayed in the dorms by myself. My confused roommate asked, "You're not going home?" I made up some lame excuse, but the truth was, the dorms were my home. The new year of 1985 coincided with my first-semester grades release, and they were awful. My subpar performance was likely the result of poor study habits and an overwhelming curriculum. I needed to maintain at least a C average to be eligible next season, and all I had were D's. To make matters worse, my schedule for the following semester was part two of all the classes I struggled with the first semester. It was imperative that I buckled down or else.

Despite being far removed from the streets of New York, I began hearing talk of a new, cheap, cocaine-based drug sweeping through the hood. They called it "Crack." I recalled that conversation I had with Steve (R.I.P.) when he bragged about exchanging sex for drugs, and it all began to make sense. Crack was yet to explode, but it was on everyone's radar. I was so grateful to be away attending school. An area like Bed-Stuy would have been ripe for a drug of this caliber. One day, I got into an odd conversation with one of the guys on the basketball team about Crack. I mentioned how crazy a person would have to be to try a drug so potent that one hit would have you addicted. To my surprise, this Division 1 collegiate athlete said, "You know what? I tried it, and it scared the shit out of me." What? Now I needed to know why it scared him. He confessed to me that, "It was so good that it was better than sex. It scared me, so I had to leave it alone." What? This guy was a muscular, 6'6" tall physical specimen who dated a hot cheerleader. I remember thinking, "Crack is better than your girlfriend?" I didn't want to try anything better than sex. That should be the limit of the human body, the absolute threshold. The year was 1985, and Crack was still in its infancy. The real horrors were yet to come.

June of 1985 arrived, and my freshman year came to an end. By this time, three things had occurred. First, my grades, which were better than my first semester, were still subpar. I landed on "Academic Probation." What a disappointment. Instead of turning my life around, I was in danger of flunking out of college. Second, there was still no sign of Larry, eight months, and counting. I began to fear he was either dead or in jail. The third development was I started dating a girl named Pam, who lived in my co-ed dormitory. She was African-American and a member of the St. Peter's College Women's Basketball Team. She was two years older than I was and hailed from Baltimore, Maryland. We were together all the time. In July, Pam threw me a bash for my 19th birthday. It was the first birthday party of my entire life. I was having a fantastic time and, you guessed it, the other shoe dropped.

Kenny's 19th Birthday

The end of the academic school year meant I had no choice but to move out of the dormitory and return to Pyramid Group Home for the summer.

After spending ten months living the life of a college student, Brooklyn looked crazy to me now. I felt like a foreigner in my hometown. Pyramid acquired some new rambunctious young residents who were fighting and running wild in the facility. I decided I could no longer be around that environment anymore. Luckily for me, I received some great news. Pam had enrolled in summer courses at St. Peter's College and chose to stay in the dorms for the summer. She invited me to stay with her for the rest of the summer instead of living at Pyramid. Perfect! I began staying with Pam in the evenings and working at the school in the daytime. Despite Pyramid, I still enjoyed the summer.

At the start of the fall semester, Coach Dukiet and my academic advisor summoned me to a meeting concerning my future. I was very nervous. My advisor informed me that although I was still on academic probation, my grades showed a slight improvement from my dismal first semester. He stressed that I needed to improve my GPA, and he would monitor me closer during the upcoming semester. Coach Dukiet then added that he would be activating my full athletic scholarship for the upcoming academic year. YES!! I was an official member of The St. Peter's College Basketball Team. No more financial aid. No more work-study jobs. It was a cause for a celebration!

Now that I was on scholarship, I made the bold decision not to return to Pyramid at all. I didn't even call to check in anymore. The group home rules stated that after thirty days, they would consider me AWOL. That was grounds for discharge. I didn't care; I planned on living in the dorms all year round. In September of 1985, I was unceremoniously discharged from Pyramid Group Home. Looking back, I should have returned one last time to say my proper goodbyes and thank the staff for all they did to help change my life. But, I couldn't stomach Pyramid anymore. I was technically still eligible for at least two more years of additional benefits from The City Of New York. However, once I got a taste of life outside of Brooklyn's mean streets, there was no turning back.

I moved back into the dorms, but this time as a member of the basketball team. I was beginning my sophomore year of academics, but my freshman year of athletics. Failure was no longer an option. I bet on myself, and I only had one chance to get it right. My girlfriend Pam, who was a senior, began asking me some serious questions about my future. She said, "What are you going to major in?" I didn't know yet. "What is your GPA?" she asked. I had to come clean and confess that I was on academic probation.

Pam sat me down for a heart-to-heart conversation. She said, "Look, I know you, you're not stupid. There is no way on earth; you should leave this school without a degree. They are paying for everything, classes, books, tutors, dorms, food; there is no excuse!" She then confessed, "I can't even go back home without a degree; my mother would kill me." I sat there listening to a person who was on track to graduate, and I knew she was right. Pam was saying things that resonated with me more than any conversation I ever had with anyone else before. She both embarrassed and challenged me at the same time. She was the voice I needed to hear at that exact moment. Almost instantaneously, I rediscovered my dedication to academics that I lost years ago. Pam was a student/athlete as well and still achieved good grades. Why couldn't I? Pam remained relentless in her interrogation, "What classes are you taking this semester?" I told her I didn't know because my academic advisor hadn't done my schedule yet. She exploded, "What? That's your problem right there. You should never let your academic advisor pick your classes. They're going to give you the most challenging courses possible. I'm doing your schedule this semester."

Pam devised a schedule for me that contained some of the core classes I needed to graduate. She mixed in some less demanding elective courses that gave me some breathing room. I was clueless. Pam scheduled my classes later in the morning, which allowed me to receive proper sleep. Between Pam's motivational speech and her restructuring of my schedule, my grades showed immediate improvement. I went from a D average to almost a B during that semester, and I never looked back. I had to learn how to become a college student first before learning the actual curriculum.

Basketball practice began in October, and it was grueling! We practiced twice a day for six weeks straight. College basketball was on a whole different level than high school basketball. I needed to re-learn every aspect of the game, passing, dribbling, shooting, defense, everything. Coach Dukiet would yell, "You're not in high school anymore!" We had to execute every drill with more accuracy because of the skill and athleticism at the college level. I wasn't tall anymore, 6'5" was nothing. I had to learn what I could and could not do against taller defenders. I struggled. I was the lowest guy on the totem pole. I felt like I couldn't do anything right. The coach cursed me out every day.

After the grueling six weeks of "boot camp," my freshman basketball season was finally underway. I moved up in the rotation from a lost freshman to the 8th or 9th man off the bench. In my first official NCAA collegiate game, I scored 4 points, all from the free-throw line. I remember thinking how incredible it would be to score in double figures one time during the season. There were seniors on our team, some better than I was, who hadn't received any playing time in four years!

Our next game was against The University Of Connecticut, AKA "UConn" of the mighty Big East, the nation's best basketball conference. Future NBA All-Star Clifford Robinson (R.I.P.) was a member of that squad. The Location was at the 16,000 seat Hartford Civic Center. Our team was in for a long night. I knew I wasn't going to receive any significant playing time in this big game. I was going to sit on the bench, watch, and learn. A few minutes into the game, I suddenly heard the coach yell my name, "Kenny Parker!" I wanted to say, "Who me?" Instead, I jumped up and ran to the scorer's table. The next thing I knew, I was in the game! I needed to settle down. I thought, "You know what? The hell with UConn! I'm from Brooklyn! (in my Ham voice) I'm gonna play my game." Moments later, I hit my first jump shot, Swish! After that, the coach left me in for the rest of the game. We lost the contest, but I scored 10 points off the bench, which for a freshman, against UConn, on the road, seemed to be a bigger deal than I thought. Following the game, Coach Dukiet informed me that he was moving me into the starting lineup, only two games into my freshman season. Wow! I had no ambition to start at all that year. My personal goals were set very low.

The next significant game was against in-state rival Seton Hall University, another Big East conference School. St. Peter's College had never beaten Seton Hall University dating back over 20 years. Seton Hall's squad was impressive. They started three future first-round NBA draft picks. Their incoming freshman class featured the New York State High School Player Of The Year and The New York City PSAL scoring champion. My homeboy from Bed-Stuy, a high school All-American named Gerald, was also on the team. To top it off, they featured The Big East's leading scorer, Andre McCloud, who I would be guarding. Our building sold out; it was standing room only!

As I was warming up, I looked into the stands, and who did I see? Coach Hartstein! He traveled from Brooklyn to watch me play. He was sitting next to Tom Konchalski, the legendary New York City high school basketball scout and talent evaluator. It was the biggest game of my young life. Two amazing things happened that night. For the first time in school history, we beat Seton Hall, and I played the game of my life, scoring a team-high 20 points along with eight rebounds. When the final buzzer sounded, everyone ran from the stands and began jumping up and down like we won the National Championship! Coach Hartstein greeted me with the biggest smile on his face. He was so proud of me, and I was happy to have that kind of game in front of my former coach. I wouldn't have been there if it wasn't for him. It was the highlight of my basketball life.

The basketball season ended in March, and I had a good freshman year. I was only the second freshman in MAAC history named conference Player Of The Week. I earned All-New Jersey honors for Division 1 Colleges, and 'The Sporting News' magazine listed me as one of the "Freshmen To Watch" in the country. It was an excellent start to my basketball career. Things were going far better than I could've imagined. I was on scholarship, my grades improved, I played solid basketball, and I was in a relationship. Although I was happy, there was still a hole in my spirit. It was now over a year and a half with no sign of Larry. I used to talk to Pam about it all the time. The worst part of the whole thing was knowing that I could help him now if he were out on

Kenny Jump Shot

the streets. Although I was only a college student with a small budget, I had plenty of food, sweatsuits, jackets, and things like that he could wear. I also had access to an endless amount of sneakers. Larry could have stayed at the dorms a couple of nights a week if he wanted to. It was the not knowing that was most upsetting. I feared the worst because there was no way Larry wouldn't come looking for me. I couldn't understand it.

1986 was also another pivotal year for my favorite music genre, Rap. Run-DMC, who was now the biggest Rap group in history, dropped their most celebrated album yet, 'Raising Hell.' The lead single, 'Walk This Way,' was a remake of a 1975 Aerosmith song and featured the band Aerosmith. The music video received heavy rotation on MTV and exposed Rap to an audience that never experienced Hip-Hop before. The song took Run-DMC and Hip-Hop to heights only reserved for the biggest stars in all of music. Their success led to an unprecedented one million dollar endorsement deal from Adidas, based on the popularity of their second single, 'My Adidas.' To me, Run-DMC weren't real humans anymore; they were music Gods.

I was still glued to the radio on the weekends, recording everything to cassette. In true Hip-Hop fashion, a competitive beef began between the two rival NYC radio station's mix shows. Mr. Magic & Marley Marl of 107.5 WBLS versus Kool DJ Red Alert of 98.7 KISS FM. I used to listen to both shows, but Red Alert was my favorite. One weekend, Mr. Magic and DJ Marley Marl premiered a new song. The track was slow with a funky bassline and an eerie whistling sound playing throughout. I was nodding my head super hard when the emcee began rapping. As soon as I heard his flow, I knew this was something different.

In 1986, almost everyone rapped very aggressively, in the loudest voice they could muster. Rappers were trying their best to outdo Run-DMC. Young Rap phenom LL Cool J had already taken aggressiveness to the maximum with his performance on the song 'Rock The Bells'. Rappers were screaming and growling by this point. Everybody loved the traditional Rap bravado, but this new rapper was different. His voice was smooth and effortless like he was having a simple conversation. The title of this DJ Marley Marl produced song was 'Check Out My Melody.' Along with the flow, the next thing that stood out was the wordplay, which was both advanced yet witty at the same time. The metaphors were next level. At that exact moment, I knew he was the best rapper in the game. By the song's end, I knew I heard the best rapper of all time. It only took me one listen to make that assessment. His name was Rakim.

The following week, I heard another song from Rakim called 'Eric B Is President,' which was more incredible than the first song. Once again, Marley Marl produced this jam featuring another funky bassline and lots of scratching by DJ Eric B. This song took the Hip-Hop world by storm, playing nonstop on daytime radio and becoming the unquestioned hottest Rap song of the year. Led by another mesmerizing vocal performance by Rakim, the Rap game had tilted on its axis. Almost every song released before 1986 was now considered old-school Rap. Although 'Eric B Is President' was the more popular song by far, I would argue that 'Check Out My Melody' was more important. That was the song that displayed Rakim's lyrical prowess and rhyme flow that everyone copied. 'Check Out My Melody' was the song that ushered in a new breed of emcee.

Not to be understated, was the rise of DJ Marley Marl, the producer of both Eric B & Rakim's songs. Marley was more than the DJ for Mr. Magic. He was already a chart-topping Hip-Hop producer best known for crafting the smash hit 'Roxanne's Revenge' by Roxanne Shante. Marley Marl was also the exclusive producer of a fascinating new beatboxer/rapper named Biz Markie. Their hit collaboration, 'Make The Music With Your Mouth Biz,' became the second hottest Rap song in NYC behind 'Eric B Is President.' Marley didn't stop there. He also produced a Hip-Hop anthem called 'The Bridge' by MC Shan. This song, dedicated to the Queensbridge housing projects in Queens, where they both resided, became arguably the third hottest record that summer. Marley Marl was on a roll. He created a new sound, and the streets couldn't get enough. Marley combined all his emcees under one umbrella and called them 'The Juice Crew.' A name derived from Mr. Magic's radio nickname 'Sir Juice.' 'The Juice Crew' consisted of MC Shan, Roxanne Shante, Biz Markie, Mr. Magic, and Marley Marl. Led by Marley's production and Mr. Magic's constant boasting on the radio, The Juice Crew became the hottest new group in the Rap game in 1986.

By this point, my obsession with Hip-Hop reached a new level. I would stay cooped up in my dorm room on Saturday nights, taping the underground public access mix shows that came on WHBI. I wouldn't go to bed until 5 am. Everyone else would be out doing whatever young college kids did on a warm Saturday night. Not me, I was a Hip-Hop nerd. What could be happening outside that was better than listening to Red Alert and Marley Marl? The answer to that question would appear in the form of a commercial on the radio advertising a new, all Hip-Hop nightclub opening up on 14th street in Manhattan called 'Union Square.' For any club to play, Rap music in 1986 was rare. There were legendary NYC Hip-Hop nightclubs like 'The Disco Fever' and 'Harlem World,' but that was before my time. Union Square was 18 and over to get in. Kicking things off for the grand opening was a live performance by Eric B & Rakim with DJ Red Alert providing the music. Oh My God! This club was the headquarter for the new Hip-Hop movement. I contemplated going to Union Square, but I didn't go because Darrell couldn't go with me. I had never been to a nightclub before, so I wasn't going by myself. Meanwhile, it was now two years since I'd heard a word from Larry, two full years! I finally accepted the fact that my brother was dead.

CHAPTER 12
LITTLE GREEN RADIO

Kicking off the fall of 1986, I received some fantastic news. Darrell was transferring to Saint Peter's College. Yes! Darrell visited the campus so often that he became very familiar with the school over the past year. I managed to pull some strings which allowed Darrell to become my roommate in the dormitory. We were going to have an absolute blast living together in college.

One Sunday, Darrell returned to campus from a weekend visit home. He greeted me with an excited tone; he said, "Yooo, guess what? Larry came by the house looking for you!" Wait a minute, WHAT THE HELL DID HE SAY? I was in absolute shock and confusion. I needed a minute to absorb the news that Larry was still alive. What a relief! I asked Darrell to repeat himself like I didn't hear him the first time. Darrell said, "Larry, came by the house; he's looking for you." I said, "You saw him?" Darrell said, "Yeah," I asked, "Well, how does he look?".... "He looks good," Darrell says. Now, the reality of what he was saying set in. Larry didn't leave a number but told Darrell he would return the following weekend. Ah man, that sucked! I couldn't travel to Brooklyn that weekend because of prior basketball obligations. When the weekend arrived, Larry indeed returned to Darrell's house, but unfortunately, I wasn't there.

When Darrell returned to campus, boy did he have a story to tell. Darrell told me that Larry was still living in The Bronx, and earlier that year, he recorded a Rap song. What? I couldn't believe my ears. Was Larry a real rapper? How? When? Darrell said, "Wait, there's more." Larry invited Darrell to hang out with him for the evening and go to a couple of clubs. Wow! A club? Like myself, Darrell had never been to a nightclub either, but unlike myself.; Darrell wasn't afraid to go. Darrell, along with Larry and some other guys, went on a club-hopping adventure. Darrell said, "Yooo, guess who I saw at one of the clubs? A couple of guys from (the Rap group) Whodini!" Wow! I was so jealous. I had never seen a celebrity before. Whodini was a major Rap group in 1986; I couldn't believe it.

I asked Darrell, "Yo, you saw Whodini with your own two eyes?" He said, "Yeah, we were in the V.I.P section with them chilling." I said, "Wait a minute, you and Larry were in the V.I.P. section?" Darrell said, "Yeah, he knew some people back there, and they let us in." I said, "GET THE FUCK OUTTA HERE!" Darrell said, "Wait, there's more....We went to another club after that. Guess who else we saw? Biz Markie!" Oh shit!! Not the same Biz Markie who had one of the hottest Rap songs in the city? I asked Darrell, "How did you know it was Biz Markie?" He said, "He was wearing a hat that said, BIZ!" We burst out laughing.

During this era, the average consumer wouldn't have recognized most recording artists. Only huge acts had music videos. Most rappers and R&B singers didn't have a picture on the cover of their singles. Your favorite artist could be standing next to you, and you would have no idea. Darrell then said, "Check this out though, Biz Markie said, 'What's up' to Larry when they walked past each other." I said, "What? Biz Markie spoke to Larry? Are you sure?" Darrell said, "I swear to God, I was standing right there, they said what's up to each other."

At that point, I couldn't take it anymore. What in Heaven's name was going on? I hadn't seen this dude in two years, and now he's hanging out in clubs talking to Biz Markie? Unbelievable! I needed to sit down and collect myself. It was more than I could comprehend. If it were anyone else in the world besides Darrell telling me this story, I wouldn't have believed them. He then said, "Larry left me a number for you to call him." Darrell gave me the number. I immediately found a payphone and called. The number Darrell provided me was to a guy named Scott La Rock, who was a DJ and close friend of Larry's. I rang the number, and Scott answered. I said, "What's up, Larry gave me this number. I'm his brother." Scott said, "Yo, Kenny, what's up! Your brother talks about you all the time. How are you? Your brother's doing so well, let me tell you what's going on." Scott begins to explain how he and Larry formed a Rap group and were recording music. Scott asked, "Do you remember that song called 'Brooklyn's In The House' by Cutmaster DC?" Of course, I did. I said, "Hell yeah, that song used to play on all the mix shows a few months ago." Scott goes, "Your brother helped write that song." No way! That song was THE Brooklyn street anthem. I was speechless.

Scott told me how they released their own single a few months earlier as well. He said it didn't do anything in America, but sold about 30,000 copies overseas. He also stated that they were about to release another single soon. Wow! Larry is doing it. He's a bonafide rapper. I was so proud of him. Scott told me to "Call this number; he's staying at the record company. I know he wants to speak to you."

I immediately hung up the phone from Scott and called the new number, "Hello, can I speak to Larry?" A guy with a pretty harsh voice said, "There's no Larry here." I said, "Are you sure? He's tall, about 6'4". The guy sounded aggravated, "I don't know who you're talking about" and hung up the phone in my ear. I immediately called Scott back and said, "Hey, I called the number you gave me, and I asked for Larry. They said no one by that name was there." Scott said, "No, No, No... You can't ask for Larry; no one calls him that, ask for KRS-One." Huh? Ok. I was a little confused. Where did the "One" in his name originate? The last time I saw him, he was only KRS. That was his graffiti/MC name. Now he is KRS-One? I was like, "Ok, I like it." It sounded so extra, so majestic. No one else had a "One" at the end of their Rap name. It was original.

When I called the number back, I said," Hello, I'm looking for KRS-One." The rude guy's tone changed. He said, "Ohhh, what's up? Kris just left a little while ago, try this number" (Kris?). I called the new number, and Larry answered! I was so happy to hear his voice that I couldn't even yell at him the way I wanted. I still had to ask, "Yo, man, where have you been for the past two years?" Larry replied, "Yo, I've been out here in these streets."

It was such a vague reply that I chose to leave it alone. I figured whatever went down with him didn't matter, Larry was here now, and I missed him.

Larry starts telling me how he finished recording a new song, and it was coming out soon. He had given DJ Red Alert an advanced copy, and Red would play it on Saturday. Wait a minute? Not the same Red Alert from 98.7 KISS-FM, who I'd been listening to religiously every week for the past three years? I flat out asked him in astonishment, "You know Red Alert?" Larry laughed and said in a very casual manner, "Of course, I know Red Alert."

I was bugging out because all of this still wasn't adding up. The last time I saw Larry was in 1984. He moved out of his group home and was hanging out with a guy named ICU. Now his name is KRS-One, and Red Alert was about to play his new single on the radio? What in the world was going on? Larry and I talked for a little while longer, and he mentioned that his group's name was Boogie Down Productions (BDP). That made sense. The nickname for The Bronx was "The Boogie Down Bronx." Larry and Scott were representing The Bronx hard with that group name. Larry told me he had to go but to listen for his new song on the radio and call him afterward to let him know what I thought of it.

We ended the phone call, and all I could think about was how unfathomable this entire episode had been. Unfortunately, at that moment, I didn't own a radio. The boombox that I purchased with a part of my financial aid money (don't judge me) had recently broken. What was I going to do? I decided to visit one of my closest friends named Faith. She was a member of the St. Peter's College Women's basketball team. She owned a small green radio with pink trim, so I asked her to borrow it. Faith said yes. Her radio was so small that it had no bass at all. Still, it was better than nothing.

When Saturday night arrived, I was sitting alone in my dorm room attached to the radio. The anticipation was killing me. At some point during his set, Red Alert plays MC Shan's song 'The Bridge.' It was one of the hottest jams in New York City. All of a sudden, Red Alert mixes in a new track. The drums were hard, with some stabbing horn sounds playing throughout. I then heard a guy's voice introducing his group while the music was playing. He mentions Boogie Down Productions and KRS-One. Oh shit! Larry's song was playing! My chest was pounding as I pressed record and began listening. Another guy starts talking, and as soon as I heard his voice, I recognized it right away; that's freakin' Larry! I would've recognized his voice anywhere. I was glad he told me in advance. Had I been listening to Red Alert on a Saturday night and heard Larry's voice without speaking to him in two years, I would've lost it!

As the song intro ended, the chorus comes in. It sounded like a group of guys chanting in unison SOUTH BRONX! SOUTH-SOUTH BRONX! Over and Over again. They kept repeating SOUTH BRONX! SOUTH-SOUTH BRONX! The chorus was very catchy and powerful. It sounded like a brand new Bronx anthem like 'Brooklyn's In The House' was an anthem for that borough. When the first verse began, it was Larry's unmistakable voice for sure. But, his attitude was way more aggressive. Larry is very laid back and reserved. This guy rapping wasn't Larry; this guy was different; he was KRS-One.

To my surprise, he immediately begins the verse by taking a verbal shot at "Juice Crew All-Star" MC Shan. He even mentions Shan's neighborhood, Queensbridge Projects, in the first verse. What is this? By the time the infectious chorus comes in again, you already knew it and couldn't help but sing along, SOUTH BRONX! KRS-One then goes into a history lesson about the origins of Hip-Hop. He explains how Rap started in The Bronx and NOT in Queensbridge Projects, as MC Shan allegedly suggested in his song. He mentions Red Alert and Chuck Chillout of KISS FM. Then, KRS-One takes a few more subliminal shots at MC Shan AND his producer Marley Marl. He taunted them by using MC Shan's vocal style. It was an obvious answer to their song 'The Bridge.' KRS-One did everything but mentioned them by name. He even insinuated that if MC Shan or Marley Marl ever came around The Bronx talking about Queens, they "might get shot!" It was crazy! The chorus repeats, and then the song ends.

I was beside myself with joy and exhilaration. To me, if DJ Red Alert played your song on KISS-FM, you made it! In 1986, it was difficult for a Rap song to receive any radio play, even on a mix show. I immediately hit rewind and listened to the recording about ten times in a row. There were a few occasions before where a rapper answered another rapper's hit record. The only notable answer songs came from female emcees responding to a male rapper. Ironically, Marley Marl entered the Rap game with Roxanne Shante answering UTFO's mega-hit 'Roxanne, Roxanne.' No male emcee ever answered another male emcee's song in this aggressive fashion before. In 1986, this type of response would be considered very disrespectful. Before 'South Bronx,' battle rhymes got directed towards an unnamed "wack" MC or some imaginary character who wasn't living up to the rules of Hip-Hop. No rapper ever implied in a song that a real person was a wack MC. KRS-One upped the stakes. I had to call him.

I dialed the number, and he picked up the phone right away. I said, "Yooo, I heard your record on the radio." Larry asked me if I liked it? I said, "Hell yeah, but it sounded like you were dissing MC Shan." He said, "Yeah." Now keep in mind, I liked MC Shan, I thought he was dope. I worried about what response Shan would have to Larry's song. My exact words were, "Are you sure? Shan is dope!" Larry said in a condescending tone, "He's alright." I was thinking to myself that MC Shan was more than "alright." This guy owned one of the hottest records, and Marley Marl was his producer. MC Shan was on fire! Anyway, it didn't matter. I was beyond happy for him. Larry told me he was staying at his girlfriend's house now. She was also a rapper, and her name was Ramona, AKA "Ms. Melodie." After we hung up the phone, I forced myself to come back down to earth. Although it was back to my regular life of academics and basketball, everything was different now. My brother was alive and well. He also appeared to have a real potential future for the first time in his life. For me, I was a Hip-Hop fanatic with a brother in the Rap game. What more could I ask?

For the next two weekends, I didn't get a chance to talk to Larry because of our schedules. Red Alert played 'South Bronx' three weeks straight on KISS-FM. Each time, he would play it immediately following MC Shan's song 'The Bridge.' Entering the third weekend, Darrell returned to campus from another home visit. He said Larry came by the house and dropped off two free passes for entry to a nightclub called 'The Latin Quarter' (LQ). They played Hip-Hop music on the weekends. They were trying to compete with the rival Club Union Square, which had quickly become very popular. The LQ was in Times Square, near the location of the New Year's Eve ball drop. Larry said he would meet us there on Saturday night. Great news!

I was super nervous, not about seeing Larry but the fact that I'd never been to a nightclub before. I began bombarding Darrell with a bunch of annoying questions. What time should we get there? How should I dress? What were people wearing when you went to that club with Larry? Darrell said, "Everybody dressed regular, wearing their most fly gear, you know." I'm like, "What do you mean regular?" I wouldn't stop pestering him. What kind of sneakers? What kind of pants? What type of shirt? Darrell yelled, "It's a club with like a thousand people in there. What the fuck?" We both started laughing. I know I was buggin' out, but so what; I wanted to look right.

On Saturday night, I finally found something to wear, and we headed to The Latin Quarter. We arrived early at around 11 pm. We presented the passes at the door and slid right in with no problems. We were so early that there was another party still in progress. It was a Latin Freestyle party. They were playing all Latin dance music like 'Silent Morning' by Noel. There were Spanish people everywhere, all dressed up with fancy shoes, dancing, and singing. After a while, they started to file out, and the Hip-Hop crowd began to arrive. The transition was complete by midnight. The Latin music was still playing, when a DJ with a deep voice gets on the microphone suddenly. He says, "Welcome to The Latin Quarter" and BAM! He drops my favorite Rap song, 'Ego Trippin' by The Ultramagnetic MC's. Since I had never been to a nightclub, I had never heard a real sound system before.

To make matters worse, for weeks, I'd been listening to my music through Faith's little green and pink radio. When 'Ego Trippin' dropped in this club, with that booming sound system, I completely lost my mind! I began yelling at Darrell like a little kid, "Yo! I'm in a fuckin' club! Can you believe it? Look at all these people!" He was looking at me in disgust and shaking his head; More laughter.

We were at the LQ for about half an hour, and I was observing everything. Everybody, in the now packed club, was Black except for this one White dude. Of course, he stuck out. He was either brave or unaware of the potential danger. Keep in mind; New York City was still America's crime capital. Times Square was a particularly dangerous place at night. Packs of thugs ran around "The Deuce" robbing and stealing from anybody they could. Many of these same hoodlums would find their way inside of the LQ, looking for more trouble. Security had to be alert at all times. Amid that environment, here's this lone White boy moving throughout the club with no problems. He appeared to know everybody. He was also a pretty good dancer (not that I was an authority). Out of the blue, this White dude walks up to Darrell and asks, "Is Kris here?" Darrell says, "Nah, not yet." The White boy continues about his business. Now I'm looking at Darrell in confusion. How does he know him? Darrell explained to me how the White dude remembered him from the night he was hanging out with Larry club hopping. Darrell said, "That White boy followed Larry all over the club that night." As it turned out, that White boy's name was MC Serch. He would later form a very successful Rap group called 'Third Bass.' Serch would also sign the rapper Nas to his very first recording contract.

Two hours passed, and Larry still hadn't shown up. I started to wonder if they were going to play Larry's new song? I didn't know if anyone liked the song. Red Alert played it for three weekends straight, but I had been living in my college dorm bubble. I didn't know what was going on in the club world. Sure enough, the DJ began playing MC Shan's hit 'The Bridge.' Everyone yelled, "Hooo!"... And began singing! Everybody was dancing when suddenly, the DJ mixed in Larry's song. The first verse comes right in, and everyone is still dancing and nodding their heads. I was watching the whole thing develop, super nervous. When the chorus came in, "South Bronx, South-South Bronx!" The entire club exploded!! They blew the roof off; I almost passed out! I was like, "Ohhhh shit! Larry's got a hit record!!" I can't begin to describe the exhilaration of being in a club for the first time, and one of the hottest songs of the night was from my brother. It was nuts! I could tell which people were from The Bronx because they were going extra crazy.

Hip-Hop originated in The Bronx. But, by 1986, all their stars, like Grandmaster Flash & The Furious 5, Kurtis Blow, Kool Herc, The Cold Crush, and Afrika Bambaataa, had all passed their primes. The other boroughs had taken over. They were now the ones with the stars and the hit records. The Bronx was dormant in 1986. Now, a group called Boogie Down Productions stepped up and began repping The Bronx in the most aggressive fashion ever. The Bronx had a new life, and they were making their presence known in The Latin Quarter. The incredible thing was, people who weren't from The Bronx were singing along with the chorus. It was a universal anthem; people were adding their neighborhoods into the chorus. I was delirious. Larry never even showed up that night. I don't remember how I got home; I may have floated back to the dorms. In my mind, there was no way it could get any better than this.

It was now two years and one month since I'd last seen Larry face-to-face. Another couple of weeks went by, and I was (what else?) listening to Red Alert on a Saturday night. I heard a commercial on KISS-FM, "Next week...Performing live at Club Union Square! Boogie Down Productions! Performing their hit 'South Bronx'!" What? Does Larry have a real show? No way! I don't know why this was surprising to me, but it never crossed my mind that Larry would be performing somewhere. I was still in denial that this song was a hit. The most unbelievable part was that they would be performing at the hottest Hip-Hop Club in NYC, Union Square. That was the very same place Eric B & Rakim appeared. Unimaginable events kept happening one after the other. I called Larry the next day, and before I could say anything, he asked me, "Are you coming to my show? I said, "Hell Yeah!!" He told me to meet him at midnight in front of Union Square. I was so excited. I couldn't wait for the following week to arrive.

On the night of the show, Darrell and I headed to 14th street, Union Square. We arrived early at around 11:30 pm. At midnight, Larry wasn't there. 12:30 am...still not there. At 1 am, people were filing into Union Square, and he still wasn't there. While we waited outside of the club, my mind began to wander. I started having doubts. What if no one shows up? What if this song isn't that hot? Meanwhile, people were still filing in. As I stood out there, knee-deep in my baseless doubts, Darrell taps me on the shoulder and says, "Look! I've found a flyer for the show on the ground!" I looked at the flyer, and it said, "Boogie Down Productions Performing Live." There was a picture of the three guys in the group, D-Nice, Scott La Rock, and KRS-One. I stood there, gawking at the flyer. This photo was the first time I'd seen what Larry looked like in two years. It looked like him, but he was wearing shades. I started buggin' out again. I couldn't believe a real Hip-Hop flyer had Larry advertised on there.

By 2 am, there were no more people entering the club. We were the only ones standing outside. All of a sudden, a limousine turns the corner and proceeds down the block. Wait a minute; that couldn't possibly be Larry, could it? In 1986, a limousine was a big freakin' deal. Most people never had the opportunity to ride inside a limousine unless they were graduating from school, going to a prom, or getting married. Limousines were very expensive; only stars rode in limos. This particular limousine slows down as it approaches the club. I could see a guy running alongside the limo wearing a white Boogie Down Productions t-shirt. Hold up; they have t-shirts too? How much more could I take?

The limo stops right in front of the club. The guy wearing the t-shirt opens the limousine door. The first person out of the limo was Ms. Melodie. Then this skinny fifteen-year-old kid named D-Nice jumps out, followed by Scott La Rock, and then...Larry jumps out. He looked at me and smiled. I was trying to maintain my composure with everything that was going on at the moment. Larry looked great!. He was a little thinner than the last time I'd seen him. His hair looked freshly cut. Larry was wearing shades, black jeans, and sporting a brand new pair of red and black Air Jordans. We hugged each other, and he said, "Yoo, what's up! We gotta talk after this. I don't have time right now, let's go!" We all entered the club together. Despite my initial fears, the club was wall-to-wall packed. There must have been a thousand people there.

My first impression of Union Square was different than that of The Latin Quarter. The LQ was an upscale club, tailored for all types of events. Union Square was far less glamorous. There would rarely be an occasion to wear a suit and tie in there. Rumor had it that Brooklyn was running wild in the club. Being a Brooklyn native myself, I could tell Brooklyn was present in large numbers. I noticed how they dressed and how they walked around. Guys from Brooklyn usually wore dark-colored clothes. They always seemed to be under-dressed for the occasion compared to everyone else. These dudes were watching people as they walked past like they were scheming on them. We would say they looked "Grimy." Brooklyn had a reputation for both traveling in large groups and robbing people. Brooklyn always posed a significant security threat.

The BDP entourage made their way to the stage area where Red Alert was deejaying. I had never seen Red Alert before, but I knew it had to be him because he was the only guy present with red hair. There was a smaller turntable set-up on the side of the stage reserved for the performance. Scott La Rock went over to those turntables and began setting up. Larry walked right up to Red Alert and started chatting with him. Once again, I couldn't believe it. Larry was talking to my number one guy! He really does know Red Alert. After a couple of minutes, Red Alert gets on the microphone and addresses the packed house. He says, "Yo...Showtime is in five minutes! I'm gonna play one more song, what y'all wanna hear?" People started chanting "South Bronx! South-South Bronx!" Red Alert says, "Nooo, I can't play that record, they're about to perform it." I'm soaking all this in like "Wow! Everyone wants to hear this song?"

Once again, I began getting crazy thoughts. Larry is minutes away from appearing in front of a thousand people. Is he going to be nervous? I had only seen him rhyme in front of Neville, Darrell, and his group home residents. I started feeling anxious. Finally, it was showtime! Red Alert fades the music and Larry walks out on stage. He grabs the microphone with a surprising amount of confidence. As I observed his body language, I could immediately tell this was not the Larry I've known my entire life. This guy was KRS-One. He wasn't nervous at all; his whole stage persona was commanding. What in the world was I thinking?

Larry greets the crowd and then says, "How many of y'all have heard the B side to 'South Bronx'?" Everyone began cheering, "Hooooooo!" I was standing there lost. What B side? Does he have another song? Larry yells, "Hit it, Dee," and D-Nice starts doing a slow beatbox with his mouth on the microphone. Larry begins performing a Reggae Dancehall routine over the thumping D-Nice beat. Everybody in the audience was nodding their heads in unison. This song, called 'The "P" Is Free,' told the story of a crackhead girl he met in the street who tried to trick him out of some money. Larry was dissing this girl in the song, and I was listening along to the verse. When Larry begins to sing the chorus, the entire club completed the hook by singing in unison, "Oooh Yeah!" Everyone knew the words except me. As if this night wasn't mind-blowing enough, now I had to process that Larry had TWO dope songs!

Right when I thought I reached my excitement limit, Scott threw on the song everyone was waiting to hear, 'South Bronx.' The club reached pandemonium levels now. I found myself watching the crowd as much as I was watching the show. Everyone was singing the song word for word, and when the chorus arrived, I thought there was going to be a riot. It looked like The Bronx was going to attack everyone else at the party! As I watched the performance, trying to remain conscious, I made an obvious observation. This rapper guy KRS-One was freakin' dope! Even if I didn't know him, KRS-One would have still been impressive. He destroyed Union Square, the hottest club in New York City.

After the show, Larry left the stage and got immediately surrounded by people wanting to talk to him and shake his hand. Darrell and I waited for the commotion to die down and the dance party to resume. Larry comes over to where we were standing. His demeanor changes, and he became regular Larry once again. He starts laughing and says, "Can you believe this?" I told him, "Since I was the very first person to tell you that you were wack, let me tell you right now, YOU ARE DOPE!" He burst out laughing, and we hugged. His dream finally came true. It was the only thing in life he ever wanted. Larry then said to me, "I'm staying in Brooklyn with Monie (Melodie) now. Let me give you my new number. You should come over to the house, and so we can talk outside of all this madness." While Larry was writing down his new number on a piece of paper, these two random girls walked right up and said: "I want the number, I want the number too!" I was looking at them like "Holy shit! He's got groupies too?" Larry laughed as more people began to crowd around again. We said a quick goodbye and faded into the background. Every single person Larry knew was calling him Kris. Somehow, calling him Larry seemed outdated, even for me. I decided I was going to address him as Kris from now on. Calling him Larry was so, 1984.

As Darrell and I exited the club, a guy blew past us, running right into the path of oncoming traffic. Being hit by a car was the least of his worries. About twenty bloodthirsty Brooklyn hooligans were chasing him. He ran towards this park across the street from Union Square with this posse in hot pursuit. He tried to scale a five-foot brick wall that surrounded the park. Unfortunately, he didn't have enough time, and that brick wall became the barrier between his freedom and impending doom. Darrell and I looked on in horror as the gang of twenty beats this poor dude senseless. It was the first time I witnessed someone getting stomped by that many people at one time. Stomping people was part of a Brooklyn specialty known as a "Bum Rush." The most vivid part of the whole incident was seeing this random guy, who was the smallest member of the crew, maneuvering himself around the pack's side to get a better position to land a blow. He found the tiniest opening between the melee and the brick wall with a clear shot at the victim. This little guy cocked his leg back and kicked that poor soul right in his head. Pow! I could feel myself gasp at the sheer brutality of this senseless act. We didn't stick around to see what became of that guy. We headed in the other direction.

The following weekend, Pam and I traveled to Brooklyn to have dinner with Kris and Melodie. Of course, I had a bunch of questions to ask him. First, how did he meet Scott La Rock? Kris told me that sometime after I saw him in 1984, he found himself homeless once again. He took residence at The Bronx Men's Shelter, where Scott Sterling, who was three years older than Kris, worked as a counselor. They met and immediately didn't like each other. Scott summed Kris up as a guy with no ambition, who was doing nothing with his life. Kris looked at Scott as a sell-out and "Handkerchief Head" who chose to look down on them like he was better than they were. It wasn't until Scott overheard a young KRS-One battling some other rappers in the shelter that Scott noticed Kris' potential. Scott revealed that he was a DJ, with a weekly gig at a nightclub in Manhattan. They soon formed a friendship, which led to a musical partnership. Scott began introducing Kris around town as his new emcee. Although Scott had the connections and the expertise to create music, he needed the right lyricist. Scott felt he found him in KRS-One.

Things started slow for the duo. They recorded and released two singles, on two different independent record labels, under two different names. Still, they didn't receive the reception they had hoped. Kris and Scott weren't discouraged. They kept searching for the right situation and song to put them over the top. I asked Kris why he decided to diss MC Shan? Right around the time that they released their second indie single, the one that sold overseas, Scott and Kris decided to show up unannounced to a studio session where radio personality Mr. Magic of WBLS was recording. They wanted to inquire about joining his Queens-based 'Juice Crew.' Mr. Magic not only turned them down but completely disrespected them to their face. He proclaimed that they could never be down with 'The Juice Crew' because they weren't on the level of MC Shan and Marley Marl. Magic cursed at them, called them bums, and instructed them to get out! As Kris and Scott rode the train back to The Bronx, they vowed revenge.

Kris felt he was a better rapper than MC Shan and set out to prove it. That diss by Mr. Magic gave Boogie Down Productions the direction they needed. They were able to craft a song that accomplished two goals, make a Bronx anthem, and diss MC Shan. BDP signed a recording contract with a small independent label called 'B-Boy Records,' their third label in twelve months. B-Boy records never released a Rap song before. This time proved to be the charm. Kris also mentioned that he was working with the Rap group, The Ultramagnetic MC's. That's the same group that made my favorite Rap song 'Ego Trippin'.' Of course, I asked a stupid question, "You know them too?" Despite all I had seen, I still couldn't wrap my head around the idea that my brother was a real artist now.

Since I knew nothing about recording Rap music, I asked him, "Who played the instruments in your song?" Kris laughed and said it was a new technique called 'Sampling.' I asked him, "What is that?" He said, "It's complicated. I can't explain it to you right now. That's a conversation for another time." I then asked Kris what it was like to have a hit record? He said it took a while to sink in because when the 'South Bronx' first hit, he was still homeless. Kris was sleeping in the basement of the record company. He was earning a little extra cash as a part-time custodian at a beauty salon. Kris was sweeping hair when he first heard his song on the radio. His backstory made everything seem even more incredible. After dinner, I returned to my college dorm. I still hadn't told anyone at school about my brother's hot song. None of my friends at school knew I had a brother.

As the weeks progressed, the 'South Bronx' continued to grow in popularity. The song got requested so much that the #1 R&B station in New York City, 98.7 KISS FM, added it to their regular rotation. Receiving daytime radio play was rare for a Rap song released on a small indie label. "The little song that could" became one of the most requested songs in New York City. It landed on the "Top 8 at 8" evening countdown on KISS-FM. The 'South Bronx' by Boogie Down Productions climbed to #2 on that countdown. It could not dethrone the R&B smash 'Shake You Down' by Gregory Abbott. With crossover success came a bunch of shows for BDP. They even traveled to other states to perform because the song began receiving significant airplay outside of New York City. I tried to go to as many NYC shows as possible. I got to witness first-hand what it was like for an artist to have a hit record. Kris was making real money now. It was great!

After about three months or so, the 'South Bronx' finally began to wind down. What an incredible run for a song like that! It was right around that time, (you knew the other shoe was coming right?) I was listening to Mr. Magic and Marley Marl on WBLS when I heard them play a new MC Shan song in the mix. Like I anticipated, MC Shan finally responded to 'South Bronx.' The battle was on! MC Shan released a song called 'Kill That Noise.' Shan explained how he never said Hip-Hop started in Queensbridge Projects and how these suckers (BDP) used his name and fame to gain recognition. He also gave a stern warning about what he would do to these suckers the next time they mentioned his name in a record. Marley Marl produced the song and dared to scratch in the chorus from BDP's 'South Bronx' while Shan yelled, "Kill That Noise" behind it. To make matters worse, at the end of the song, MC Shan mentions KRS-One and Scott La Rock by name while laughing....."Hahaha!" As you can imagine, I was very concerned after hearing this song. He actually said KRS-One's name! Everyone in NYC was going to listen to this song. Marley Marl played MC Shan's song about three times on his show that same night. Ah, man! This situation was terrible.

The following weekend, Union Square scheduled Boogie Down Productions to perform once again. I spoke to Kris, and he told me to meet him in Manhattan so we could all go to the club together. As soon as I saw him, I said, "Yoooo, you heard 'Kill That Noise'?" Kris said, "Yeah, I heard it." I then said, "I told you not to mess with Shan, I told you!" I felt like this was the beginning of the end for Boogie Down Productions. I was still very proud of him. There is nothing wrong with being a so-called "One-Hit-Wonder." That's more than most artists will ever achieve in their lifetimes. Still, MC Shan, backed by Marley Marl and Mr. Magic, would be too much to overcome.

After I reminded Kris that I warned him about tangling with MC Shan, he looked at me and smiled in his usual calm demeanor, and said, "I got the answer already." What? It had only been one week since MC Shan debuted his song. Kris elaborated a little more; he said, "I have a song called 'The Bridge is Over.' I'm like, "The Bridge Is Over? How does it go?" Kris said, "Well, it's to a Reggae beat. The bass line goes…" and he begins to mimic the beat with his mouth "Dum Dum Dum Da Dum…Dum Dum Dum Da Dum." I immediately cut him off and said, "Ah, man, that shit is wack! It's over!" Kris started laughing and said, "We're gonna do it tonight at Union Square, come and see." We all headed over to a sold-out Union Square. As usual, Brooklyn was running wild. Security had to break up about three fights. Darrell and I found a spot right next to the stage. I remember seeing DJ Eric B standing right in front of me wearing a custom-made Gucci jacket designed by the legendary Harlem tailor, Dapper Dan. Red Alert was deejaying. We were standing in the capital of Hip-Hop.

KRS-One and D-Nice hit the stage. They go into their rehearsed routines as usual, but when the time came to perform 'South Bronx,' there was an unexpected twist. As they started doing the chorus "South Bronx, South-South Bronx,"…You could hear a sizable portion of the crowd chanting, "Kill That Noise!" I don't know if they were either some of MC Shan's crew, people from Queens, or a very knowledgeable Hip-Hop crowd. But, the chants were audible and on time, like they were in MC Shan's song. Kris could hear them chanting as well, but his next maneuver completely shocked the hell out of me. Kris said, "Oh, I see Shan has his people in here; Say It Louder! Say It Louder!" I became confused. Is he encouraging the audience to diss him? Now, D-Nice chimes in, "Kill That Noise! Say it louder!" People began yelling, "Kill That Noise" even louder!

Kris stops performing the 'South Bronx' and says, "This is for all the MC Shan fans out there!" He points in Scott La Rock's direction and says, "Hit it, Scott!" Scott throws on a beat that comes blasting through the speakers. It was one of the most thumping drum beats I ever heard. The whole Union Square was quiet now, waiting to see what was going to happen next. The tempo of the track was slower than most of the Rap songs of that era. As the drums were thumping, a simple little piano riff begins to play., Kris paused to let the crowd absorb the track. All of a sudden, the piano riff morphs into this haunting rendition of the Reggae Dancehall smash 'Boops' by Jamaican artist Super Cat. It was the same melody Kris was singing to me earlier in the day. Now I finally understood what he was trying to explain to me. The track sent a chill up your spine. People's heads were beginning to nod and bounce in unison to this new hybrid blend of Hip-Hop and Reggae Dancehall. Kris moves the microphone closer to his mouth. You could tell by the look on his face that he was about to say something crazy. Confidence was dripping off of him like sweat. Kris opens his mouth, but instead of rapping, he caught everybody off guard by chatting in a Jamaican-styled accent, "The Bridge is over! The Bridge is over! Buda Bye Bye! - The Bridge is over! The Bridge is over!... OHHHHH SHIT! Everybody lost their collective minds! The whole place started yelling "HOOOOO!!" Kris then proceeds to alternate back and forth between rapping traditional American style, "chatting" in this Jamaican-styled accent, and singing in a sort of nursery rhyme style. He managed to blend all three of these styles perfectly.

Using this new technique, KRS-One unleashed the most vicious verbal attack towards another artist ever heard in recorded music history. He was cursing in this song, which was rare in 1986, even for a Rap song. Not only did he attack MC Shan and Marley Marl, but Mr. Magic and the entire borough of Queens. He disrespected Roxanne Shante, who had nothing to do with the beef but was also a "Juice Crew" member. There were no subliminal jabs like previous songs. Kris mentioned the names of everyone he had a problem with several times and called them disrespectful slurs. He even implied that Mr. Magic could basically "suck his dick!" Kris then upped the stakes by dragging DJ Red Alert into the beef. KRS proclaimed that Red Alert was now down with Boogie Down Productions, and his rival Marley Marl of WBLS was not on Red Alert's level. Red Alert now had a mouthpiece to defend himself against the relentless verbal attack of Mr. Magic. There was now an official beef between the two radio stations as well. Oh, the drama! By this point, along with everyone else, I was screaming to the top of my lungs with sheer excitement! You knew at that moment something new had happened in the world of Hip-Hop. It was similar to when you heard 'Check Out My Melody' by Rakim or 'Sucker MC's' by Run-DMC. You could tell that this was not only a dope song but a game-changer. A new Hip-Hop genre was born; "The battle record." It was also a coming-out party for a new lyrical Juggernaut, KRS-One.

The following week Red Alert played the official 'The Bridge Is Over' song on his radio show. He muted out the curses live on the air. Everyone in New York City heard this new "diss song." It became the talk of the town. Red's mix show gave me another chance to analyze what I had listened to at the club. Not only were the vocals revolutionary, but the track itself was groundbreaking. In the '80s, all the different music genres were separate. R&B, Hip-Hop, Reggae, and Rock were rarely mixed. Despite Hip-Hop borrowing some of its backing music from R&B songs, the genres still weren't linked at all. Both genres disliked each other. R&B artists and journalists showed zero respect for Rap Music. They felt Rap wasn't authentic music because they used a DJ instead of a live band, and rappers weren't singing any real notes. Hip-Hop was considered a fad that would be over soon enough. Hip-Hop felt R&B music was soft music that did not respect or reflect what was going on in the streets. R&B Music could not match the energy and rebelliousness of Hip-Hop culture. Rap was like R&B's illegitimate black sheep child. Likewise, traditional Reggae music had its misfit offspring in the newly created "Dancehall Reggae." This rebellious style of Reggae music had risen in popularity during the early 1980s, in locations where there were large West Indian populations. New York City, owned the second-largest West Indian population in America, outside of Florida.

By 1986, Dancehall Reggae was massive in the streets of New York. There were underground Dancehall mixtapes everywhere. Yet, with each music genre considered separate, every style had specific radio stations and nightclubs. Nowadays, when you go to a club, you can expect to hear various music genres. In 1986, R&B clubs only played R&B. Hip-Hop Clubs played Hip-Hop, and Reggae clubs only played Reggae. You chose what kind of music you wanted to hear before you left your house to go clubbing. Run-

DMC merged Rock and Rap with their hit' Rock Box' and then with their monster pop hit 'Walk This Way.'

A few months later, here comes Boogie Down Productions with 'The Bridge Is Over.' BDP mixed Dancehall Reggae with Hip-Hop in a way that started a lasting trend visible to this day. A couple of Rap artists attempted to do Reggae earlier, but it sounded more like a parody or joke. BDP's version of Hip-Hop/Reggae was the one that struck a chord with the Hip-Hop audience. Only a person with a complete understanding of both Reggae and Hip-Hop culture could pull it off. Enter KRS-One. I look back to our childhood experiences with Rastafarian Joe. All the years of Reggae music and culture that he exposed us to significantly influenced Kris' love and understanding of the West Indian art form. At least Joe was good for something.

Another small but important observation I made about 'The Bridge Is Over' was the sneaky subliminal shout-out given to Brooklyn in the song. KRS-One was not shy about the feeling of dominance he felt The Bronx had over Queens, in particular Queensbridge Projects. But, he added a line in 'The Bridge Is Over' that stated, "Manhattan makes it, Brooklyn takes it, The Bronx creates it, and Queens keeps fakin' it." The phrase "Manhattan makes it, Brooklyn takes it" is an old Brooklyn street slogan. Manhattan, AKA "Uptown" was legendary for having the flamboyant 'hustlers' who wore expensive jewelry and drove fancy cars. Brooklyn's specialty, as I mentioned earlier, was robbing people, especially Uptown dudes. The fact that KRS-One acknowledged Brooklyn, and what they did best was very strategic. Brooklyn ruled every party in NYC by their sheer numbers and brutality. If you could somehow bring Brooklyn over to your side of the argument, you couldn't lose. Kris, who was very familiar with Brooklyn, was crafty by saying, "I'm from The Bronx, but I see you Brooklyn, and I respect you." He managed to align Brooklyn with The Bronx in that way. It was brilliant!

Suppose you take into account the inventiveness of the Reggae/Hip-Hop blended track. Add KRS-One's never before heard Rap/Reggae flow and the unprecedented viciousness of the lyrics, 'The Bridge Is Over' might have been as unique a song as there was in the entire world.

After a couple of weeks, Kris went back into the studio and made a clean version of 'The Bridge Is Over,' featuring Red Alert doing his signature "YEEEAAAHHH!!!" in the middle of the song. Red Alert stamped it a

KISS-FM song now. Kris added an intro part where he says the line, "Yo Red, I'm getting sick and tired of this!" That's a phrase my mother used to say all the time when she got mad at us. I laughed when I heard it. Kris stole my mother's line. Only he and I could understand how funny that was. Red Alert played the new clean version for about fifteen minutes straight on his radio show. 'The Bridge Is Over' electrified New York City. It became the hottest record in the streets. Every person with a radio was walking by playing the song.

I still hadn't mentioned any of this to anyone at my school. By this time, I no longer had the words to describe how happy I was for my brother. I was a complete KRS-One fan too. I couldn't believe I doubted him like that. Although in fairness, no one could've seen this coming. As great a song as it was, 'South Bronx' showed no signs that Kris was capable of raising his Rap skills to this extraordinary level. It was like a brand new emcee subbed into the battle. My only question now was; how many styles does he have?

By the end of January 1987, 'The Bridge Is Over' was a bonafide smash. The song even eclipsed the popularity of the 'South Bronx' despite receiving no daytime radio play, for obvious reasons. Yet, there wasn't a peep from MC Shan. What was going on? BDP dropped a first of its kind, cold-blooded verbal attack, disrespecting Shan in every way imaginable, and he hasn't said a word? KRS-One answered MC Shan's response in one week. It was now over two months of complete silence from the Queensbridge emcee, strange.

With back-to-back hit records, Boogie Down Productions was now one of the hottest groups in the Hip-Hop world. That meant more events for me to attend. Although school work and basketball had me swamped, I tried my hardest. One evening, Kris invited me to a studio session in midtown Manhattan, where he was recording. I was finally going to get a chance to see how they made a Rap song. Darrell and I met Kris and Scott in the city and headed over to the session. We entered a studio filled with recording equipment, a long mixing board, a vocal booth, and an engineer. I found a spot in the corner and sat there for hours watching everything. I was happy to be there despite having no idea what was going on. I was grateful that Kris was allowing me to experience the entire ride with him. Every time I asked him to tag along, he agreed without hesitation. Even though I asked many questions, even dumb ones, it never seemed like I was getting on his nerves. None of this Rap star life seemed to phase him at all. I do think he enjoyed watching me lose my mind over every little thing, though.

After my first studio session, I decided I could no longer keep these fantastic experiences to myself. I began telling some of my college friends that my brother was KRS-One, and as expected, they couldn't believe it. Every one of my friends who listened to Hip-Hop was very familiar with the songs and the battle itself. They couldn't understand why I hadn't said anything in the past five months since 'South Bronx' took off? Partly, I was hesitant in the beginning out of fear. If Kris' dream didn't pan out, all the jealous haters would have something negative to say. That would have caused me to end all my friendships in the process. After things took off, I would have then sounded like a braggart. I despise braggarts. I never wanted to attract attention to myself by going around, saying, "My brother did this, and my brother did that." Also, revealing my brother's success would've raised some obvious questions like, how come you've never mentioned him before? Why has he never come to visit you? Did I want to reveal that I hadn't seen Kris for two years before his musical explosion? I decided during my freshman year not to disclose any parts of my family dysfunction. Now, things were becoming too crazy; I had to say something. I only told a couple of my close friends, but the news spread like wildfire. Everyone began asking me when BDP was performing next so they could come with me to the concert. I may have been trying to avoid that too.

By February, things were beginning to happen at a rapid pace. B-Boy Records decided that the success of 'The Bridge Is Over' warranted investing money in a music video to take the song to the next level. In true indie fashion, they spent the least amount of money possible. B-Boy Records decided to rent out Union Square and advertise BDP shooting a video in front of a live audience. On the day of the video shoot, partygoers filled Union Square. Since the video concept was a live performance, BDP performed the song about six or seven times. With each take, the crowd went crazy like it was the first time the music played. The video budget was so small that the director shot in black & white film. That was subpar even in 1987. A New York-based, public access video show called 'Video Music Box,' hosted by Ralph McDaniels, premiered the grainy, black & white, off-synched video. The Hip-Hop world got its first real look at Boogie Down Productions. All my friends were saying I looked like Kris. How many times have I heard that before?

'The Bridge Is Over' was now at its peak in popularity. MC Shan still hadn't responded. By this time, it was a moot point anyway. The battle was over. Boogie Down Productions defeated MC Shan and The Juice Crew in the most embarrassing and unprecedented fashion. BDP changed the way emcees would battle each other from that point forward. Before 'The Bridge Is Over,' emcees would compete against each other face-to-face. They were either surrounded by a small crowd called a "Cypher" or on a stage with a live audience judging who won the contest. In 1987, if someone told you that two known rappers had battled, the first thing you would ask was, who won? Where was it held? Did anybody tape it? If you weren't there, you missed it. Even the most famous Rap battle up until that point…The legendary Kool Moe Dee vs. Busy Bee battle at The Harlem World Club in December 1981, had only a few hundred spectators. It took years for the cassette tape of that particular battle to circulate in the Hip-Hop world. I first heard it in 1983, at Pyramid. That was a full two years after the competition had taken place, and I lived in New York City the entire time! After 'The Bridge Is Over,' all major rap battles were now settled on wax. The dynamic shifted to who made the best diss song. Everyone in America now had the opportunity to hear a battle at the same time. Every radio DJ could play competing songs, and anyone could buy the music as well. The "Diss Record" and "Beef" is now considered a staple in Hip-Hop culture. 'The Bridge Is Over' was a game-changer.

Midterm exams approached, and I was knee-deep in school work. Still, I made an effort to check in with Kris at least once a week to stay updated. During one call, Kris sounded frustrated for the very first time. He said, "You know Kenny, I'm getting tired of people saying that all we can do is battle. They act like we can't make real songs. I'm working on my album now, and I'm going to show everyone what I can do." Of course, I had to ask stupid questions, "What? An album? Do you mean like a real tape with your picture on the cover"? Kris said, "Yes, it's called 'Criminal Minded'." I loved the title. It sounded rough and grimy. I was eager to hear more music from him anyway. I was a real KRS-One fan.

Afterward, I traveled out to Brooklyn to meet Kris. He gave me a cassette featuring two new songs from his album, 'A Word From Our Sponsor' and a rough version of 'Poetry.' The lyrical styles on both tracks were once again different from the previous BDP releases. On 'A Word From Our Sponsor,' KRS debuted a Rapping technique called the "Offbeat Style." Instead of rhyming on time with the beat's tempo, he would sometimes pause, leave a gap between the words, and catch up to the rhythm in the next bar. Kris would break up the phrase as he rapped. The listener would have no idea where the word would land next. Then, he might speed up his lyrical pace and then slow it back down for effect. It sounds complicated, but Kris made it look easy.

I had now heard five songs from KRS-One, and each one of them featured a different style. As a Hip-Hop fanatic, I felt like something special was happening here. Kris promised me a copy of the album upon its completion. I was bursting at the seams.

Meanwhile, my academics were going well. After completing one of my required classes, Psychology 101, I found studying human behavior fascinating. I decided to choose Psychology as my major. On the athletic side, things weren't going so well. My coach, Bob Dukiet, left to accept the head coaching position at Marquette University. The assistant coach became the new head basketball coach. I liked him as an assistant and was happy with his promotion. Unfortunately, I soon learned the feeling wasn't mutual. Almost immediately, our relationship changed. As head coach, he began criticizing me all the time. The conflict was over the style of play. During stretches of my freshman and sophomore seasons, St. Peter's College led the entire NCAA in the fewest points allowed per game and defensive field goal percentage. I played for one of the top defensive schools in America. But, I was a kid from the playgrounds of Brooklyn, scoring was my forte. Playing defense was, ah, not my strong suit. That's what the coach said anyway. During my sophomore season, I alternated between starting and playing well and "The Doghouse," not playing at all. To say my demotion was disappointing would be an understatement. I contemplated transferring to another school, but I couldn't. I already "redshirted" during my academic freshman year. I was stuck. All I could do was try to make the best of the situation. My disappointing sophomore basketball season ended in March with a loss in the N.I.T. Tournament's first round. With the season finally over, I could go back to concentrating on my studies and having fun.

The first full weekend of March 1987, I found myself in a familiar position, listening to the Hip-Hop mix shows in front of the radio. It had been about two weeks since I'd spoken to Kris, and I was still waiting for my copy of his new album. As I listened to 'The Awesome Two Radio Show' on WNWK FM, to my surprise, they premiered a new Boogie Down Productions song called 'Dope Beat.' It had a funky Rock sample along with KRS-One's now-signature aggressive tone. Kris boasted about how different he was from everyone else and took a subtle shot at the great RUN-DMC. After the song ended, Special K of The Awesome Two announced that the new Boogie Down Productions album was arriving in stores this week. Huh? How is the new album coming out, and I haven't heard it yet? Damn it, Kris! I decided I wasn't going to wait any longer; I'm buying myself a copy.

That following Wednesday, I went to the local record shop and asked for the new Boogie Down Productions album 'Criminal Minded.' The store owner, Stan, (R.I.P.) kept a box of the cassettes right by the cash register. He said, "Man, this is the hottest album in my store. As soon as I get a delivery, it sells out." My "anti-bragging" policy went right out the window. I said, "That's my brother's album!" Of course, Stan was skeptical. He handed me a copy of the album, and the first thing I noticed was the cover. It was dark, with the title 'Criminal Minded' plastered right across the front in bright red and white lettering. There was a picture of Scott La Rock and KRS-One under the lettering. But wait, they were both holding guns on the cover of the album! It was the hardest album cover in music history. There was an actual grenade on the table in front of them. A row of real bullets draped across Kris' shoulder. I pointed to KRS-One on the album cover and said to Stan, "That's my brother right there!" He looked at the picture, looked at me, and then uttered that all too familiar phrase, "You look like him."

I rushed home and popped the cassette into my radio. What came through my speakers was a masterful combination of some of the rawest lyrics ever heard, mixed with the Reggae-influenced chatting, the "OffBeat" rhyme style, and an advanced (for Hip-Hop) Vocabulary. There was even a little singing from KRS-One. Incredible! The music was equally impressive. 'Criminal Minded' pioneered a new technique called "Sampling." Sampling is recording bits and pieces of old songs and combining them using a drum machine to create a new instrumental track. This musical technique was state of the art in 1987. Ironically, DJ Marley Marl's innovative production is the origin of Sampling as we know it today. 'Criminal Minded' is the first full-length album to have most of its music derived from Sampling. The album featured a mixture of Funk, Rock, and Reggae samples. It blew me away.

Never, in my wildest dreams, could I have imagined the Hip-Hop journey I had the pleasure of witnessing over the past six months, culminating with this masterpiece's release. I investigated the cassette further and found the liner notes. Along with an assist from Ced-Gee of The Ultramagnetic MC's, Scott La Rock produced the album's music. Also, to my surprise, was the icing on the cake; a nice, big shout out to me in the credits. They even spelled out my full name, Kenneth Parker. Ha!

March of 1987 brought Boogie Down Productions to the Latin Quarter. It was their first show since the 'Criminal Minded' album dropped. Like the rest of NYC, I was bursting with anticipation. On the day of the show, Kris instructed us to meet him right in front of the club at a specific time. Considering his penchant for lateness, that could be a serious problem combined with the cold weather. When we arrived, the line was down the block and around the corner. My first inclination was to wait for Kris to arrive as instructed. But, Darrell convinced me to ask the manager of the club to let us in without Kris. The manager of The Latin Quarter was a colorful character named Paradise. He had a dark-skinned complexion, sported a shiny wet Jheri curl, and wore blue-colored contact lenses. I walked up to him and said, "How are you doing? I'm a guest of KRS-One." Paradise looked at me and said, "Oh yeah, you're Kris' brother, right?" Yes! What a relief. He then said, "Well, Kris isn't here; you have to wait." Huh? He then turned to walk away. In desperation, I said, "Wait! Is Scott here?" Paradise replied, "Scott already went inside, and he had fifteen people with him." I knew any chance of an early entrance was over after that. Darrell and I waited outside in the cold for over an hour until Kris finally arrived. Right when we were about to enter the club, I spotted three guys coming across the street, moving in our direction. As they closed in, I recognized one of them; it was MC Shan. Uh oh! Kris recognized him too, and we all paused right in front of The Latin Quarter. I thought to myself, "Well, this is it! The showdown! We're all about to be fighting out here." Shan comes across the street, walks right up to Kris, and said, "Yooo, Kris, what's up?" in his distinctive high pitched voice. Shan had a big grin on his face with his arms stretched out like he was ready to give a warm hug. Wait a minute! What's going on here? I couldn't believe my eyes. KRS-One is about to enter the LQ and disrespect you in front of a sold-out audience, and you greet him like this? They embraced, exchanged some brief pleasantries, and then MC Shan left. As a Hip-Hop fan, I felt disgusted. I immediately turned to Kris and asked, "How could Shan hug you like that after what you said about him in 'The Bridge Is Over'?" Kris looked at me and said in classic KRS-One fashion, "He knows he can't beat me, so he has to get down with me." We both burst out laughing and went inside the club. Showtime!

After that night, I knew MC Shan had no chance of competing with KRS-One from the very beginning. Shan wasn't built like that. Kris was living in The Bronx Men's Shelter, barely getting by. Meanwhile, Shan was presumably running around spending money, buying clothes, and eating well. The only thing Kris ever dreamed about was becoming a Hip-Hop artist. He was desperate, not only to become a successful rapper but to sustain himself day-to-day. If you put those two individuals in a winner-takes-all competition, where the desperate man could have everything he ever desired if he defeated the well-fed man, the desperate man would have the advantage. His whole mentality would be different. That's precisely how the entire scene unfolded; Kris smelled Hip-Hop blood. Shan brought a freakin' spoon to a rusty knife fight. Shan was playing checkers, and Kris was playing three-card monte. Kris later told me that he actually wrote 'The Bridge Is Over' first. He then decided to hold that particular song for later and released the 'South Bronx' instead. KRS-One set MC Shan up. Kris used the 'South Bronx' as the bait to get Shan to respond. Releasing 'The Bridge Is Over' afterward made it more potent and effective. That's why Kris had such a quick response to MC Shan's 'Kill That Noise.' He was waiting on Shan to make a move. Kris controlled the entire narrative. He strategically assigned everyone a role in the saga, and MC Shan played his part to perfection. In some ways, I felt sympathy for Shan. He had no idea what was happening. Shan was an unsuspecting pawn in beef he didn't even start. That distinction would belong to Mr. Magic, who Kris cast as the villain, allowing BDP to align themselves with Red Alert and KISS-FM. The "Production" in Boogie Down Productions could have been a metaphor for the masterful Broadway-level play that Kris & Scott created. The plot was flawless. The acts were well-timed. The cast of characters couldn't have been chosen any better. Everything lined up exactly as anticipated. The entire Hip-Hop audience was sitting back in the theater, eating their popcorn, awaiting the next act to begin.

A couple of weeks passed since the release of the album. I still felt like I wasn't getting the full impact of the album's success because I was in my dorm room cocoon most of the time. I took another trip to Brooklyn to catch up with Kris and chat for a bit. We walked for about three miles down Flatbush Avenue, laughing and talking like we used to do as kids. We even passed by our old comic book store, which was now a VHS video rental store. Kris told me that he ran into Juice Crew member Roxanne Shante at a bank in Manhattan. The very same Shante he dissed in 'The Bridge Is Over.' As expected, she was furious! Kris said she started yelling at him about his disrespectful comment towards her. Shante explained how she had nothing to do with his beef with MC Shan. I asked Kris what did he say in response? He said, "I asked her if she was a member of The Juice Crew? She said yes. I told her, well, I was dissing everybody in The Juice Crew, so I suggest you make your own reply then." Sheesh, this whole beef thing seemed stressful.

Kris and I got some food and then rode the subway to 34th street in Manhattan so I could catch the NJ Path Train back to Jersey City. Kris decided to ride with me to New Jersey and then turn around and go home. Right when we got to the Path Train entrance, Kris pulled out a square sticker and tagged 'KRS-One' in graffiti. He then slapped the sticker high up on the Path Station wall. The entire deed took about five seconds. I burst out laughing; he was forever the graffiti artist. That sticker remained on the Path Train station wall for years before it got taken down.

When we reached the Journal Square station in Jersey City, Kris and I exited the train. We proceeded up a long escalator to the street-level entrance of the station. As we were riding up, a young black guy was riding down the opposite escalator. He was staring in our direction with a confused look on his face. When we reached the top level of the escalator ride, we stood there for a minute, saying our official goodbye's. The guy jumped back on the escalator at the bottom level and rode up towards where we were standing. When he reached us, the guy still looked puzzled. He said, "Excuse me, I know this sounds crazy, but, you look like that guy from the album cover." Before Kris could say anything, the guy said, "Nah, it couldn't be" and went back downstairs. We both chuckled. It was the first time I had seen someone recognize Kris outside of a nightclub, from the album cover no less. I thought it was so cool. We said goodbye, and I went back to school.

In a few short weeks, 'Criminal Minded' captivated New York City. The imagery and subject matter were so raw that many consider it the first "Gangster Rap" album. DJ Red Alert was playing almost the entire album on his weekly mix show. The lead single, 'Poetry,' premiered on regular daytime rotation on KISS-FM. Even Mr. Magic and Marley Marl were playing selections from the album on WBLS. Who would've thought that was possible. BDP was doing interviews on the radio and in magazines. Scott did the majority of talking; Kris played the background. It was evident that Scott La Rock was the leader of the group. From watching him speak in interviews and being around him, I made two observations. Scott La Rock was a very charismatic, fun-loving guy. He was also super confident, almost to the point of arrogance. When Scott would arrive at the club, everyone knew him and showed him love. He was very popular with both men and women. Kris made a hilarious tribute song on the album dedicated to Scott and his love for the ladies called 'Super Hoe.' They seemed to have the perfect partnership and friendship.

As far as creativity, 1987 may have been the most critical year in Hip-Hop history outside of the formative mid-1970s. Quite a few Hip-Hop blueprints got handed down in 1987. Along with 'Criminal Minded,' the Hip-Hop world was also blessed with the debut of Eric B & Rakim's groundbreaking monster album 'Paid In Full.' While KRS-One changed the Rap game with his new styles, Rakim unleashed the most effortless flow in Hip-Hop history. His next-level wordplay set the bar. Rakim required several rewinds per song to appreciate the complexity of his lyrics.

Although KRS-One had lyrically castrated MC Shan, his DJ, Marley Marl, managed to recover historically. While still producing hits for Biz Markie, he also introduced the Hip-Hop world to Biz's partner, The Big Daddy Kane. Kane was an elite new emcee out of Brooklyn. He combined the best traits of Grandmaster Caz of The Cold Crush and Kool Moe Dee of The Treacherous Three but with more flair and charisma. Kane displayed a rapid-fire delivery and the wittiest "Dolemite" level punch lines ever heard before. These three emcees would set the standard for legions of rappers to follow for decades to come. Adding to Marley Marl's stable of new emcees was another gifted MC named Kool G Rap. Sprinkle in a radical new group called Public Enemy and 1987 was a fantastic time to be a Hip-Hop fan.

After rising to become the epicenter of the new Hip-Hop revolution, in less than a year, Hip-Hop's premier nightclub, Union Square, finally chose to distance itself from Rap music. The story I heard was of a massive riot in Union Square led by who else but Brooklyn. Packs of thugs created so much havoc that the hired security became overwhelmed. The bouncers had to surrender the club to these hoodlums. After that night, Hip-Hop at Union Square was no more. The Latin Quarter, the only other real competition to Union Square, became the undisputed capital of the NYC Hip-Hop world in 1987. Unfortunately, all the Brooklyn hooligans who terrorized Union Square made their way over to The Latin Quarter. This extra dose of undesirable partygoers added to the already volatile Times Square area. Traveling to The LQ became an adventure in itself.

The summer of 1987 arrived. I met up with Kris and Scott in the city, and Scott seemed to be in a happy mood. I remember him declaring out loud in true Scott La Rock super confident fashion, "You know what? I think we're the hottest thing in New York City right now, and nobody wants to tell us!" I remember laughing at his declaration because it was so bold. No one asked him anything either; he chose to blurt that out. Scott was half-laughing but half-serious at the same time. Kris had a different announcement; he was getting married to his girlfriend, Melodie. I was so happy for him. He surprised me by asking if I would be his best man at the ceremony? Of course, I would! The wedding was coming up fast though, the second weekend in July. I would have to get fitted for a tuxedo immediately.

A week before the wedding, Boogie Down Productions had yet another show at The Latin Quarter. Darrell and I decided to go as usual. We did our routine of going to the club entrance and having Paradise make us wait outside until Kris arrived. We finally entered the club with Kris, who headed backstage while Darrell and I hit the dance floor area to find a spot to watch the show. I didn't see what happened backstage, but this is what Kris told me. Scott, who was already inside, immediately goes up to Kris and starts whispering something in his ear. It appeared that the legendary Melle Mel of Grandmaster Flash and the Furious Five fame showed up at the LQ. He walked into the backstage area and, without provocation, declared that he was the greatest rapper alive. Melle Mel challenged any emcee to battle him on the spot for $1,000. Scott La Rock, never one to back down from a challenge, told Melle Mel, "Ok, wait till my boy gets here!" The whole evening took on a different tone. I've always felt that although Melle Mel made his challenge to anyone who was within earshot of his voice, the fact that he came to a BDP show at the LQ meant he was looking for only one person, KRS-One.

Melle Mel, from The Bronx, was once considered to be the best rapper in the game. Now, there was a new young gun claiming The Bronx and Melle Mel came to regain his crown. When the show began, we in the audience had no idea what happened backstage. Kris went through a few songs off the album, and the audience sang along to every word. Right when he started to perform his latest single 'Poetry,' Melle Mel walked right out onto the stage in the middle of the concert. He was holding a roll of money in the air, issuing a lyrical challenge to KRS-One. It didn't take long for the audience to figure out what was going on. Kris, who was facing the audience and performing the song 'Poetry,' turned and began directing the song's lyrics at Melle Mel. He pointed right at Melle Mel's face. Oh, man! It was about to go down right now.

Shortly after that brief exchange, the music stops. The show got interrupted by Melle Mel prancing around on stage. The crowd began to get annoyed by Melle Mel's antics. It appeared like they were in no mood to see this potentially legendary battle. They were more interested in seeing BDP perform the 'Criminal Minded' album. I could hear some people becoming restless and yell "Get off the stage!" Somehow Melle Mel found his way over to a spare microphone and jumped right into a full-fledge battle rap right on the spot. The next thing I knew, his mic completely shut off. I don't know if it was Scott or Red Alert or someone else controlling the sound, but Melle Mel's mic cut off right in the middle of his rhyme. The crowd was becoming more agitated now; people started booing. Somehow, someone from the audience threw what appeared to be a bicycle chain at Melle Mel. I don't know how they managed to sneak a bike chain into the club, but I saw it, wiz, right past Melle Mel's head. Melle Mel was now pleading for someone to turn his microphone back on but to no avail. He turned and left the stage. Kris might have performed one or two songs after that, but the crowd's electric energy all but diminished.

Over the years, I've heard people talk about this mythical battle between

KRS-One and Melle Mel at The Latin Quarter. In reality, that battle never happened. In Melle Mel's defense, there definitely would have been a battle if someone hadn't cut off his microphone. Melle Mel's lyrics might have been devastating, but we'll never know. There was a rumor of some agreement made between the two emcees for an official battle the following weekend at the LQ. That didn't make sense because Kris was getting married that weekend. The follow-up battle never happened either.

The day of the wedding finally arrived. July 11th, 1987, was two days after my 21st birthday. I was a grown man. The plan was for the groom and groomsmen to meet at Darrell's house in Brooklyn. Afterward, we would drive to the wedding location together. I have no idea what they were doing the night before, but the entire BDP crew arrived at the house looking disheveled. Scott forgot to bring his shoes. He asked Darrell if he could borrow a pair of shoes to wear to the wedding. Darrell lent Scott his favorite pair of 'Clarks' shoes, which Scott never returned. We arrived at the wedding location, and of course, I was nervous because I had the ring. What if I lost it? I kept checking my pockets the entire time. Before the wedding commenced, we were all relaxing in a church section designated for the groom. Scott was holding court telling funny tour stories. Somehow, the conversation turned to sports and then to basketball. Out of nowhere, Scott began talking trash to me out of the blue about how I couldn't play ball, and he would bust my ass. What? Scott never saw me play ball before. Does he know who he's talking to right now? Scott was tall, about 6'3", but I now stood a 6'6". I competed against players 6'8" or 6'9" every single day. I considered Scott a little dude. I was also four years younger than Scott and just played an entire season of Division 1 college basketball. I was in the top basketball shape. Scott, who played Division 3 college basketball, had been sitting behind a desk for four years. What was he thinking? He was even talking trash to Darrell, unprovoked. Things became so heated that we agreed to play ball against each other after the reception.

Both Darrell and I were so mad that we traveled back to New Jersey and changed into our basketball gear. We then headed to the reception in long Island. Darrell and I showed up at Kris' wedding reception wearing shorts and sneakers! Scott did too. Kris' new wife Melodie was not happy. Imagine the best man showing up at the wedding reception in shorts, sneakers, and a t-shirt? She had every right to curse us out. There was a park with a basketball court located near the reception. I wanted to not only beat Scott but embarrass him. All I could think of on the way over there was the different ways I was going dunk on him. Darrell, Scott, and I left the reception and walked over to the park to play our grudge match. However, we couldn't find a ball. There was no one on the court when we got there. Damn! We never got to play ball on that hot, steamy July day after all. We walked back to the reception and chilled out for the rest of the afternoon. Scott was lucky that day.

About two weeks had passed since the wedding, and the 'Criminal Minded' album was still scorching hot. BDP got booked to perform yet another show at the Latin Quarter. This show was shaping up to be the craziest one yet! That very same week, Roxanne Shante had taken Kris' advice. She released a new song written by Big Daddy Kane called 'Have A Nice Day' that featured a BDP diss in the last verse. To her credit, at least she dared to respond to KRS-One.

On the night of the show, I decided to switch up my routine, something a superstitious athlete would rarely do. I should've listened to my gut. We met Kris in front of the club as usual. I didn't waste my time approaching Paradise for my typical rejection. When we entered the club, I decided to venture into the backstage area for the first time. I weaved through the crowds of people back there, and I found a seat in the dressing room area. The next thing I knew, I felt an intense, burning pain in my left thigh. Arghhh!! I jumped up. What is this? To my surprise, Scott La Rock had shocked my leg with a stun gun! Everybody was laughing, but I was not amused.

It appeared Scott was going around shocking people with an illegal stun gun that he recently purchased. I knew the stunt was all in fun, but I still didn't know how to respond. Everybody loved Scott, and he didn't seem to have any malicious intent behind his prank. Still, I recalled the way he challenged me a few weeks earlier at the wedding reception. I started thinking, "If I don't put a stop to this right now, I will have a real problem with Scott in the future." I knew he was playing around but, was he? If it were anybody else other than Kris' best friend, I would've had a different reaction. My lifelong history with bullying caused this incident to raise an immediate red flag. Bullying always starts as a "harmless" joke. Angrily, I decided to leave the backstage area altogether and go out into the crowd. The vibe in the LQ had changed in only a few short weeks. There were way more thugs roaming around now, like wolves on the prowl. The ratio of criminals to partygoers was never this high before Union Square closed down.

As I surveyed the club, I noticed a tall, light-skinned figure appear on the dance floor wearing a custom-made Dapper Dan Gucci jacket with matching pants and a hat too! He was also sporting a thick, shiny gold "dookie" rope chain around his neck. Who could that be? It was none other than the "Prince Of Rap," LL Cool J. He recently released his double-platinum album 'Bigger And Deffer', and his single 'I need Love' was tearing up both the radio airwaves and MTV. LL Cool J was a bonafide superstar. He was five feet away from me, along with another guy, standing on the dance floor, nodding his head to the music. The song that was playing happened to be the first Rap song I ever heard at The LQ, 'Ego Tripping' by The Ultramagnetic MC's. It didn't take long for the Brooklyn wolves to notice him and begin closing in. I could see them approaching from the right as the music blasted. LL noticed them too. As they got closer, one of them yelled something derogatory at LL, but he didn't seem bothered by the taunt at all. He shrugged his shoulders and raised his hand in the air, rubbing his thumb and index finger together, making a gesture like "I'm getting money though."

This slick hand gesture made the Brooklyn dudes furious. One of them picked up a chair and was about to throw it right at LL when security intervened in the nick of time. They pushed the goons back, and the music stopped. Red Alert got on the microphone and said in an aggravated tone, "Yo L, why don't you just come up to the DJ booth?" I have to give LL Cool J enormous credit; he didn't appear rattled at all. I gained a lot of respect for LL for choosing to come onto the dance floor and party with everyone else instead of staying backstage. Still, he should've known better.

After Red Alert resumed playing the music, I could tell there was still a restlessness in the air. My instincts told me something terrible was going to happen. Shortly after the LL Cool J altercation, it was showtime. KRS-One hits the LQ stage to a raucous crowd. The energy was insane. He started things off by saying, "Yo...I heard Roxanne Shante tried to diss me! Ok, check this out...." Kris had an answer to Shante's song already. Scott threw on a hard beat, and Kris began singing a jingle detailing his encounter with Shante at the bank a few months earlier. Trust me when I tell you, it was crazy! Fortunately for Shante, it was the first and only time he did that routine. For some reason, Kris chose not to release his response as a single.

After the Shante routine, Kris began performing songs off of the 'Criminal Minded' album. Once again, during the performance of the song 'Poetry,' things went south. An all-out brawl broke out between Brooklyn and a crew from The Bronx called 'The Violators.' It looked like an old-fashioned saloon fight in a western movie. Chairs were flying, and glass was breaking. People were screaming and running everywhere. Kris continued performing the lyrics to the song as he looked down at the chaos from the stage. Finally, the music had to stop. It was an all-out war in the club. Darrell and I ran through some doors leading to the backstage area and right into the DJ booth. Red Alert closed and locked the door behind us and declared, "No one is coming in or out of this room, period!"

Inside the DJ booth were Me, Darrell, Kris, Ms. Melodie, Scott La Rock, Red Alert, and some wild young boy named Chris Lighty. It appeared, Chris Lighty was part of The Violator Crew that was fighting against Brooklyn. He tried to open the booth door and join the melee, but Red Alert blocked the door. Chris Lighty then attempted to leap from the DJ booth onto the dance floor. That was about a two-story jump! Red Alert tackled him and was holding Chris Lighty in a bear hug. Chris was screaming, "Let me go, Red! Let me Go! I have to get down there! My boys are out there fighting!" Red Alert continued holding onto him saying, "You're not going anywhere." I was looking down at the absolute mayhem taking place on the dance floor. I was thinking, "This guy Chris must be a lunatic to want to go out there and get involved in that madness." As I'm watching Chris Lighty, screaming at the top of his lungs, I saw a guy on the dance floor get whacked in his ribs with a metal pole, CRACK!

It was so disappointing and embarrassing to see our Hip-Hop crowd destroying this beautiful nightclub. The police came rushing inside the club, spraying pepper spray to regain law and order. The lights came on, and the remaining partygoers began to emerge from out of hiding. The Latin Quarter was in shambles. Glass, debris, and broken chairs were everywhere; it was a mess. But wait, without warning, a guy appeared in the middle of the dance floor, surrounded by all kinds of debris, and started dancing! What the hell? It was the rapper, Biz Markie. Everyone recognized his signature dance moves, and the remaining crowd started chanting, "Go Biz Mark! Go Biz Mark! Go Biz Mark! It was hilarious. I was looking at him from the DJ booth laughing my ass off, thinking, "This guy is nuts!"

Before the police allowed anyone to leave, they searched us on the way out. People were shooting guns outside, so the cops wanted to make sure nobody inside the club had a firearm. The police felt the need to protect the general public visiting Times Square from the patrons of a nightclub; imagine that? Darrell was wearing a gold, three-finger name ring that night. I yelled at him to take it off. He refused. I told him, "This is no time to be macho. Do I have to explain to you what's going to happen if we go outside and those hoodlums see you wearing a gold name ring?" Darrell appeased me and took off the ring. The entire situation was a mess. I knew it wouldn't be long before Brooklyn's antics would cause yet another club to shut down. This brawl felt like the beginning of the end of The Latin Quarter.

During the middle of August 1987, Kris hit me with some magnificent news. Boogie Down Productions would be performing at "The World's Most Famous Arena," Madison Square Garden. WOW! A huge Rap show was taking place there featuring several of the hottest Rap groups and headlined by none other than LL Cool J himself. BDP was in such demand that the promoters added them to the bill. Unbelievable! It doesn't get any better than Madison Square Garden. Of course, I wouldn't miss this show for the world. I tried to imagine what it would be like to see 20,000 people singing along to my brother's music. I couldn't even picture what it would look like in my head. I had spoken to Kris at the top of the week. He told me he had a show in Ohio over the weekend and would be back on Monday (that sound you hear is the dreaded "other shoe" dropping).

That following Monday, I gave Kris a call. He immediately answered the phone. I asked him, "How was your show in Ohio?" He said, "What? You didn't hear about Scott?" I said, "No, what about Scott? Kris said in a somber tone, "He's dead, he got killed on Thursday." WHAT?? I know Kris would never joke like that. I asked him what happened? Kris told me that on Thursday, he received a phone call from D-Nice, but Dee was crying so uncontrollably that he was incoherent on the phone. Someone else took the phone from Dee and told Kris the story. D-Nice got into an altercation in The Bronx with some guy over a girl. Dee called Scott, who was like a father figure to him, for help. Scott arrived with a few other members of the BDP crew with intentions of peacefully resolving the situation. There are many different versions of the story. The consensus was everyone talked it over, and the beef got settled. As Scott and the other crew members got back into the car, bullets rang out from a rooftop above hitting the vehicle. Scott was the only one hit by the gunfire. Some say he wasn't even the intended target. Scott succumbed to his gunshot wound at the hospital shortly after that.

Over the years, I've heard conflicting stories about what happened that day and what became of the perpetrators of the crime. One thing was for sure, Scott was gone. Kris told me that he didn't want to go to the hospital and see Scott lying there in that condition. Kris said Scott was his hero and felt that Scott would always be there with him. That's how he wanted to remember him. The death of Scott La Rock was devastating to the Hop-Hop community. It was the first time in music history that a senseless act of violence took a prominent Hip-Hop artist's life. There were vigils held for Scott all over New York City. Multiple news outlets carried the story, and radio mix shows from around the country paid tribute to the fallen star. Scott left behind a short but remarkable musical legacy. His innovative production was the perfect backdrop for KRS-One's lyrical onslaught. Together, they crafted a body of work called 'Criminal Minded.' The record was so influential that in 2003, the most prestigious music publication in America, Rolling Stone Magazine, named 'Criminal Minded' to its list of 'The 500 Greatest Albums Of All Time.' Considering an estimated 1.8 million different albums have been released worldwide, that's a pretty impressive feat for an independently released project with limited distribution, recorded in only two weeks! Having been sampled dozens of times by artists ranging from Rihanna and Jennifer Lopez to The Notorious B.I.G., 'Criminal Minded' became one of the most sampled Hip-Hop albums in music history. In 2017, The Borough of The Bronx renamed and dedicated a street in his honor. Long Live the great Scott La Rock!

CHAPTER 13
PARKER BROTHER

"*Fame is a weird one...People see a value in you that you don't see yourself*" - Benedict Cumberbatch

The Death of Scott La Rock left Boogie Down Productions with a dilemma, what happens now? It was a multi-layered question with limited time to figure out. There was still a Madison Square Garden concert pending in less than two weeks. All of the group's decisions fell on the shoulders of KRS-One, who decided to continue the group. Kris worked his entire life to reach that point, quitting now was not an option. Scott wouldn't have wanted that either, that's not the type of person he was. Kris decided to perform a tribute to Scott La Rock at Madison Square Garden. Kris had a colossal mural erected of Scott placed behind the turntables, which he left empty. It was going to be an emotional night for everybody involved. On the day of the concert, Kris told me to meet him at the artist's entrance on 33rd street at 7:30 pm. BDP's scheduled time to perform was 8:10 pm. I arrived by myself at 7 pm sharp.

As I stood there, observing the concert-goers walking by, who did I see?

None other than Paradise, the manager of The Latin Quarter. Surprisingly, he stopped and spoke to me. He asked me why I was standing there? I told him I was waiting for Kris to arrive so I could receive a pass. Paradise reached into his pocket and pulled out a ticket to the concert. He said, "Here, I have an extra ticket for the show; You can have it." What?? I didn't see that one coming. Paradise had no problem denying me entrance to The Latin Quarter, but he would volunteer to help me get into Madison Square Garden? Go figure.

I thanked Paradise for the ticket, and he left. As 7:30 pm approached, Kris hadn't arrived, but I bumped into one of his good friends, the rapper Just-Ice. He and Kris had been friends dating back to The Bronx Men's Shelter days. "Juss" was an accomplished rapper in his own right. He had several New York City club bangers under his belt, including the hit single 'Latoya.' I've always liked Just-Ice, and my face lit up when I saw him, "Yo Juss, what's up!" He stopped, and we talked for a little while. He mentioned that he was waiting for a friend who had a ticket for him, but the guy was late; sounded familiar. As we waited, I noticed an odd-looking character across the street, speaking very loud to another fellow. Something about this guy stood out to me. He was very dark-skinned, sporting a baseball cap turned sideways on his head. He wore a matching tracksuit with a stopwatch around his neck. He was moving his arms in a very animated fashion and had a nasal voice. He said to his friend, "Yeah, Gee! We about to rock The Garden tonight, Gee!"

I could not take my eyes off of this dude; he was different. Just-Ice noticed me staring at him and said, "That's Flavor Flav from Public Enemy." No way! Public Enemy was my favorite group! I loved their debut album 'Yo! Bum Rush The Show!' Their latest single 'Rebel Without A Pause' was on fire in The Latin Quarter. Although I was familiar with their music, I had never seen them in person. Flavor Flav looked like the embodiment of everything Hip-Hop to me. Public Enemy was on the bill as well as Eric B & Rakim. This concert was the Hip-Hop show of the year; I couldn't wait.

It was now about 7:40 pm, and of course, Kris was late. The person Just-Ice was waiting for didn't show up at all. I decided to offer him the ticket Paradise had given me. I wouldn't need it once Kris arrived. Juss asked me if I was sure? I told him "Yes," so he took the ticket, thanked me, and left to go inside The Garden. Meanwhile, 7:45 no Kris. 7:50 no Kris. 7:55 no Kris. 8 pm, No, Kris! Suddenly, I see Kris, his manager "Mo," and a few other guys from the crew running down the block at top speed. Kris yelled at me, "Yo! Get in that van over there, and it'll take you inside. We gotta go now!" I ran over to a van that held Ms. Melodie and her sister "Harmony" and jumped into the vehicle. We drove down the entrance ramp about to proceed inside when suddenly the van stopped. Security wouldn't allow us any further without "all-access" passes. They instructed us to wait until the manager of Boogie Down Productions returned with our laminates. Uh oh!

While we were sitting outside in the van awaiting our passes, I could hear the sold-out crowd's roars coming from inside The Garden. Damn, I was missing the show. The next thing I knew, the sound of 'The Bridge Is Over' was coming through the arena walls, to more cheers. Ah man, they're on stage right now! As I sat there, disappointed with my current plight, I couldn't help but be reflective at that moment. What an unbelievable journey my brother had traveled to reach this point. Less than a year ago, Kris was homeless, sleeping in an abandoned freezer in the record company's basement. Now, he's rocking a sold-out Madison Square Garden. If you watched a movie and this had been the plot, you would have called the unrealistic flick, trash! Yet, it was all true. How unfortunate was it that Scott La Rock wasn't there? With his massive ego, he would have been in all his glory at Madison Square Garden.

My introspective daydreaming got cut short by the yelling of security, "This van has to move out the way! Whodini's limousine has to get by!" Security backed us right out onto the sidewalk and made us exit the van. Things were not looking good. We stood on the sidewalk for about an hour before realizing "Manager Mo" was not coming back outside to get us. To add insult to injury, I had a ticket to the show and gave it to Just-Ice. Sometimes you have to laugh at a situation and move on. Lesson learned.

The fall of 1987 meant classes resumed, so there was little room in my schedule for club hopping. However, a new Hip-Hop song called 'Top Billin' by The Audio Two was tearing up the airwaves. Of course, The Latin Quarter booked the duo to perform. I could not miss this show. Neither Darrell nor myself had any money to pay for admission. Would my new "friend" Paradise decide to let us in The LQ? I wasn't counting on that happening. We only had one sure option, call Kris. By this time, he had moved into a luxury apartment building on 34th street in the heart of Midtown Manhattan. I put in the call, and Kris answered right away. I hadn't seen him since the MSG concert. We talked for a bit, and then I slipped in my real purpose for calling. Can he help us get into The Latin Quarter to see The Audio Two?

After laughing at me for about a minute straight and calling me a "Superfan," Kris confessed that he hadn't gone out at all since Scott died. He didn't know if he was ready to deal with people asking him questions about Scott if he went to The LQ. In a somber tone, I told him I completely understood. Kris must've sensed my disappointment because he agreed to help us, after all. This performance would be the first time I would see a Rap show by a group not named Boogie Down Productions. Darrell and I met Kris in front of the club, and we went right in. No sooner did we enter the club, we lost him. Kris turned right, and we turned left, and that was it. We didn't see him anymore for the rest of the night. We watched the show and went home afterward. That turned out to be my last visit to The Latin Quarter. After three people got shot leaving the club one night, the LQ officially closed its doors to Hip-Hop.

It was a sad end of an era. Brooklyn's ruthless behavior had ruined another club. The LQ would leave a lasting legacy as one of the most influential nightclubs in Hip-Hop history. Every weekend, the cream of the Hip-Hop crop socialized there. It became a training ground for countless Rap legends. Future rappers, who would later rise to stardom in the '90s, also reminisce about their time sneaking into the legendary nightspot as teenagers. Even my "buddy" at the door, Paradise, would become a founding member of the insurgent Rap group X-Clan. I was fortunate to have experienced this short-lived, but iconic moment in Hip-Hop.

The year was 1988—a pivotal year for Hip-Hop and Boogie Down Productions. Right before Scott's death, BDP was all set to sign a brand new recording contract with a major label. When Scott died, the company's A&R representative felt they were no longer receiving a full group without Scott. In his opinion, Boogie Down Productions died with Scott La Rock. They were no longer interested in signing the group. I've always felt like this was an odd conclusion for a record company executive to make if he analyzed the entire situation. Sure, Scott was the main driving force behind the 'Criminal Minded' musical sound. But, KRS-One was 100% responsible for the lyrical content. With a little investigating, the A&R rep would have also discovered that KRS produced the smash hit 'The Bridge is Over.' With those credentials and obvious talent, you had to take a chance on KRS-One. They could have paired him with another established producer if they weren't sure about the music. Still, the major label passed on Boogie Down Productions.

Luckily, that old timeless proverb always applies, "One man's trash is another man's treasure." After years of considering Rap Music a fad and predicting its imminent demise, the major labels finally came to a different conclusion. Hip-Hop had become wildly popular in many urban cities. Rap music was putting up financial numbers that the music industry could no longer ignore. The major's wanted in. They started gobbling up all the smaller independent labels. They either bought their hottest artist outright or gave national distribution deals to the indies. These acquisitions raised the quality and output of Rap music tenfold.

For KRS-One, the record company that came calling was Rap/R&B label Jive Records, distributed by RCA. Their roster included DJ Jazzy Jeff & The Fresh Prince, Kool Moe Dee, and R&B star Billy Ocean. Jive saw potential in KRS-One/BDP and signed Boogie Down Productions to a recording contract. They also signed Ms. Melodie and D-Nice, who replaced Scott as the new DJ for BDP, to solo deals. Armed with a new major label deal, Kris headed back into the studio to record a new album, but with question marks. First, could he succeed without his musical partner, Scott La Rock? Second, after the runaway success of 'Criminal Minded,' what would KRS-One do for an encore?

As for myself, my junior basketball season came to an end during "March Madness," which allowed me a little more free time. I continued to tape DJ Red Alert every weekend. I also spent a portion of my scholarship stipend money on various Rap albums that I liked. My closest friend on the basketball team, also named Larry, would swap cassettes with me of the albums I didn't own to make a copy (called a "dub"). I was up to date on almost every Rap release coming out of New York City in 1988. Despite all my radio monitoring and cassette dubbing, I missed one weekend, and some new music got past me. I traveled to Baltimore to visit my girlfriend Pam. When I returned, I got bombarded by several friends saying the same thing, "Yoooo, your brother has a new song out, and he said your name in it!" What? A new song? Did he say my name? Are you sure?

It didn't take me long to get to the bottom of this. The new Boogie Down Productions song 'My Philosophy' was playing everywhere. It was the lead single from the forthcoming BDP album. When a person received a "Shout-

Out" from a rapper, it was a big deal dating back to the earliest days of Hip-Hop. If an emcee in a club or park jam mentioned your name, they acknowledged you as special or relevant. A shout-out separated you from everyone else attending the party. Getting 'shouted' on a record was more significant because your name became part of the song's lyrics.

After listening to 'My Philosophy,' I discovered that not only had I received a shout-out from one of the hottest rappers in the game, but Kris took the acknowledgment to another level. The song's actual line goes, "My brother's name is Kenny, that's Kenny Parker, my other brother ICU is much darker." WOW! Not only did he mention my name, but he repeated it and said my last name as well. To add to the line's enormity, Kris recognized me as his actual brother, not a homeboy or group member. I had no idea Kris was going to do that. It blew me away. Everyone in school was buggin' out. If I told people KRS-One is my brother, that's one thing. If KRS-One tells people, I'm HIS brother, that's a whole different animal. When I finally got in touch with Kris, I immediately expressed my shock and happiness, "Yo! You shouted me out on your new song!" Kris replied in his usual carefree tone, "Yeah, of course." His response made it seem like it wasn't that big of a deal, but it was. I didn't realize how big, though.

It didn't take but a couple of weeks for my life to change dramatically. Word spread like a virus around Jersey City that KRS-One's brother is a student at St. Peter's College. I began hearing whispers when I went to the grocery store like, "Is that him? It looks like him." Some of the African-American students who never spoke to me, began saying, "What's up?" It felt a little weird, to be honest. I received accolades from time to time based on my play on the basketball court, but this was different. I was getting a ton of attention, and I hadn't done anything to deserve it. People would ask me if KRS-One was my brother? I would say yes, and their faces would light up. What was I supposed to say after that? "Um, I have to go now. I have a term paper due tomorrow." It was surreal.

Not to be forgotten with the hype surrounding my shout-out was the brilliance of the new single 'My Philosophy.' The first thing that caught your attention was the beat. The song featured an up-tempo, drum-driven track with a haunting saxophone rift playing throughout. Some spoken word samples were scratched in the intro by (now DJ) KRS-One for added effect. After the listener absorbed the track for a few bars, the lyrical assault of KRS-One begins. Kris opens the song with a reintroduction of sorts about who he is and what he stands for, along with a recap of the previous year's events. He also introduces the Hip-Hop world to the official expanded BDP roster (D-Nice, Ms. Melodie). He includes Scott La Rock, who Kris speaks of in the present tense, signaling that Scott will always be there with him in everything he does. Kris also establishes a new persona for himself. No longer is he the "Poet" from the 'Criminal Minded' album; he is now "The Teacher," and all of Hip-Hop is his classroom. Kris reveals to his "students" his current opinion on the state of Hip-Hop. Without mentioning any names, he scolds many rappers about their public image and lack of substance in their music. There's another subliminal shot at the great RUN-DMC. The trademark KRS-One vocabulary is present along with a sprinkling of battle rhymes. 'My Philosophy' is the one song an unfamiliar listener would need to hear, to sum up, KRS-One and Boogie Down Productions in a nutshell. The song became an instant hit. The Rap audience so well received it that in 2008, VH1 ranked 'My Philosophy' #49 on its list of 'The 100 Greatest Hip-Hop Songs Of All Time.' With the success of the new single, any thoughts of a sophomore jinx got squashed. Boogie Down Productions was poised to become a bigger force in Hip-Hop in 1988. After digesting the first single, I was thirsty to hear more of the new BDP album.

I was able to track Kris down at Power Play Studios in Long Island City, Queens. He was doing some last-minute final mixes before turning in the album. D-Nice, who was also present at the mixing session, asked me if I heard the new album yet? Of course not. He played me a song called 'I'm Still #1,' and it was incredible! It might have been more impressive than the hit single 'My Philosophy.' After I recovered from having my head musically blown off, D-Nice then played another new track off the album called 'Jimmy.' This song was a witty and hilarious warning about unprotected sex and the use of condoms. 'Jimmy' was also the second BDP song to feature vocals from the now official crew member, DJ Red Alert. Unfortunately, I was only able to hear two new songs that night, Damn!

After a long, hard-fought journey dating back to 1973 and the slums of The Bronx, Hip-Hop was on the verge of an explosion in 1988. The whole Rap industry was sitting on a powder keg, one spark away from detonation. That spark's ignition came from the unlikeliest of sources, MTV. As with the major labels, MTV finally concluded that Rap music was worth taking a gamble on. However, they still wouldn't completely dive into the Hip-Hop water yet. Led by Ted Demme (R.I.P.), MTV created a weekly Rap show called 'Yo! MTV Raps'. MTV beamed Rap music videos into the living rooms of homes where Hip-Hop never appeared before. Before 'Yo! MTV Raps', Hip-Hop was regional. If you didn't live in a major city, you had minimal access to Hip-Hop. Let's say you were fortunate enough to get your hands on a morsel of Hip-Hop. You would still be months behind everyone else due to the indie labels' poor marketing and distribution. With the combination of major label distribution and MTV's coast-to-coast programming, the lid finally blew off the Hip-Hop pot in 1988. 'Yo! MTV Raps' became the most-watched show in MTV history. The youth of America, both Black and White, couldn't get enough of the Hip-Hop culture, to the horror of their parents.

The timing of YO! MTV Raps couldn't have been better for Boogie Down Productions. Jive Records decided to shoot a music video for the single 'My Philosophy.' The director was none other than the soon-to-be host of 'YO! MTV Raps', Fab 5 Freddy. It was perfect! The video shoot took place over two days. Kris invited me down to one of the video locations. Awesome!! I met up with Just-Ice, and I got a chance to witness the making of an actual music video. That consisted of fifteen takes of the same scene, followed by fifteen takes of another seen, rinse and repeat. After spending all day on the set, I only received five seconds in the video's final cut. During a crowd scene, no less. Ha!

Regardless of my "don't blink or you'll miss me" cameo, BDP's first "real" music video turned out to be a huge success! Fab 5 Freddy captured KRS-One's persona to a tee. The way Kris communicated to the camera, the custom-made leather BDP suits he wore, and the background imagery of The Bronx made the video an instant Hip-Hop classic. The 'My Philosophy' video exposed Boogie Down Productions to a whole new nationwide audience. The anticipation for the new album reached a fevered pitch.

On May 31st, 1988, Boogie Down Productions released their sophomore album 'By All Means Necessary' worldwide on Jive/RCA Records. The first thing that jumped out about the album was once again, the cover. There was a picture of KRS-One, once again holding a gun, a rifle to be exact, like the 'Criminal Minded' album cover. This time the symbolism was different. The cover was a re-creation of the famous 1964 photo of Malcolm X looking out of the window, holding a rifle. KRS bared a slight resemblance to "Brother Malcolm" on the album cover. Even the album title 'By All Means Necessary' came from the iconic Malcolm X battle cry "By any means necessary." If you guessed based on the imagery, that the new BDP project appeared to be a theme album, you would be correct. Produced, directed, and mixed by KRS-One, 'By All Means Necessary' was an "in your face" commentary about the African-American experience in America. The album seemed to pick up where Grandmaster Flash & The Furious Five's 'The Message' left off back in 1982. It was an entire album dedicated to a socially conscious theme, a first of its kind in Hip-Hop. Coincidently, right around the time that KRS-One & BDP were cooking up their new offering, another group was working on a socially conscious gem. The group's name was Public Enemy.

On June 28th, 1988, Public Enemy dropped their masterpiece 'It Takes A Nation Of Millions To Hold Us Back.' Together with 'By All Means Necessary,' these two albums ushered in a new Hip-Hop era dubbed "Conscious Rap." Although 'The Message' was the first recording to introduce this Rap style, no trend followed in 1982. There was a sprinkling of "problems of the world today" type songs, but Hip-Hop stayed in its familiar territory; partying, boasting, and battling. Now in '88, a couple of rebel groups decided to raise Hip-Hop to new thought-provoking heights. Public Enemy represented a Black Panther Party styled group approach. KRS-One, still part of a group, presented himself more as a solo activist and leader of the new movement. Both KRS-One and Public Enemy leader Chuck D had something in common. Grandmaster Flash's 'The Message' described the daily struggles African Americans experienced living in the ghetto. Chuck & Kris expanded on the topic, identifying the core root of the problem, the culprits responsible, and possible solutions. BDP and PE upped the ante quite a bit.

'By All Means Necessary' was another runaway success for Boogie Down Productions. The Recording Industry Association Of America (RIAA) certified the album gold. A tremendous accomplishment for a Hip-Hop album in the 80s.

With back-to-back groundbreaking albums, KRS-One was now considered an elite emcee. Once again, he was at the forefront of another Hip-Hop movement. When I got a chance to speak with him, I had questions (what else is new?). Why did he change his style this time compared to the 'Criminal Minded' album? Kris explained to me that actually, he hadn't changed his style at all. Kris revealed that the conscious style was how he intended to come out in 1987. It was Scott La Rock who convinced him otherwise. Scott felt Kris needed to establish himself first. His message would resonate more if he had a bigger audience. The plan all along was to drop the "Criminal Minded" style first and then release a conscious album. When Kris wrote the 'Criminal Minded' album, he also composed half of the 'By All Means Necessary' album too. Unbelievable! My next question was, what's next?

The answer to that question was a tour. BDP was taking its act on the road. A gigantic 50 city arena tour called 'The Dope Jam Tour' was heading out for the entire summer. It would feature Eric B & Rakim, Doug E Fresh, Kool Moe Dee, Biz Markie, Ice T, and Boogie Down Productions. Hip-Hop had come a long way. Gone were the days when only Run-DMC, The Fat Boys, and LL Cool J could sell out arenas. Kris invited me to come on tour with him and hang out for the summer. That sounded like a fantastic summer vacation, but I had to decline. I was enrolled in summer classes and on track to graduate. I needed those extra credits. Oh well, maybe next time.

The summer of 1988 moved at a pretty fast pace. My 22nd birthday was in July. I spent most of my time either cooped up in hot summer classes or in the gym working out. I was preparing for my final year of college basketball. During the second week of August, I received Kris's message asking if I still wanted to come on the road with him and hang out. He had an open spot on the tour bus. The fall semester didn't start for another three weeks, so my answer was an emphatic, HELL YEAH! Kris sent me some cash, and I flew out to Ohio to catch up with the tour there. I didn't know what to expect. I had never been on a tour bus, and I'd never seen an arena-sized concert either. The closest I came to an arena show was sitting in a van outside of Madison Square Garden. My goal was to observe everything. I wasn't going to miss a thing.

I arrived in Ohio in time to head over to the arena with the crew for a soundcheck. Everyone I met was acting friendly towards me, "Oh, you're Kris' brother, right? Kenny Parker." Everybody there already knew who I was. We returned to the hotel, and I met my assigned roommate. Who could it be? None other than DJ Red Alert! He had taken some time off from KISS-FM to join the tour and perform 'Jimmy' with BDP. He was super cool. I didn't dare tell him that I had been listening to him every weekend for five years straight and he was my absolute favorite DJ in the entire world.

It didn't take long for showtime to arrive. As we gathered in the lobby to ride back to the arena, I saw the rapper Biz Markie sitting on a couch chilling out. He was also enjoying great success with his debut album and hit single 'The Vapors.' He looked over at me and said, "You're Kris' brother, right? Kenny Parker." That seemed to be the ongoing theme of my life. Biz and I immediately hit it off. It was like we had been friends for years. I asked him how the tour was going? He said it was great, but he felt like he didn't have enough time to perform the way he wanted to. "How much time do you have?" I asked. Biz told me he only had fifteen minutes. I asked him how many songs would he perform? He said, "About seven." What? How can you perform seven songs in only fifteen minutes? I told him that was impossible. He challenges me to a bet. I had only known Biz Markie for roughly ten minutes, and we already had a friendly wager.

I rode over to the venue, preparing to see my very first, arena-sized concert. When we arrived, I walked around the backstage area absorbing the scenery. I noticed a stunningly beautiful woman about twenty feet away, having a conversation. One of the guys from our crew spotted me gazing in her direction. He said to me in a stern tone, "Don't even think about it, that's Darlene. That's Ice-T's girlfriend!" Oooh ok. I told him I had no intention of saying anything to her at all. She happened to catch my eye, for obvious reasons. He explained to me that not only was Ice-T friends with the entire BDP crew, but he was also a known street dude out in Los Angeles. He warned me not to disrespect Ice-T. Sheesh. Ok, I got it.

After a while, the arena began filling up, and it was showtime! I found a spot right next to the stage. When the lights went out in the building, the whole crowd roared in anticipation. The cheers reminded me of when the home team would score at a basketball game. The sound system was thunderous. Ice-T was up first. He had a hit single and video called 'Colors.' He had the crowd rocking in no time. Next up was Biz Markie. Now, this I had to see. Seven songs in fifteen minutes? Yeah right. Since I hadn't seen many concerts before, I didn't know that sometimes an artist might not perform a hit in its entirety. I was naive enough to believe that if the song was four minutes long, that's how long it took to sing it. Biz Markie breezed through a medley of his biggest hits. Not only did he perform the seven songs, but he had enough time to do a funny routine, talk to the crowd, do the "Biz Dance" and still have time left to perform his smash hit 'The Vapors' which brought the house down. I lost the bet.

At long last, it was time for Boogie Down Productions. BDP had twenty minutes to perform. As I watched D-Nice set up behind the turntables, I looked around the arena, and it was a complete sell-out, 18,000 plus. Once again, I became nervous about the show. After all the fantastic things I witnessed Kris do over the past two years, somehow, I still had doubts. Ohio wasn't like New York, would they know his music? Could BDP rock as hard as Biz Markie did? What if there are technical difficulties? I was tripping out. Before I could have a full-blown anxiety attack, the music begins. A bass-heavy Reggae beat comes blasting through the two-story-high stack of speakers. KRS-One walks out on stage, and the crowd roared in approval. I started feeling a little bit better about the whole thing. To my surprise, as the show progressed, they knew every single song, even the album cuts! What the hell was I thinking? BDP crushed that arena like it was The Latin Quarter in New York City. The problem I was having was the Kris I knew, and the rapper KRS-One were two different people. I kept expecting to see my brother Kris walk out on stage, but KRS-One would show up in his place.

After the show, I congratulated Kris on an excellent performance. I never revealed my illogical doubts and insecurities. I stayed at the arena to watch the rest of the show. Everyone was on their A-game. I saw Kool Moe Dee perform 'Wild, Wild, West' and Doug E Fresh perform all of his hits and do "The Dougie" dance. Ha! One of the highlights of the night was seeing Rakim perform my favorite jam 'Microphone Fiend.' It was an unforgettable night for a Hip-Hop fan like myself to experience.

After the concert, I headed back to the hotel to wind down for the night. What I didn't know was, the real party started after the show was over. When I arrived at the hotel, there were hundreds of people roaming around. There were dozens of people in the hotel lobby; the majority of them were women. As soon as someone would walk into the hotel, you could hear them murmuring, "Who's that! Who's that!" If it were one of the rappers, you would hear gasping and yelling from the girls. It was a circus. The same guy from our crew who schooled me about Ice-T pulled me to the side and said, "Ok, here's what you do. Pick the girl you want and take her upstairs, don't hang in the lobby for too long." What? Pick the girl I want? It's that easy? He said, "Yeah, but there's one rule. If someone else scoops the girl you picked before you can get her to your room, you can't be mad. That's how it goes." He then stepped off to partake in the "festivities" and left me standing there bewildered.

It didn't take me long to figure out that what he said was true. Anyone and

I mean anyone, who was part of the tour, had access to various girls posted in the lobby. It didn't matter if you were a manager, dancer, security, or part of the entourage. If you were wearing a backstage pass, you were all set. As I was standing there with my mouth open, I started to hear rumblings, "That IS him. He looks just like him. That's his brother right there!" People started surrounding me, singing the line from 'My Philosophy,' "My brother's name is Kenny, That's Kenny Parker." I was more surprised to see them; than they were to see me. "You know who I am?" I asked. "Hell yeah! Can I have your autograph?" Huh? The next thing I knew, I was signing several autographs and answering a lot of KRS-One questions. I became a little overwhelmed by the entire situation. I needed to regroup. I decided to go straight to my room. I got on the elevator and rode up to my floor. When the elevator door opened, a gang of people made noise and ran through the hallways. I was familiar with traveling on the road during college basketball away games. After the game, you would go to your hotel room, and that was it. We had rules and a curfew. Now, I felt like I entered the movie 'Animal House.'

I went to my room and took a minute to let it all sink in. I made a decision right then and there that I wasn't going to try to be someone other than myself out there. I had a girlfriend back in the "real" world. The actual test of a man's faithfulness was for him to remain loyal in an environment like this. I only had two and a half weeks to stay focused. My only real purpose out there was to spend time with my brother and enjoy the music. That was the goal anyway. The following day, I took my first tour bus ride to the next city. When we arrived, I decided to ride with D-Nice over to the soundcheck. I wanted to see how everything worked. When we reached the arena, some of the other groups were already there. About twenty feet away from me was Ice-T and his crew. He walked right over to me and said, 'What's up! You're Kris' brother, right? I'm Ice-T." He was so cool. He introduced me to his entire crew. As friendly as he appeared to be, I knew this was the same guy who had a "whole arsenal in his trunk" out in Los Angeles.

Moments later, Darlene walked past, smiled, and said hello. She was pleasant, as well. Still, I was a little apprehensive about replying to her after my warning from the previous day. She was standing there, talking to another beautiful girl. Let's call her Diana. As we sat there watching the soundcheck, Diana and I struck up a friendly conversation. She possessed one of those infectious personalities. After she left, the same BDP member who filled me in on all the gossip told me that Diana was dating one of the artists on the tour. She had been traveling with him for a while. Ok, fine, I didn't think anything of it.

Before showtime arrived, I stopped by Kris' hotel suite to chat for a bit. He gave me some authentic Boogie Down Productions tour t-shirts to wear. As I was about to leave, he said, "Wait"...He then took off the custom-made leather BDP hat he was wearing and placed it on my head..."Now you are official," he said. This was the same hat he wore on the cover of the 'By All Means Necessary' album. It didn't get more official than that. Wearing that hat raised my profile. There was no doubt in anyone's mind that I was part of the group, even though I wasn't. After that, I couldn't go out into the crowd to watch the concert anymore. People were all over me. I feared someone might try to snatch my hat. I hated watching the show from backstage. I couldn't get the real impact of the concert from behind all the action.

After watching one show backstage, I had enough. There was a concert in Indiana the following night. I discovered a separate, roped-off V.I.P. section in the middle of the arena, near the soundboard, so I decided to watch the concert from there. When I arrived in the V.I.P. section, I noticed that they were selling merchandise and taking pictures nearby. Someone stopped me while I was walking and asked if I would take a polaroid picture with them over by the photo area. I agreed. When we posed for the picture, the photographer looked surprised and charged the person $10. They paid the money, and he took the photo. Suddenly, another person stepped up and wanted a picture too. Sure, I took another picture. The next thing I knew, there was a line about thirty feet long! People were coming from everywhere. I thought to myself, "There must be some mistake. These people think I'm KRS-One. I have to put a stop to this before it's too late."

I turned to the next waiting patron and said, "Do you know who I am? I'm not KRS-One." He smiled and said, "Yeah! You're Kenny Parker. My brother's name is Kenny, that's Kenny Parker." I couldn't believe it. How could people in Indiana know me like this from one line in a song? Regardless, the photographer began rushing people along like an assembly line. He was trying to photograph every single person before the show started. I took pictures for about fifteen minutes and then the concert began. The photographer asked me if I would come back after the show to take more photos. I told him, "No!" He made enough money off of me for one day.

After a few tour dates, we arrived in Atlanta, Georgia. Red Alert told me he was staying with family in Atlanta, so I had the entire room to myself for the night. Nice! After the concert, I headed to my room, and who do I see in the hallway? Diana. She and I had become friends over the week. We often spoke, both during soundcheck and backstage at the concerts. I said hello to her, but this time something was wrong, she was crying. I asked her what was wrong. Diana told me that this "guy" she was traveling with kicked her out of the room, a thousand miles from home with no money and nowhere to sleep. She didn't know that I already knew who she was dating on tour. Being the gentleman I am, I told her I had an extra bed because Red Alert stayed with relatives. Her face lit up! She hugged me, said thank you, and left to retrieve her bags. She returned to my room shortly after that.

Now I know what you're thinking. Here we have a beautiful woman, alone in my room, in a vulnerable position. I would have been a fool not to take full advantage of the situation, right? Most men would have, but I chose to stand on my moral ground. I wasn't going to disrespect my relationship with my girlfriend. Even if I were single, Diana was still a friend in need. Right then would've been the sleaziest of times to proposition her. It cost me nothing to let her sleep in the vacant bed. Diana looked exhausted and went straight to sleep. The next morning, she thanked me once again and left. I don't know how it happened, but somehow Kris found out Diana stayed in my room overnight.

Immediately upon entering the tour bus, Kris and his wife Melodie summoned me to the bus's private back room. Kris instructed me to sit down. He said, "I heard Diana was in your room last night." I told him, "Yeah, but I was only helping her out." Kris then said, "Let me tell you a story." Kris explained how a couple of years earlier, he was hanging out in a club. He saw Diana enter the bathroom with a famous rapper (whose name you would know). When they exited the bathroom, the rapper blurted out in front of everybody, "Guess what, that girl right there sucked my dick!" Kris explained to me that this was the type of girl I had in my room. He warned me to be careful; he didn't want me to fall in love with her. At first, I felt annoyed. What kind of guy did he think I was? I told him I didn't love her; he knows I have a girlfriend; I was only trying to do something nice for somebody. Kris looked at me with one eyebrow raised and said, "Ok, I'm just warning you." After I thought about it for a second, I realized Kris didn't mean any harm. He was only trying to look out for his little brother, a naive one at that. The whole situation could have gone in the wrong direction. What if her "man" had gotten the impression that I was interfering in his personal life? It could have created a potential conflict between BDP and another group on tour.

Who needed that drama? I thanked Kris for looking out for me and assured him it wouldn't happen again. As I should have expected, Diana and her "man" got back together the following night. Lesson learned.

During one of the concert dates, The Dope Jam Tour had a surprise visitor. It was none other than the legendary DJ Jam Master Jay of Run-DMC fame. Despite the influx of new talent and Hip-Hop's elevated status thanks to 'Yo! MTV Raps', Run-DMC were still the biggest name in the game. They had recently released their platinum-selling 'Tougher Than Leather' album. Jam Master Jay was the most famous DJ in the world, and there he was backstage, standing three feet away from me. After the show, somebody mentioned that there was a basketball court not far from the hotel. After some friendly trash-talking, We all decided to play some ball. The opposing teams were Kool Moe Dee's crew versus the BDP crew. Jam Master Jay wanted to play with Kool Moe Dee's team, but he didn't have any basketball shorts. I stepped up and told him I had an extra pair of shorts back in my hotel room. JMJ said, "Dope! Let's go to your room and get them."

We jumped on the elevator and began riding up to my room. The whole situation was surreal. There I was, alone on an elevator with THE Jam Master Jay riding up to my room to retrieve some basketball shorts. How could this be? Run-DMC weren't real human beings in my mind. They were like The Beatles to me. Even though KRS-One had taken lyrical jabs at Run-DMC on his albums, JMJ was still super cool. We arrived at my room, and I dug out an extra pair of Saint Peter's College basketball shorts I had in my bag. As JMJ begins changing his clothes into basketball gear, he said, "Hold this for a second" and hands me this big fat gold Run-DMC rope chain he was wearing. It featured an impressive solid gold, miniature shell toe Adidas sneaker hanging from the chain. It was the very same gold chain Run-DMC wore in their latest video 'Run's House.' The Hip-Hop fan in me was going crazy! I was holding the rope chain and staring at it in amazement. Jay changed his clothes, and we went back downstairs to head to the park. The BDP team featured me, Kris, Red Alert, McBoo, and Manager Mo. Kool Moe Dee's team had JMJ, DJ Easy Lee, LA sunshine, and some of the crew's dancers.

We played ball for over an hour that night. During the game, the ball got loose and rolled near some water. D-Nice, who wasn't playing but came along to hang out, was standing nearest to the puddle. Somebody from our crew yelled, "Yo, Dee, get the ball!" D-nice was reluctant. He replied, "Nah, I don't want to get my sneakers dirty." Jam Master Jay said, "Don't worry, I can get you a brand new pair of Adidas on a trade-in." D-Nice then replied in a condescending tone, "That's alright, I don't wear Adidas!" Everyone's eyebrows raised a little. It was a blatant diss to Run-DMC. A calm Jam Master Jay looked over at D-Nice and said, "You would for a million dollars." Ooooh Shit! Nobody said a word, but the silence was deafening. I glanced over at Kris, and he had a look on his face like, "Well, alrighty then." By this time, someone else retrieved the ball, and we resumed playing. Touché Jam Master Jay. (R.I.P.)

After two weeks of traveling to different cities and watching a legendary concert, I didn't want the tour to end. I was having the time of my life. I met and befriended most of the other artists and their entourages. Unfortunately, the Labor Day weekend meant there were only a couple of tour dates left, Philadelphia and New York. Philly has always been a particularly strong Hip-Hop town, so there was considerable anticipation for this show. To make things more exciting, the ultra-hot Public Enemy got added to the bill. Their album 'It Takes A Nation Of Millions To Hold Us Back' had exploded beyond the Hip-Hop audience. The record was on its way to double-platinum status (two million records sold). I would argue that Public Enemy created the album of the year in any musical genre.

I arrived at the soundcheck as per my usual routine and found a seat in the empty venue. The legendary Spectrum in Philadelphia was a storied basketball arena with the jerseys of NBA greats hanging from the rafters. As I sat there taking in the sights, I looked over my right shoulder, and standing only a few feet away from me was the leader of Public Enemy, Chuck D. Wow! The first thing that came to my mind was lyrics from his song 'Rebel Without A Pause.' To my surprise, he didn't possess the physical stature of someone with such a booming voice. He should've stood about seven feet tall based upon his vocal tone. Chuck must've sensed someone staring at him because he turned and looked right at me. Damn, I got busted! He smiled and uttered what turned out to be the summer's most familiar phrase, "You're Kris' brother, right? Kenny Parker!" Oooh shit! Well, yes, I am! Chuck D actually walked over to me and introduced himself. It was a classy move on his part. In my lifetime, I have encountered many artists with far fewer credentials than future Rock & Roll Hall Of Fame inductee Chuck D. Some of them made it difficult for me to extend my hand to them no less. Meeting him was one of the highlights of the tour.

CHAPTER 14
PEACHES & HERBS

As the summer of 1988 came to an end, so did The Dope Jam Tour. What an incredible summer vacation! I traveled to ten different cities, saw a spectacular concert, and met several Hip-Hop stars. Everyone treated me like a celebrity. I signed autographs, took pictures, and spent two and a half weeks hanging out with my brother. Red Alert gave me an open invitation to visit him at KISS-FM, Yes! When I said goodbye to Kris, he couldn't understand why I was leaving. He said, "Man, where are you going? You need to come rock with us; we're living the life out here." As accurate as that statement was, I explained to him that this was my final year of college, and I was on track to graduate with a degree. It would be foolish and irresponsible to drop out now. He agreed, and I headed back to school in time for the start of the fall semester. Unfortunately, Darrell informed me that he was transferring from St. Peter's College. The tuition was too expensive. I completely understood, but it still sucked. Damn.

1988-89 was my final year of college, so I decided to set two goals for myself.

First, to graduate from Saint Peter's College with a degree in Psychology. Second, to have the finest basketball season of my career. I worked out every day during September and October and came into practice in excellent shape. I had a strong pre-season and not only earned a starting position, but the team voted me co-captain. Everything started well, but soon, the all too familiar pattern returned. I once again lost my starting job after a couple of games. We then flew out to Montana for the 'Forest Industries Basketball Classic.' I performed so well that I made the 'all-tournament team' despite coming off the bench, a rarity in the sport of basketball. But, after a few games, I was right back in the "doghouse" not receiving any playing time at all. Still, I continued to persevere. I managed to play my way out of the doghouse and back into the starting line-up. Unfortunately, my rejuvenation would be short-lived as once again; I found myself receiving no playing time at all. This entire nightmare roller coaster ride took place before the season was even halfway over. After my latest benching, I finally had enough of the coach's politics and favoritism; I mentally checked out. I lost all my love for the sport of basketball, something I thought could never happen. From that point on, I counted down the days until the season was over.

Meanwhile, my popularity off the court continued to grow. People recognized me everywhere I went. It reached a point where players from the opposing teams approached me during warm-ups asking if I was THE Kenny Parker. I couldn't understand it. I was still having problems adjusting to the notoriety. Instead of enjoying the attention, it felt awkward to me. I hadn't done anything to deserve it. I have always believed that you earned respect based on your actions. Yet, I struggled to get playing time on the court, and guys were treating me like I scored 40 points. People who rarely spoke to me were now telling others we were good friends. I needed to find a way to cope with this new superficial environment. I decided my best course of action would be to remain myself. If other people chose to change their behavior towards me, that would be their prerogative. Their whole perception of me was an illusion. In reality, my life hadn't changed at all.

One weekend, I had some free time, so I decided to take Red Alert up on his offer to visit him at 98.7 KISS-FM. I didn't have Red's number, so I hopped on the train, rode over to the city, and went to KISS-FM's location. When I arrived, the receptionist asked me if I had an appointment to see

Red Alert. He was live on the air, and the station didn't allow unauthorized guests. I told her no and was about to leave, but the receptionist decided to call the DJ booth and inquire if Red would see me unannounced. I waited a short time, and during a commercial break, Red came out to the reception area and walked me into the station. That was very gracious of Red; he didn't have to do that for me. Red escorted me right into the broadcast booth with him. I was in heaven. I was standing there watching DJ Red Alert do his legendary mix-show in person! I would've been at home taping this very show. A couple of other guys were in the booth as well. One of them I recognized. It was Chris Lighty. The same guy who Red Alert tackled to prevent him from jumping out of the DJ booth window during the brawl at The Latin Quarter. This time, we were properly introduced. I struck up a friendship with the future Hip-Hop mogul that would last for many years. R.I.P. Chris Lighty.

During one of the commercial breaks, Red Alert got on the microphone and announced to the entire New York City Hip-Hop world that I was "in the house!" Unbelievable! By the time I returned to the dorms, everyone in the school knew I visited KISS-FM. They immediately bombarded me with "Damn, man! Why don't you ever bring us with you? We want to go too." Now I'm not an entourage type of guy, and I would never overextend my invitation. The only person I ever went to Hip-Hop related events with was Darrell. Still, I didn't want to be selfish, so I relented. On future visits to the radio station, I would bring various friends to meet the legendary Red Alert. On one occasion, I introduced a friend of mine to Red Alert. This guy asked Red, "How come when there's a commercial on KISS-FM, and I turn the dial to (rival) WBLS, they have commercials playing at the same time?" What a dumb, inappropriate question. Red Alert looked at him and didn't reply. I was so embarrassed. I should've trusted my gut and left that fool home.

A few months passed since The Dope Jam Tour, and besides visiting Red Alert, I hadn't gone to any Hip-Hop events. I was itching for some excitement. As luck would have it, I stumbled across a flyer promoting a nightclub in Newark, NJ, called 'Club Sensations.' 'Sensations' happened to be one of the most popular Hip-Hop clubs in the tri-state area. All the hottest acts that appeared at the now-defunct Latin Quarter would head across the Hudson River to perform at Sensations. Newark was only a fifteen-minute train ride from St. Peter's College. When the weekend arrived, I scraped my coins together and headed to a club by myself for the very first time.

I arrived at Sensations to find a long line outside, and several fancy cars cruised the block. It felt like NYC for a second. I waited in line for what seemed like forever. Finally, I reached the club's front entrance. The security guard looked at me, and to my surprise, said, "Kenny Parker, what's up? Come with me, and I'll introduce you to the manager." The security guard escorted me past the remaining patrons and right to the club manager who knew "who" I was. He said, "It's an honor to meet you, go right in. Who are you with?" Huh? Did he mean I could get in for free, and bring a guest too? Now that was something I could get used to in a hurry. Club Sensations was smaller than The LQ or Union Square, but the energy was electric. The song that brought the house down that night was 'The 900 Number' by The 45 King. As I strolled through the club checking out the scenery, I bumped into a familiar face...Biz Markie! I hadn't seen him since the tour ended. Our conversation picked up right where it left off during the summertime. He asked me where I lived, and I told him I was still attending St. Peter's College and living in the dormitory. He gave me his number and suggested we hang out. He even claimed that he would swing by the dorms and pick me up. Yeah right! This big Rap star would travel to my little college and pick me up? That sounded more absurd than his claim of performing seven songs in fifteen minutes.

Nevertheless, I had a great time at Club Sensations and became a frequent visitor. I also brought some of my college friends with me. I saw EPMD, The Ultramagnetic MC's, Special Ed, Kool G Rap, Redman, and other legendary artists perform there.

Thugs from Brooklyn would have the audacity to travel out to New Jersey with the same intentions of causing mayhem as they did in The Latin Quarter. This time, they would get a taste of their own medicine. Guys from Newark would outnumber guys from Brooklyn. They would chase Brooklyn back to the train station. Still, Brooklyn would return week after week, like some locust.

Throughout my life, I've spoken to many college graduates about our shared college experiences. There always seems to be one consistent theme; time flew by at warp speed. One moment you're a bumbling freshman trying to find your way around campus. The next moment you're a "too cool for school" senior not wanting the experience to end. My senior year was no different. One moment I was on a summer tour with BDP living like a rock star, and the next moment, it was December, and the semester was coming to an end. Where did the time go?

One lazy evening, I decided to stroll downstairs to another level of my dorm building to check out one of my friends. They happened to have recently installed a rare private phone line in their room. This friend allowed me to make one short phone call. Great! Who better to call than Kris. I hadn't spoken to him in a while. I dialed his number, and he answered right away. When he heard my voice, he sounded enthusiastic, "Yooo Kenny, what's up? I have someone here who wants to speak to you." Really? Kris' excited tone piqued my curiosity. There was a pause, and then I heard a woman's voice say, "Hello, Kenneth." I became confused because I didn't recognize her voice at all. I asked, "Who is this?" The lady responded with a deep southern drawl, "Well, who calls you Kenneth?" I still had no clue. "No one calls me Kenneth," I replied. She finally confessed, "It's your mother!" WHAT??

I was speechless for a few seconds. It had been four and a half years since I had that brief phone conversation with my mother at Dee's apartment. I didn't know what to say. I uttered the first thing that came to my mind, "Why does your voice sound so country now?" She explained that she had been living in the south for a while, so her accent changed. Kris jumped back on the phone and proclaimed his happiness, "Isn't this great! Our mother is back!" Well, that wasn't my sentiment at all.

As I regained my composure, my feelings of anger began to recur. Kris explained that she would be staying with him in Manhattan for a while. I didn't want to say too much more after that. I told Kris we needed to talk, he agreed, and we set up a day to meet. I hung up the phone and returned to my dorm room, stunned. I needed to figure out how I was going to deal with this unexpected development. I was 22 years old now, not some scared little teenager from 1983. Still, it would be a lot easier to deal with her if Kris wasn't involved. I decided to act like an adult and tell Kris the truth about how I felt.

On the day of our scheduled "sit down," I met Kris in Manhattan, ready to clear the air. First, I had to ask the obvious question, how did you find her? Kris told me that actually, he didn't find her, she found him. My mother was on her way to Georgia from Florida and decided to make a quick stop in New York City first (Huh?). Kris continued explaining that while in New York, she wanted to reconnect with her sons. It appeared that her old friend Dee (R.I.P.) had told her about Kris' success. So, my mother went to Tower Records Store and found the latest Boogie Down Productions album. On the back of the album was the name of Kris' record label. She then called Jive Records and told them she was KRS-One's mother. Jive directed her to Kris' lawyer, who, in turn, put her in touch with Kris. By that point, I had heard enough. I told Kris that although I thought it was great to see him so ecstatic, I didn't share his happiness. His relationship with our mother was very different than mine. Kris told me he already knew how I felt. He told her that if she wanted to be back in the picture, she would have to deal with me because I was going to be around as well. Um, that's not exactly what I had in mind.

I told Kris that I didn't want to be the one to spoil his reunion. I suggested that he continue to establish his newfound relationship with his mother, and I'll stay out of the way. He and I could have a relationship apart from her. Kris didn't care for my suggestion. He then revealed to me that they were in discussions for her to become his business manager. What? I asked him if he trusted her to deal with his finances. Kris said yes. We didn't see eye to eye at all. I decided to raise the stakes.

I told Kris that not only didn't I trust her, but I felt like her story was inconsistent. Frankly, I thought it was bullshit. First, no one on earth would travel from Florida, headed to Georgia, and decide to make a quick detour over a thousand miles to visit New York City. Second, if she were looking for her "sons" like she claimed, it would've been easy to find me. I was still close friends with Darrell. He lived in the same house, with the same phone number. Had she called him, she would have found out right away where I was and received Kris's number. Instead, she chose to go through that whole album credits adventure. To me, she was never looking for her "sons" at all; she was looking for KRS-One.

After explaining to Kris what I considered the obvious truth, he looked me right in my eyes and said, "I don't care. It doesn't matter to me why she's here. I'm tired of our family being all over the place." Once he said that I knew this was something important to him. Damn, what was I going to do? This situation had me torn between my love for my brother and my complete disdain for this con artist. I decided to compromise. I would be cordial with my mother for Kris' sake, but I wouldn't drop my guard. I didn't trust her, and I knew she would show her true colors sooner or later.

Winter break arrived, one of the most cherished times of the school year rivaled only by spring break. I couldn't travel on vacation because of basketball obligations. So, I finally decided to call the number Biz Markie had given me at Club Sensations. He answered right away, "Who's this?" I told him it was Kenny Parker. He said, "Yo, where are you?" I told him I was in the dorms at St. Peter's College. He said, "I know where that is, I'm on my way." What? There was no way on earth Biz Markie would come to my little school to scoop me up. I was wrong. Not only did Biz come to my dorm building, but he showed up in a brand new BMW, blasting music. His arrival prompted a few students to look out the window to see who was causing all the commotion. When they saw it was Biz Markie, it created quite a stir. Biz parked his car, entered the dorm building, walked up to the third floor, and into my apartment. One of the guys on the basketball team came down the hall and knocked on my door. He wanted to get a better look at "The Inhuman Orchestra."

Biz suggested I come club-hopping with him that night. Sure! I had no problem riding shotgun in a brand new BMW. Biz went downstairs a little ahead of me while I gathered my coat. My teammate confided in me that Biz Markie was his favorite rapper. Ok cool. He then proclaimed, "Man, I love Biz so much I would suck his dick!" What the Hell??? I burst out laughing! Is he for real? I looked right into his starry-eyed face, and he was dead serious. Keep in mind; this guy was 6'4" and a known heterosexual (allegedly). But, he was so starstruck that he lost all sense of his sexuality. Even if he was trying to use an analogy to express his admiration for Biz, he knows damn well straight guys don't play like that! Regardless, I didn't have time to figure out why my teammate would say such an outrageous thing. I had a fantastic night ahead of me. Biz and I went to several clubs that night and had a blast. This would become the first of many nights hanging out with The Biz. Our adventures would need a separate chapter.

Biz Markie wasn't the only rapper to visit our small Jesuit college. One day, I bumped into one of my brother's friends on campus. She was a young female rapper from New Jersey who I recently met at a party. She had dropped her debut single, 'Wrath Of My Madness.' It was none other than

Queen Latifah. We were both surprised to see each other. I found out we had mutual friends who attended St. Peter's College. Latifah had an infectious personality and a great smile. We chatted for a bit, and I told her I was a senior on the basketball team. She mentioned that she also played basketball and then asked, "Do you start on this team?" With shame, I told her no. She looked confused and asked, "You're a senior, and you don't even start?" What could I say? That was my sad reality. She shook her head, and we moved on to another topic. I would see Latifah a few times in the area over the next few months, and we developed a friendship. All Hail The Queen!

The day finally arrived for my "reconnection" with my mother. I was calm, traveling to Kris' house. I had no real expectations, so I chose to play it by ear. Surprisingly, the whole ordeal turned out to be anticlimactic. We exchanged pleasantries and engaged in some small talk. We never addressed any of the real issues between us. It seemed like we were both trying to be on our best behavior, knowing that any deep, meaningful conversation might lead to an argument. Kris seemed pleased that we were "getting along," which was the ultimate goal, I guess. I went home afterward thinking about all the things I should have said to her but didn't. Was this going to be the extent of our new relationship? Will we pretend the past twenty-two years never existed and act like we met each other as adults? How long could that charade last? How long could I pretend to be indifferent? How long could she?

The year 1988 ended on a high note for KRS-One and Boogie Down Productions. The rising comedian, writer, and producer Keenen Ivory Wayans commissioned the group to create a theme song for his new comedy film entitled 'I'm Gonna Get You Sucka.' Contributing to a movie score was another rarity for a Hip-Hop act in 1988. The name of the song was 'Jack Of Spades', and The BDP Crew even got to appear in the movie. Kris invited me to attend the movie premiere in Manhattan, red carpet and all. Nice! The plan was to meet at Kris' apartment on 34th street, and then we would all ride over to the theater together.

I arrived early, and only Melodie and my mother were there. When I saw my mother, I gave her a cordial greeting, but this time I could tell something was different. She looked at me and rolled her eyes without saying anything. Her attitude was much different than the last time I saw her, which confused me. Based on our previous meeting, I thought we were at least going to be civil towards one another. Did Kris say something to her? I doubted that. I tried to hide my confusion by moving on and talking to Melodie for a while. Afterward, we all rode over to the movie premiere in separate limousines and found our theater seats.

After the movie ended, I ran into my mother again in the lobby. This time she looked at me with more disdain and walked away. What? Oh ok, that was all the confirmation I needed that somehow a "beef" had arisen between us. It appeared to me like she was acting one way when Kris was around and another way when we were by ourselves. Regardless, it didn't matter how it started; I was going to finish it. I didn't mention our confrontation at all with Kris. I wasn't going to let him talk me out of my feelings this time. All I knew was the next time I saw her; I would unleash a fury that she had never seen from me before. I directed some of my anger towards myself. I had chosen to swallow my pride, allowing myself to be in a position to have to deal with her crazy behavior once more. I vowed it would never happen again.

Right around the new year of 1989, I reached out to Kris and found him in a somber mood. It was rare to hear Kris sound less than optimistic about most situations, so his tone had me concerned. I asked him what was going on, and he revealed to me that our mother had abruptly left. "What do you mean she left?" I asked. Kris explained that she approached him complaining about how she no longer wanted to stay at his apartment. My mother wanted Kris to buy her a brand new house in New Jersey. A house? What? Kris then told me that he agreed to buy her the house, but she would have to wait two weeks. He was expecting a sizable check, and he would purchase the home at that time. My mouth was hanging wide open as Kris continued this plot-twisting story. I couldn't believe he was going to do it. "Well, what did she say?" I demanded. Kris said she gave him an ultimatum: "If you don't buy me a house right now, I'm leaving New York and going back to Florida!" The audacity of this woman.

Kris pleaded with her to wait out the two weeks. He tried to explain to her that he had money tied up in other ventures at the moment. He couldn't pull it out to buy her a house. Ultimately, the same person who Kris wanted to hire to run his business affairs, didn't care much about his finances at all. Since he could not buy the house for her at that exact moment, she indeed packed up and left New York.

My first reaction upon hearing the news of her latest exploit was, "I knew it! I told you so." However, after hearing the disappointment in Kris' voice, I felt more empathy for him than I did vindication for myself. Kris attempted to welcome her into his world with open arms and reunite our family for the first time in seven years. Instead, what he received was a continuation of the same family dysfunction that separated us back in 1982. Kris tried to assume his rightful position as the family patriarch but, everybody wasn't on board. There was plenty of blame to go around. I reluctantly agreed to embrace his plans for our family reunion despite the wrongs perpetrated against me in the past. My undercover pessimism would have created problems sooner or later.

As for Kris, despite having the best intentions, he was so blinded by his desire to create a cohesive family unit that he either couldn't or wouldn't accept reality. Unfortunately for him, the truth is always present, whether you like it or not.

My mother's motives are a little harder to understand. Based on her actions, it would be reasonable to assume that she had no intention of being part of any family structure. My only question was if her return was only a money grab, why wouldn't she "play the game" a little longer? Was the strain of trying to act friendly too much for her? All she needed to do was smile for two more weeks, and she could've had a brand new house. Who knows what else would've been in store had she grinned for a few more months after that. Maybe, the thought of having to be part of a real family structure wasn't worth the potential windfall awaiting her on the back end. Perhaps she didn't like Kris' wife or mother-in-law or cat, who knows? I know one thing for sure, she had a hard time stomaching me, and I only saw her twice. Our rocky relationship was bound to fall apart. I had planned on giving her a piece of my mind the next time I saw her.

After my mother left, Kris moved on from the whole saga, which was good. I don't know if there were any lessons to be learned from this ordeal. Somehow, things seemed to have worked themselves out this time, bullet dodged.

After the whole "Mother" episode, I settled back into my routine. I was finishing up my academics and winding down my horrible basketball career. By this point, all my excitement resided off-campus. Ever since Darrell's departure, I tried to invite a friend or two with me whenever possible. I wanted other people to share in this once-in-a-lifetime experience I was having. Because I was new and somewhat naive to my newfound fame, I never anticipated the arrival of the ugliest of the Seven Deadly Sins, Jealousy. The jealousy wasn't directed towards me but at each other. My friends dared to bicker amongst themselves about who I should invite to hang out with me. Things became so petty that some guys stopped speaking to each other. Dudes were whispering in my ear how I should hang out with them instead of another close friend. In no time, the anger became directed towards me.

For example, KRS-One created a new organization named after one of his songs called "The Stop The Violence Movement." The idea originated after a concertgoer got killed during the very last show of The Dope Jam Tour. Kris decided to organize some of the Rap world's biggest names to record a benefit song called 'Self Destruction.' This project would be the first of its kind in Hip-Hop. Considering KRS-One's respect amongst his peers and his "Conscious Style" of music, he was one of the few artists who could pull it off. Produced by BDP member D-Nice, 'Self Destruction' was a huge success. The all-star collaboration spent ten weeks at number one on the Billboard Rap Singles Chart and earned a gold certification. Kris recorded 'Self Destruction' over several days with different artists recording each day.

I called Kris at Power Play Studio during the recording process and asked him who was recording on that particular day. He told me Heavy D (R.I.P.) and MC Lyte. I told him I was stopping by. I hunted down my homie, who mentioned that Heavy D was his favorite rapper, and invited him to come with me to the studio. He got to meet his favorite rapper and get an autograph too. About a week later, I chose to invite someone else instead of him to another event. That ungrateful bastard became so angry that he stopped speaking to me. Unbelievable!

Another time, I brought a good friend with me to Power Play Studio to meet Kris. This guy had the nerve to follow Kris into the bathroom and ask Kris to let him come on tour with BDP. When Kris replied that if he were going to bring anyone extra, it would be his brother, this so-called "friend" responded with, "Don't bring Kenny, bring me! I'll work harder than he would." What a cutthroat move. I used to bring this guy with me everywhere. Of course, Kris told me what he said, and I cut him off completely. After that, I needed to reevaluate my friends.

My final basketball season had dwindled to a few precious weeks remaining. One day I found myself at practice, running drills and dripping with sweat like I'd done hundreds of times before. This time, a rare visit from the head athletic director, Mr. Stein, halted the practice. In front of the entire team and coaching staff, he announced that "Kenny has to come to the office. 'People Magazine' is on the phone, and they want to speak to him." Huh? We were all puzzled. Why would the prestigious People Magazine wish to talk with me? Our head coach made a sarcastic joke, "Well, Kenny, don't just stand there. You can't keep People Magazine waiting." Everyone laughed as I headed toward the athletic office. I realized by this point that it must have had something to do with Kris.

By the time I arrived at the office, the journalist had been on hold for at least ten minutes. A guy with a pleasant voice greeted me as I answered the phone, "Hello, is this Kenny Parker?" "Yes, it is," I replied. The journalist explained that he was writing a piece for the following week's issue of People Magazine. The article detailed KRS-One's rise from homeless teen to Hip-Hop superstar. Kris had already completed the interview, but the journalist needed my confirmation on specific aspects of the story. Kris told him what college I attended, and he tracked me down at practice. The phone call was brief. My answers to the journalist's questions were consistent with what Kris had told him. Afterward, the practice was over, and I hit the showers.

The following week, the February 27th issue of People Magazine hit the newsstands. It was a fantastic moment for Kris and a milestone for Hip-Hop in general. Few Rap artists had the opportunity to grace the pages of such a reputable mainstream publication in 1989. KRS-One's journey to success was so unique and inspirational that it transcended music. The article was very uplifting and tastefully done. I read it and thought, "Man, they don't even know the half of it." Within days of the issue's release, my mother got wind of it and went ballistic! She called Kris furious over the way they portrayed her in the article. She threatened to sue the magazine for slander and demanded they took it off of the shelves. If anything, she should've felt embarrassed. Everything in the article was accurate, even understated. Only three people could have confirmed the accuracy of the story. Two of them were unanimous that the piece was factual. I'm no lawyer, but what legal ground did my mother have? Unfortunately, sometimes your dirty laundry gets aired in public without your consent. Deal with it.

At long last, "Senior Day" finally arrived in my basketball career. That is the term given to celebrate the final time the seniors would ever play on their home court in front of family and friends. It was the unofficial countdown that your basketball career was coming to an end. Every college in America has a ceremony before the game to honor the seniors on the team. The school invites family members to attend the ceremony; it is an emotional event. Three seniors were graduating that year. Unlike the other two, I had no family to invite to the presentation except for my brother. I was thinking about asking Kris, but I was too embarrassed knowing that I wouldn't receive much playing time. I didn't want the first basketball game Kris ever attended of mine to be disappointing, so I chose to go it alone. I walked out to half court during my part of the ceremony and smiled for a picture, unaccompanied by anyone. Was I the only college basketball player in NCAA history to walk out to half-court on 'Senior Day' by themselves?

As part of the Senior Day celebration, it is customary for the head coach to insert all the seniors into the starting line-up. It's a show of appreciation, even if they only play for five minutes. However, my relationship with the head coach was so strained that I didn't receive one second of playing time on Senior Day, and I was the team captain. Our feelings towards each other were mutual. I didn't give a damn what he did; I wanted it to be over.

During the second half of the game, some of my college friends in attendance became frustrated by my lack of playing time on Senior Day. To my surprise, they began chanting, "We Want KP! We Want KP!" Other fans in the crowd picked up on the cheer, and it started to grow louder "We Want KP! We Want KP!" My teammate Matt, who was sitting to my left, said, "Do you hear that?" Of course, I did. At first, I felt embarrassed, but then it became comical. I looked over at one of the assistant coaches who also heard the chanting because he had a funny smirk. I found it so amusing that I put a towel over my mouth so no one could see me laughing! Even still, with the crowd chanting "We Want KP" on Senior Day, my coach refused to budge. He was not putting me in that game, no matter what.

A week later, at The Brendan Byrne Arena in New Jersey, we lost the MAAC Conference Championship to 14th ranked Lasalle University. Their leading scorer was All-American forward Lionel Simmons. I happened to run into Lionel at an NBA party a few years later. By this time, he had won both The John Wooden Award and The Naismith Award as the 1990 NCAA college basketball player of the year. Lionel was an NBA draft lottery pick and runner-up to Derrick Coleman for the 1991 NBA Rookie Of The Year Award. When I saw him, we struck up a conversation, and he gave me some fascinating insight. Lionel said, "You know, we could never understand what was going on with you at Saint Peter's. In our scouting report, the coach told us to 'watch out for Kenny Parker if he gets in the game. We don't know why he's in the dog house, but he's killed us in the past.'" For a player of his caliber to know my name and associate it with a player who at least required attention, it was a compliment. It was also a bittersweet revelation coming from someone on the outside looking in. It made me think about what might have been under different circumstances. You can't change the past, though. All you can do is learn from it and move on.

"Time flies when you're having fun."

On March 15th, 1989, I played the last game of my college basketball career. St. Peter's College lost to Villanova University in the N.I.T. tournament. Over my four years of college, I have seen many guys play in their last collegiate game. With about a minute left on the clock, some would begin to cry. It's like the entire four years of college would flash right before their eyes. About 99% of all college basketball seniors will not make it to the NBA. Some may continue their playing careers overseas, but for the most part, this was it; the end of the line. All the admiration you received over the past four years as a college athlete was over. Your head coach usually substitutes you out of the game. You accept that final standing ovation in appreciation for all the years of service you've provided to the school and community. As the sounds of your adoring supporters in the crowd begin to fade, you can hear the sounds of the real world, and its lofty expectations start to grow. I've seen 6'8", 6'9" guys crying like babies at the end.

My experience was a little different. After the game, teammates, journalists, and the assistant coaches came over and hugged me. Some of them were teary-eyed as they bid me farewell saying, "We're gonna miss you, KP." After all, that's what the whole collegiate experience is all about, right? Education and cherished friendships that you'll never forget. As much as I was going to miss my guys, I was glad this chapter of my life was over.

If I could do it all over again, I would have chosen a different school to play ball, but I still feel there was a reason my journey brought me there. Everything about Saint Peter's College was the right decision for me except for my relationship with the head coach. During my freshman year, the other head coach was also verbally abusive, but at least he didn't have one set of rules for one guy and another set of rules for another guy. That's all you can ask.

Off of the court, I did a lot of growing up. I entered college as a naive, eighteen-year-old teenager, straight from Brooklyn. Now I was leaving as a twenty-two-year-old young adult preparing to face the world and all its challenges.

Now that my college basketball career was over, Graduation was only weeks away. During one of my random conversations with Kris, he asked me if there were any concerts thrown at my school. In my four-plus years at Saint Peter's, I didn't recall any recording artist ever performing at our school. Kris suggested we throw a rap concert at the college. Great idea! We approached the athletic director, Mr. Stein, about doing a show in the gymnasium. After some negotiations, he agreed. We signed a contract and set the date. Kris hired private security, off-duty police officers, and brought in a professional stage complete with an extensive sound system and lighting. I made colorful flyers and plastered them all over Jersey City. Red Alert allowed me to announce the concert on 98.7 KISS-FM. The admission fee was $15. This show was going to be epic. Not only was Boogie Down Productions scheduled to perform, but we added our boy Biz Markie to the bill. There had never been anything like this in Jersey City before.

On the day of the concert, a large and raucous crowd filled the gymnasium. All my hard work paid off. My first venture into concert promoting was a success. I came out onto the stage and introduced the show to a cheer from the crowd. I was in all my glory. After the show, Kris gave me a portion of the proceeds and went on his way. It was an excellent final send-off for me, almost like a going-away party. Saint Peter's College never had a student generate as much excitement as I had before. I can say I left a small mark on that school before I left.

The arrival of May signaled the end of my final semester of college. With my classes completed, I had more time to hang out with Kris and experience the Hip-Hop lifestyle vicariously through him. He was busy recording the third Boogie Down Productions album called 'Ghetto Music, The Blueprint Of Hip-Hop.' One weekend, the entire BDP Crew was heading to Washington, DC, for a massive arena concert featuring several popular Rap groups. Kris invited me to travel with the group. Nice! This trip would be my first time traveling to a show in several months.

By the time we arrived in the nation's capital, the general public was already entering the arena. Since several groups were on the bill, the promoters set-up a makeshift holding area for the artists outside of the building. We had to travel up a long truck ramp and walk over to some tents about 50 feet away. Hundreds of fans had already begun to gather, held back by security. They were trying to get a glimpse of a rapper or an autograph. When we reached within the crowd's range, they began to cheer and yell, "Yooo KRS, What's Up!" All of a sudden, a powerful voice cut right through the commotion, "Make room! Let her through! It's KRS-One's sister!" WHAT? Kris and I both stopped in our tracks, looked at each other, and then turned in the voice's direction. My first reaction was, "Now, that was a good one. People will try anything." When we turned around, I saw a security guard escorting a tall, young, light-skinned teenage girl over to our location. Accompanying her was an older woman who yelled, "Look, Larry! It's your sister, Chanele!" Oh shit! It WAS her! There was no doubt about it either because she looked like my mother.

It felt like time was standing still. I could no longer hear the hundreds of people still yelling and shouting in our direction. Everything was silent now. Kris was a little more composed than I was; he walked over and hugged Chanele. We hustled her over to our dressing room so we could talk away from the noisy crowd. Chanele had a shy demeanor, almost like she was afraid. That would be understandable considering the environment. The lady who accompanied her did most of the talking. There was an endless amount of questions that needed answering and limited time because Kris still had a show to do. We hadn't seen or heard a peep from Chanele since her kidnapping in 1980; it was now 1989. Chanele was five years old the last time we saw her. Now she was a fourteen-year-old teenager. I thought I would never hear from her again.

It turns out when her father Joe abducted her; they didn't move that far away, only about two miles or so. In 1980, in a city as densely populated as Brooklyn, two miles might as well have been twenty miles. Our sister grew up with Joe and his girlfriend Jane, with whom he had two more children. Joe was a chronic marijuana smoker during the 70s. It was only a matter of time before he graduated to the devastating new, cocaine-based drug that was now sweeping the nation, Crack. Because of her parent's addiction, Chanele's life deteriorated to the point where she found herself having to take care of her younger siblings despite only being a child herself. The unimaginable daily horrors she experienced at her parents' hands reached a point where The Bureau Of Child Welfare had to remove her from that environment for her safety. Chanele was living in Maryland, under the custody of her aunt (Joe's sister), who brought her to the concert.

Chanel's story was heartbreaking. I always knew something like this would happen when I was thirteen years old and tried to question my mother's decision to let her live with her father. Chanele had been stuck between a rock and a hard place because our upbringing was no picnic either. Anyway, the story gets crazier.

A few months before the concert, Chanele, a thirteen-year-old Hip-Hop fan, watched television. She saw the Boogie Down Productions video 'My Philosophy.' She sat there confused, saying to herself, "I know this guy from somewhere." A short while later, she saw rapper KRS-One on the popular television show 'Video Music Box,' and it finally came to her, "That looks like my brother!" Her grandmother happened to have an old photo of Kris holding Chanele as a baby. After studying the picture, she became convinced that KRS-One was her brother. How could she come to that conclusion from watching a video? The last time she saw him, she was only five years old. Kris was only fourteen at the time and looked different than he did at twenty-three. In 1980, his name wasn't KRS-One or even Kris, for that matter.

Chanele explained that during those years apart, she never forgot about her brothers. She recalled places and events that I had forgotten about, like her favorite nickname for me, "Yuckie Kenny." Still, her bond with Kris was different. My mother left us alone countless evenings while she either worked late or attended night school. Kris was her primary caregiver in those early years. He sort of raised her. Imagine the childhood trauma Chanele must have experienced at that age. Not only was she separated from her close siblings but her mother as well. She didn't know if she would ever see her family again. Even still, her memory was astounding.

After seeing Kris on television, Chanele began telling anyone who would listen that KRS-One was her brother, to no avail. Finally, she bought a Rap magazine featuring KRS-One and took it to the one person who might know for sure, Joe. He looked at the picture and said, "Yeah, that looks like him." After doing some research, she discovered Kris' last name was Parker. That was all the confirmation she needed.

When the radio announced that BDP would appear in Washington, DC, Chanele persuaded her aunt to drive her to the concert. She became determined to make contact with her brother. What a story! Add in the fact that I happened to have attended that particular concert. Even the best Las Vegas oddsmaker would have trouble not concluding that we were all somehow destined to reunite on that day. After the show, which became secondary, Kris invited Chanele to spend a couple of weeks with him in New York City. Awesome! Kris also had contact information for our mother, so there was that too. It looked like Chanele's life was finally about to change for the better. Good for her, she deserved it.

A few weeks after "the great sibling reunion," I made a trip to Baltimore to visit Pam. I made a promise to Chanele that when I was in Maryland, I would call her. True to my word, I gave her a ring. As it turned out, Chanele didn't live too far from Pam, about twenty minutes away. Pam suggested we take her out to dinner. Great idea! Chanele agreed, so we drove to her house and picked her up. As we headed back to Baltimore for dinner, Chanele asked if we could make a quick detour. What kind of detour would a 14-year-old girl want to make at 6:30 pm? Chanele then hit me with a bombshell. Her father was staying in a halfway house for recovering addicts right there in Baltimore. What? I didn't know how to respond to her request.

Chanele began pleading with me about how she hadn't seen her father since The BCW removed her from their home several months earlier. She claimed to still love him despite everything she had gone through. Damn! What was I going to do? She put me in a tough spot. Chanele had no idea how much I despised her father. She was only three years old when he moved out.

My first inclination was to tell her no, which I did. She looked so heartbroken that I relented and agreed to take her but on the condition that I would wait in the car. For some reason, it never occurred to me why her own family, who also lived only twenty minutes away from Baltimore, didn't take her to visit her father either?

When we arrived at the rehab facility, it was already nightfall. We parked the car, and Chanele immediately hit me with, "Can you come with me to the front door while I ring the bell?" Ah man, why was I allowing a teenager to manipulate me? My sympathy for the suffering Chanele endured, along with my eagerness to reconnect with her, caused me to disregard my better judgment. I agreed to something that would've been inconceivable an hour ago. I had no choice. When I picked her up, I became her legal guardian. I'm the one who agreed to bring her to this potentially dangerous situation in the first place.

I escorted Chanele to the front door of this residential building, turned halfway house, and rang the bell. A guy, presumably the supervisor in charge, opened the door. Chanele announced herself and asked for Joe. They yelled upstairs, and within thirty seconds, Joe descended the stairs. I stood in the corridor, halfway between the doorway and the hallway. I watched as the monster of my childhood approached me. Chanele said, "Hey, Daddy! Look who I brought with me!" As Joe reached the ground level, I was now looking eye to eye with The Devil. He looked completely different. The last time I saw him was in 1978. I was a scared little eleven-year-old boy. Now, I was a 6'6", 210 pounds athletic twenty-two-year-old looking down at a frail, 5'8" crackhead.

Joe was only about forty years old, but the years of drug abuse made him look much older. Rage began to consume my entire being. The eleven-year-old child that still dwelled inside of me was thirsty for revenge. All I could think of was how I could crush this puny little child abuser with my bare hands. Let him see how it feels to be brutally beaten by someone who completely towers over him. As I stood there staring at him, contemplating committing a crime, his face lit up as he gushed in his Jamaican accent, "Hey everybody, look at my son!" What? I'm not your fucking son! He reached out to shake my hand, and out of the corner of my eye, I could see Chanele smiling in approval. Once again, like a complete sucker, I suppressed my own emotions for the sake of a sibling and greeted him with a handshake. It was more than I could take. Luckily, the supervisor in charge said, "Ok, that's it. It's past visiting hours." Chanele hugged her father, and we left.

As we rode back to her house, Chanele confessed to me that she had actually spoken to Joe earlier in the evening and told him I was coming to pick her up. She also mentioned to him that she would ask me to bring her by the facility. Joe was expecting to see me. I was not thrilled with how the night had transpired. I didn't blame Chanele because she thought I wouldn't have any reservations about seeing Joe again. Still, her ignorance of the past, mixed with my passiveness, left a bitter taste in my mouth. At fourteen, Chanele was old enough to know the truth.

Part of me felt like I needed to see Joe as an adult to truly understand his horrific actions. At his healthiest, Joe was still only a slim-built, 5'8" man. He posed a minimal physical threat to most adult men in New York City. Joe was no tough guy or Jamaican badman, but a coward, who could only impose his will on women and children. He had no reputation in the neighborhood. I never heard of him getting into an argument with another man, not even once. What I saw that day was a glimpse behind the curtain. The Wizard Of Oz was a fraud, a scoundrel who tricked my gullible mother into believing he was more than an ordinary bum. Unlike my mother, I saw right through his facade way back when I was eight years old. Although unexpected, I needed that night more than I ever realized. Closure can be a funny thing. Sometimes you don't know you need it until you receive it. Through the innocent, but no less persuasive "game" my little sister played on me, I received confirmation about something I had already known for a long time, but needed to see for myself. The Devil is a liar.

The arrival of May brought the climax to my entire college career, Graduation. I had completed my academic requirements. Considering this was the biggest day of my life, I decided to invite Kris to my Graduation. He agreed to attend. But, Kris already had a concert booked out of town and wasn't sure he would return in time. I completely understood. The mere fact that he agreed to attend was good enough for me. On the day of my Graduation, I rode with Pam to The Brendan Byrne Arena in New Jersey, the commencement ceremony site. I was sporting a blue cap and gown with white trim. I played basketball at that arena several times, but of course, this time was different.

As we walked to the students' holding area, I couldn't help but reflect on this most joyous occasion. The enormous odds I overcame to reach this milestone in my life were mind-boggling. I recalled my freshman year when Coach Dukiet (R.I.P.) sat down all six incoming freshmen and predicted that most of us wouldn't graduate from college. Sadly, his prophecy was true. Only two of the six freshmen who were present that day graduated with a degree from Saint Peter's College. As an academic institution, my coach shouldn't have been proud to have that graduation rate under his tenure. I was also on my way to becoming one of those collegiate sports casualties, if not for that life-changing pep talk courtesy of Pam.

I wished Coach Hartstein was there so I could have thanked him for setting me on the right path. He was right; education is the key. College isn't only about trying to achieve the highest GPA to secure a future job after Graduation. It's about creating the best possible environment for a young adult to grow as a person. It's for meeting like-minded people who come from different parts of the country or world. It's for learning how to handle deadlines, pressure, and showing yourself and the world that you can see a task through to its completion. Your particular major doesn't matter as much as the fact that you persevered. That's all a college degree is. One study found that more than 40% of college graduates take positions out of school that don't require a college degree at all. According to The Washington Post, only 27% of college graduates have a job related to their major. Attending college doesn't ensure success, and it sure isn't for everybody, but it was essential for me.

The boisterous cheers grew to a fevered pitch as the time arrived for the graduation commencement to begin. I laughed with my friends as we exited the tunnel and entered the vast arena area for the ceremony. You could see dozens of family members waving at their loved ones from the upper deck. I happened to look up into the cheering crowd, and I saw this tall figure wearing dark shades and a suit, smiling from ear to ear. Wait a minute! Could that be who I think it is? Yes! It was Kris in the audience! He began proudly waving at me like the other families were. I had no idea he was coming. What a surprise! It was so ironic because I had been in the audience cheering for the past three years as I watched Kris fulfill his dream. Now, he was there in the audience cheering as I fulfilled mine. The fact that Kris managed to return from the road and arrive early on a Sunday morning made it more special. I hadn't even told him the exact location of the ceremony. Kris literally came to my college dorm in the morning looking for me and rang one of my friend's doorbells, "Yo is Kenny here?" he asked. They said, "Nah, he went to the graduation." Kris asked, "Do you know where it is?" They said, "Yeah, it's at The Meadowlands." Kris arrived in time to see us exit the tunnel. It was perfect timing.

After the graduation ceremony, all the students and their families gathered in the arena's parking lot. Kris created quite a commotion when he entered the post-graduation area. He then offered to take me out for a celebration meal. Of course, I accepted. Kris said, "Well, our ride is over here" and pointed to a grey stretch limousine a few yards away. Wow! Nobody had a limo out there. The chauffeur opened the door, and we jumped into the limo in style. I stuck my head and body out of the sunroof like I was a superstar. We settled on a place to eat, Kris ordered a champagne bottle, and we spent the next few hours having a great time. He turned what would have been a great day into a spectacular one that I will remember for the rest of my life.

Kenny and Kris at Graduation

The good times continued to roll as Chanele traveled to New York City to spend two weeks with her big brother Kris and his wife. It was a joyous occasion. Kris lavished her with gifts. It was like he was trying to make up for all the time he had missed in just a few days. Melodie even took her to the hair and nail salon. It was a whole production. I dropped by the apartment a couple of times and had a chance to spend some more quality time with Chanele. Everyone seemed pleased with her visit, and there was talk of her returning to stay for an extended period. Here's the part of the story where they say, "And they lived happily ever after." But… (cue the other shoe drop).

A couple of weeks after Chanele returned to Maryland, I received a rare message from Kris through my same friend from the dorms who owned the private phone. Kris requested I call him ASAP! Instead, I traveled to Manhattan to see what was so urgent. When I arrived, Kris asked me to take a walk with him. Once outside, Kris said, "Yo! Guess what?" His rhetorical question came with a rare sound of anger and disappointment. What could have happened? Well, it appeared that Joe had the audacity to crawl out from under his crack rock and contact Kris with a threat. If Kris doesn't pay him a large sum of money, Joe was going to the newspaper with an accusation from Chanele claiming that both Kris and myself had molested her as a child. What?? I couldn't believe my ears. I was so shocked that I had to ask Kris if he was sure? He said, "Yes, and there's more…."

Not only did we molest our sister as a child, but Kris continued to sexually assault her when she stayed at his home a couple of weeks earlier. By this point, I was beside myself with anger. I couldn't believe this degenerate would use his daughter to extort money from her brother in some disgusting plot. I knew this man was the absolute scum of the earth, but I didn't see this one coming after all these years. Unfortunately, there was more.

Joe also threatened to reveal that Kris' wife, Ms. Melodie, tied Chanele to a chair and tortured her while Kris was in the studio. Now any sane person would say, "You can't make this up," but it appeared that wasn't the case. My vexation seemed dwarfed by Kris' anger as he told me the sordid details. These accusations seemed so outlandish that I had to question whether anyone would believe this trash? Sadly, the answer is, who knows? People can be fickle sometimes. They can build you up only to tear you down. Part of the allure of KRS-One was his integrity. He had risen to become not only a leader in the Hip-Hop world but in the African-American community as a whole. An accusation like this, true or false, would be devastating for any artist but most disastrous for KRS-One.

The next obvious question now after hearing of this felonious plot was, how are we going to handle this? Kris was already on top of it. He instructed his lawyer Jay to respond to Joe's sick scheme. Whatever Jay told this bastard was enough to ensure that Joe wouldn't dare try to execute his plan or contact Kris ever again. Once again, Joe folded like the punk he was and always will be. One phone call was all it took to defeat this clown. While that was fantastic news, there was still a tragic sidebar to this whole mess. With considerable aggravation in his voice, Kris declared, "I can never be put in a situation like this ever again. I have to distance myself from Joe's entire family, including Chanele." His decision seemed harsh, but who could blame him? Kris could have lost everything, including his freedom, over this concocted story. Big brother tried to bring little sister into his world, and unwittingly brought her morally deficient father along for the ride—what a shame. With Kris' money and resources, he could've given Chanele the best education and opportunities available. She would have had a legitimate chance to recover from her parents' poor decision-making and reached her full potential in life. Instead, her father's greed condemned her to a life filled with hardships and uncertainty. In his desire for the "quick high," he disregarded his daughter's future financially and emotionally. What can you expect from a crackhead? Whether Chanele was aware of her father's actions became irrelevant. Joe sealed her fate. We would not see Chanele again for many years.

CHAPTER 15
THE VOICE

"There will come a time when you believe everything is finished; that will be the beginning" - Louis L'Amour

With my college basketball career and graduation completed, it was time to embark on the next chapter. My only question was, what would that be? My options were to enroll in graduate school or search for employment. Spending at least another two years in grad school, which would also require taking out a student loan, didn't appeal to me at the time. I was burnt out and needed a break. Regardless, I had to vacate the dormitory by the end of June, which was only a few weeks away. I needed a job ASAP. I began circulating my resume and searching the newspaper want ads every day, to no avail. As the days turned into weeks, I became more desperate. I missed the June deadline and had to ask for an unprecedented extension of my dorm occupancy. The school allowed me to stay but at a prorated weekly fee. I had a small amount of money saved from my share of the concert earnings, but I didn't want to spend it on dorm fees. It was time to accept whatever entry-level job I could find.

Finally, I found an opening at the administrative office of a trucking company. The job interview went well, and the only thing standing between me and employment was a mandatory physical exam, no problem. I found an apartment in Jersey City. Everything was moving along nicely and then, (The other shoe).

I arrived at my scheduled routine physical exam, and after a few preliminary tests, the doctor instructed me to drop my pants and cough. After some brief probing, The doctor said, "Wait a minute, you have a hernia. I can't clear you to work. You're going to need surgery." What? How can this be? I had a physical exam before the basketball season, and I was fine. This injury must have happened recently. Although I felt no pain at the moment, I knew this was serious. After a follow-up exam, the doctor scheduled surgery for August 10th. The unexpected hernia diagnosis and forthcoming medical procedure derailed all of my immediate plans. Not only was I concerned about my health, but I also faced the prospect of being homeless once discharged from the hospital. Most people would ask, "Why didn't you call your brother?" Well, up until that point, the only thing I ever asked of Kris was to be allowed to tag along with him on his musical journey, that's it. I was an adult now. The least I could do was attempt to find a solution to my problems before running to my brother for financial help. That was my rationale anyway.

After successful hernia surgery, I relocated to Baltimore to stay with Pam while recuperating and planning my next move. However, after staying in Maryland for only a week, I needed a change of environment. Every part of my being was telling me that I needed to be back in New York City. Baltimore is a splendid town, but I felt like a fish out of water there. Darrell extended me an invitation to stay at his home in Brooklyn until I found employment. I accepted his offer and returned to The Big Apple. My hometown happened to be on the verge of breaking 1988's record of 1,896 murders with a staggering 1,905 murders in 1989. Plus, robberies rose almost 8%, making New York City the worst in the nation. Great.

Right around the time I was returning to "The Concrete Jungle," Boogie Down Productions was releasing its highly anticipated third album, 'Ghetto Music: The Blueprint of Hip-Hop,' led by the uplifting single, 'You Must Learn.' Here, KRS-One gives the listener an untold historical breakdown of many unsung African-American inventors and their contributions to society. 'Ghetto Music' became the group's fastest-selling album, being certified gold by the RIAA in two months. With three consecutive gold albums in three successive years, BDP was proceeding at a historic pace. Kris turned out to be a prolific songwriter and producer. I had the opportunity to watch him write several songs at home and at the studio at an unusually rapid speed. On occasion, I would sneak a peek into Kris' rhyme books. They contained dozens of songs that were unfortunately never recorded. What I found amazing was how Kris could listen to and enjoy other styles of Rap music. Kris introduced me to the game-changing N.W.A. album 'Straight Outta Compton.' We both enjoyed De La Soul's equally groundbreaking 'Three Feet High And Rising' album. Still, Kris managed to stay true to his music style and the image he wanted to project in true artist fashion.

Despite relocating between Baltimore and New York City, job hunting, surgery, and hanging out with Kris, I still managed to catch up with my main man Biz Markie. One day, we cruised around in his new Pathfinder Jeep when Biz turned to me and said, "Yo, I wanna play you this new song I'm working on, tell me what you think." Sure! I would love to check out some new, exclusive music from Biz before anyone else did. He pops the tape into the cassette deck. The song begins with Biz Markie rapping over some thumping drums accompanied by a funky piano riff. My head was bopping hard. When the chorus arrived, all hell broke loose. Biz was singing, loud and proud! It sounded hilarious and dope at the same time. Biz named the tune 'Just A friend.' I told him with confidence that this song was going to be a hit. Biz and I drove to the recording studio, and I watched him mix 'Just a Friend' and record another track for his album. He even gave me a shout-out at the end of the song. Nice!

By September of '89, I started to feel somewhat recuperated from my hernia surgery. I decided to go 100% full steam ahead with my job search after the Labor Day holiday. I caught up with Biz once again for a night of club-hopping. I somehow managed to find myself in the middle of a high-speed car race on the New Jersey Turnpike between Biz Markie's BMW and his cousin Cool V's Volvo. I sat petrified in the passenger seat, as the speedometer hit 100 mph. After the race (which Biz lost), he mentioned that he was shooting a video for the song 'Just A Friend' the following day. We hung out all night, and the next morning, we rode to the video location, which was on the C.W. Post campus of Long Island University. During the previous night, I began to feel a sharp pain in my stomach that hurt in a way I never experienced before. It felt like a rock got stuck in my stomach. I decided to stop off at the store and buy a laxative—wrong decision. As the day progressed, the laxative began to take effect. Biz invited me to appear right next to him and his entourage at the video shoot. Excellent! Unfortunately, every time the director (Lionel Martin) yelled cut, I had to run to the bathroom. Biz found this quite amusing and teased me to no end. Still, the pain in my stomach persisted. After a few hours, I could no longer endure the agony. The production staff called 911. I left the 'Just A Friend' video shoot in an ambulance, headed to the local hospital. After a few hours of waiting and then a brief examination, the doctor determined that I had a food poisoning case. He told me the symptoms would subside in a day or so and sent me home.

I returned to Darrell's house the following morning and laid down on his couch. Everyone had gone away for the holiday weekend, so I was there alone. Despite the doctor's prognosis, the pain did not subside. It grew worse. I became so ill that I could not stand up. I had to crawl up the stairs to use the bathroom. After a day and a half, the family returned. I was barely coherent by this time. I told them I had food poisoning, and the doctor instructed me to rest until it subsided. As I lay on the couch by myself, I suddenly heard a voice say, "You know why you're so sick? It's because we put poison on this couch. It was meant for the whole family, but you received most of the poison since you were the only one home." What the Hell? I could hear this ominous voice speaking to me as clear as day. I had to do something. I needed to warn the family of this potential danger. I called out to Darrell's mother, who left the kitchen area and came into the living room to see what I wanted.

I tried to talk to her, but my speech began slurring. I mustered up all of the energy I could and told her, "Don't sit on the couch! Someone put poison on the couch!" Darrell's mother looked right into my eyes as I spoke, then she gradually turned around and screamed in horror at the top of her lungs, "Darrell!!" She then proceeded to go upstairs and vanish. About a minute later, Darrell came downstairs. He sat right next to me, and in a calm voice, said, "So, tell me your story." I repeated my warning about the poison on the couch. Darrell asked, "Who told you this?" I said, "A voice." At that moment, I realized what I just said. A voice? From where? I knew something was wrong with me. Darrell said, "We are going to the hospital right now!" He called our friend Kurt, who came immediately and drove us to the hospital.

After a two-hour wait, a doctor finally examined me. He asked some routine questions and then decided to do a test on my stomach. He took his two middle fingers and pressed into my abdomen; I didn't feel anything unusual. Suddenly, the doctor let go of my stomach, allowing it to snap back on its own. Oh My God! The pain was excruciating! I screamed in agony. The doctor said, "Let me try that again." I grabbed his hand and yelled, "Man, if you do that again, I'm gonna break your arm!" The doctor said, "Ok, relax, it might be your appendix, but I'm not sure. I'm going to go ahead and schedule you for surgery anyway. I'd rather be safe than sorry." The doctor transferred me to another ward of the hospital then he left.

Meanwhile, my condition continued to deteriorate. About six hours after my abdominal examination, the initial doctor, who had gone home for the evening, called the hospital out of pure curiosity. He asked, "Whatever happened with the Parker kid?" A nurse told him I was still lying there awaiting surgery. The doctor went into a rage and began screaming at the hospital staff to schedule me for immediate surgery. When they finally cut me open, my appendix had long since ruptured, and pus was everywhere. The time-lapse between the onset of the initial symptoms, my slurred speech, hallucinations, and weakened state was about 84 hours. One can only assume that the life-threatening condition called sepsis had developed as well. The mortality rate of septic shock is over 50%. In particular, abdominal sepsis exhibits the highest mortality rate, with 72%. I was dying. Had that doctor not been sitting at home wondering about his diagnosis of some random patient, I would not have survived.

I woke up in the Intensive Care Unit of the hospital with a five-inch surgical incision on my stomach's right side. Along with the incision was a tube leading from inside my stomach out to a drainage device by the bed's side. There was another tube inserted into my stomach through my nose that was draining more fluid. Also, there were two intravenous bags connected to my left arm. A team of doctors came in and out of my room every hour. Darrell was right there, comforting me and explaining how serious my situation was. Pam arrived the following day and gasped when she saw my condition. I wasn't allowed to eat any food or drink water. The doctor informed me that although the appendectomy was successful, my kidneys were failing. I was in bad shape. I spent two weeks in the hospital recovering from my second surgery in less than a month. I lost an enormous amount of weight and became so weak that I had to learn how to walk all over again. I was extremely fortunate to be alive. I consider this my third and most serious brush with death.

During my two-week hospital stay, several of my friends from college and Brooklyn visited me, which was a pleasant surprise. Kris and the rest of the BDP Crew were already in Los Angeles to tape their first-ever nationally televised appearance on the top-rated 'Arsenio Hall Show.' My hospital room had a color television mounted high on the wall. From there, I watched my brother reach another remarkable career milestone. Watching Arsenio Hall introduce the group to a nationwide television audience was both exhilarating and nerve-racking. It had been three years since the release of BDP's first single, and for some reason, I still hadn't quite come to grips with everything that was happening.

After two weeks in the hospital, I got discharged. Darrell came to pick me up and take me back to his place. As soon as I returned to Darrell's house, I resumed my position on his "poisonous" couch. My movements were very restricted for the first few days, and the doctor gave me a special diet to follow. Darrell's mother prepared my meals every day until my strength returned. After a week, I returned to the hospital for a scheduled follow-up exam. I was greeted by the same doctor who had examined me in the emergency room. I embraced him and said, "Doctor, you saved my life." He became emotional and asked me to follow him down the hall to another room. We arrived at a lounge where a few other doctors were relaxing. He said, "Tell them what you've just told me." I repeated my statement to his colleagues that this doctor had indeed saved my life. He had a big smile on his face. It was almost like he'd been waiting his entire life to hear someone say that to him. My gratitude was genuine, though. Had that doctor not gone beyond his call of duty, I would have died. I will forever be grateful to him.

As soon as I returned home from my follow-up visit, I received a phone call from Kris, who had returned from California. He informed me that he would be embarking on a one-month tour starting the first week of October to support his latest album, and there was a job opening if I was interested. The position was a production assistant. Kris was revamping the entire Boogie Down Productions crew from top to bottom. He hired new professional staff for the tour. If I wanted the job, I would be training under sound engineer Rebekah Foster. Kris allowed me a couple of days to make a decision. It was a fantastic offer, but I needed to take my time and weigh my options. First, I was in no condition to travel out of the state, much less endure the rigorous demands of a tour. Still, I figured I would have an additional week of recovery time before the tour started. My next scheduled doctor's appointment was also in one week to remove the staples from my stomach. If I accepted the job, I would be cutting it close. Second, I took into consideration that I still had no source of income. I spent almost two months in and out of the hospital. As gracious as Darrell's family had been, I was still an adult who at least had to contribute something to my well-being. Add that I also knew the boss very well and toured with him before, and there was only one logical choice, accept the offer. I called Kris and informed him that I would take the job and, thank you.

On October 4th, 1989, I joined the Boogie Down Production Crew as part of the staff. A host of new faces greeted me. Most of the members who were present since the group's beginning weren't there. Even founding member D-Nice departed the group to pursue a solo career. The only holdovers were Ms. Melodie (R.I.P.) and a colorful character named Willie D (R.I.P.). The first stop was in Detroit, and I soon learned what my job description entailed. As a production assistant, I had to aid in all aspects of the tour, including setting up and breaking down the musical equipment and props, loading and unloading the tour bus, running errands, carrying bags, and filming the show. The hours were long, but I learned a lot and still managed to sneak in some fun. I was being recognized at every concert and treated like a celebrity. I met several interesting people along the way, including a budding producer named DJ Premier in Chicago. For the first time, I traveled to Los Angeles and saw some real Crips & Bloods up close and personal. I was soaking everything up like a sponge.

Kenny & Kris in 1989

Meanwhile, my homie Biz Markie had exploded with his single 'Just A Friend.' After MTV aired the music video, Biz Markie's career rose to new heights. 'Just A Friend' would sell a staggering one million copies, an enormous feat at the time. It became one of the biggest Rap songs in music history. For me, watching the video was bittersweet. Although I looked happy and received several cameos in that classic video, I was in severe pain and left the shoot in an ambulance. That could have been the last time I was seen alive. Fortunately, it wasn't, and now I was on tour, earning money and having fun. Sadly, Biz Markie succumbed to an illness in the summer of 2021. Rest in peace, my friend, until we meet again.

At the tour's end, I met with Dave, the group's tour manager, who previously worked with Anita Baker, Cameo, Too Short, and ran a theater in Chicago. He said, "Ya know, Kenny, when I first heard that Kris hired his brother, I thought you were going to come on the road and do nothing because your brother was the boss. You surprised me with how hard you worked., I want to bring you with me on my next tour." It was a nice compliment coming from a seasoned professional like himself, but I had no interest in making my permanent gig production assistant. Still, I enjoyed touring with Kris and was open to working with him in the future.

When we returned to New York City, Kris asked me where I was headed and told him back to Darrell's house. I needed to regroup and figure out my next move. Kris said, "You should be staying here with me. I'm your brother." It was a generous offer for Kris to extend his home to me. I also wanted to establish a closer relationship with him. Although I was quite comfortable staying with Darrell, it would've been unfair to his family if I ran around with Kris until the wee hours of the morning and then returned to Darrell's house. I might have disturbed people who had to work in the morning. I decided to, once again, accept an offer from kris and relocate to the Murray Hill section of Manhattan, at least for the time being.

I settled into Kris' apartment in early November and began shadowing him as a self-appointed apprentice, going to meetings, interviews, and photoshoots. Kris was working on several music projects, including the fourth Boogie Down Productions album called 'Edutainment.' I went to every studio sessions I could. Kris worked on a remix for Reggae music icon Bob Marley's son Ziggy; I "crashed" one of those sessions too. I wonder what punk-ass Joe would've thought about Kris working with the Marley's?

Inside Kris' apartment was a designated music room/mini-studio where he set-up his DJ equipment. Kris owned an extensive vinyl collection with thousands of records, including all of the latest Hip-Hop jams. I realized that if I could learn how to make mixtapes, I wouldn't have to wait until the weekends to record from the radio anymore. I asked Kris to teach me how to deejay. He walked me through the basics and made a mixtape right there on the spot so I could see how he did it. After that, I began practicing every day.

For the next month and a half, I traveled with BDP as a production staff member and spent all of my spare time making mixtapes. I soon realized that if I wanted to get better, along with practicing, I needed to observe more deejays in action. I decided to pay a visit to my favorite deejay and friend, Red Alert, at KISS-FM. I didn't mention to Red that I was dabbling in the art of deejaying. I just stopped by like I'd done several times before. This time, I watched his every move like a hawk. How did he scratch? How did he mix? What kind of headphones did he use? What kind of needles did he use? How did he clean the dust off of his records?

I visited Red on a couple of occasions, taking mental notes each time. What I never realized was, Red Alert had been inspiring me for years. I had been recording, buying, and swapping music to entertain my friends, just like a real deejay would. My thirst for music even drove me to pluck a roach-infested radio out of the garbage. With basketball being out of the way, deejaying became my number one passion. I felt the same feeling about deejaying that I did about basketball when I first made my junior high school team. Everything else became secondary.

During the Christmas holiday, Boogie Down Productions got booked to perform at "The World Famous" Apollo Theater in Harlem along with Rap duo EPMD. The Apollo sold out four straight shows. The energy in that venue was like no other. This show was going to be dynamic. On the day of the first concert, I was at the soundcheck, setting up the stage. D-Nice was there chatting with Kris. During their conversation, Dee said to Kris, "You know what would be dope? You should have Kenny as your deejay. Having the two brothers up there rocking together would be incredible!" Without batting an eye, Kris said, "Yeah, but Kenny would have to be dope. I'm not just going to put him on my set." I agreed with Kris 100%. I wasn't thinking about deejaying for BDP at all. I just wanted to make my little mixtapes, that's it.

Meanwhile, the backstage area was buzzing about this new deejay EPMD had acquired named DJ Scratch. Everyone was saying, "Have you seen Scratch yet?" DJ Scratch had won the 1988 New Music Seminar 'Battle

For World Supremacy.' Being a brand new DJ myself, I was anticipating watching Scratch do his thing. During EPMD's set, right in the middle of their show, they paused and left the stage to allow DJ Scratch to showcase his skills. He began "cutting" two James Brown records ('Funky Drummer') back and forth faster than anyone I had ever seen before. Scratch then raised the stakes by simultaneously cutting the records back and forth while also spinning himself around, then between his legs, then with his back, and even with his eyes completely shut. Wow!

The EPMD hype man on the microphone said, "Wait a minute, Scratch, you have to show The Apollo what you can really do!" I was like, "What? That wasn't it?" DJ Scratch then began cutting the records back and forth once again while simultaneously taking his shirt off of his body! The audience was going crazy! But wait, he then stopped the record from spinning with his foot! The Apollo crowd was now in a frenzy. No one had ever seen anything like that before. The hype man then said, "Yo Scratch, kick that shit!" and DJ Scratch took his foot off of the record, and the music began playing from the exact spot where he had stopped it! I almost fainted.

When I regained my composure, I thought about how absurd D-Nice sounded, suggesting that I could deejay for one of the world's most popular Hip-Hop groups. What was he thinking? But, upon further analysis, I realized that what I witnessed wasn't the norm. I had seen dozens of Rap concerts with legendary deejays, and none of them "walked on water" like DJ Scratch. Some of them didn't stand out at all. I recalled the lesson I learned back during my freshman year of high school when I was discouraged from trying out for the varsity basketball team because I was afraid of the #1 basketball player in the city, Jerry "Ice" Reynolds. Here I was all over again, just getting started at a craft and being discouraged by seeing the undisputed best DJ. This time, I decided to focus on simply being the best Kenny Parker that I could be and stop worrying about what anyone else was doing. Besides, I had zero aspirations of entering a "Battle For World Supremacy." That wasn't my personality. Now my brother, on the other hand.

At long last, The Nineties had arrived. The start of a new decade always brings the added expectation of the beginning of a new era. For me, 1989 had been a rollercoaster ride filled with both tremendous highs and crushing lows. I graduated from college with a bachelor's degree in Psychology, the highlight of my life. What followed was two consecutive surgeries and barely escaping death, the lowest point of my life. I reunited with my sister, only to lose her once again. Unfortunately, my longtime relationship with Pam came to an end with the close of the decade. 1989 also had me stumbling into the art of deejaying only to discover it had been a passion of mine for many years, and I didn't realize it.

1990 arrived with me still trying to figure out what I was going to do with my life. After a quiet start to January, BDP was scheduled for a string of shows on the west coast, starting in Oakland, California. The night before our long cross-country flight, I packed up all of the musical equipment and stage props and prepared for the trip. It was about 3 am when Kris strolled into the music room and said calmly, "So...Tomorrow night in Oakland, you're deejaying the show." WHAT? He handed me a piece of paper and said, "Here's the show list of the songs, study it." With that, he added, "Ok, goodnight," and left me in the music room alone with my mind completely blown. He didn't ask me if I wanted to deejay the show or felt like I was ready for such a huge responsibility. Kris handed me the assignment with the same demeanor as if he was sending me to the store to buy a tuna fish sandwich. I had to ask myself, am I ready? After some soul searching, my answer was, Yes! I knew the show back and forth. I knew every song by heart. Sometimes, I used to play around and practice the show routines in the music room by myself to see if I could do it. Kris had precise timing; I knew where he wanted the songs to drop, down to the millisecond. I studied his subtle cues and hand gestures that most people didn't notice.

In concert, we used turntables and vinyl records to play the music, along with a new format called Digital Audio Tape (DAT). Boogie Down Productions was among the first, if not THE first Hip-Hop act, to use this format for live concerts. In 1989/90, most deejays had never seen a DAT recorder before. I was familiar with this device because I was the one who used to test it at the soundcheck before every show. Although I had only been deejaying for two months, having me fill in as the temporary deejay made sense for Kris. Of course, I got no sleep that night. We left for Oakland in the morning.

The following day we arrived in Oakland and headed to the venue for soundcheck. I went through my regular set-up routine, but this time, I introduced myself to the sound engineer as "The DJ." After soundcheck, I went back to my hotel room and took a nap, feeling confident. A few hours later, it was showtime! We arrived at the theater as a group, and I headed for the stage. Instead of setting up the camera equipment, I walked up the ramp and onto the elevated DJ set-up. I put on the headphones, cued up the music, and waited for the curtain to start the show.

I could hear the announcer warming up the crowd as the show was only seconds away. Finally, the announcer said, "Make some noise for Boogie Down Productions!!!" When the curtain rose, a giant spotlight beamed directly on me, and I could see 3,000 rabid BDP fans cheering in anticipation of the show. It was now my time to perform and, I froze. The enormity of the situation paralyzed me. I wasn't in Kris' music room anymore; this was for real. I said to myself, "I can't do this, I quit." My next thought was, "You can't quit; it's too late now." I needed to regain my composure. I switched my mind into athlete mode. I've played basketball in front of large crowds like this before. Many of the games were at the other team's building, surrounded by hostile mobs who wanted to see me fail. This show was like a home game, in front of an adoring crowd. I had trained for years to block out all external noises regardless of their affiliation and "run the offense." That's what I decided to do, run the offense. I focused on the show list and the sound of KRS-One's voice, period. I started the music, Kris walked onto the stage, and the crowd erupted! For the next hour, I "ran the plays" to perfection. The show was a success, and we walked off the stage "victorious."

After the show, I chilled out in the dressing room, and none of the crew said a word to me. That was odd. I rode back to the hotel with the production staff in complete silence. I was expecting at least a "congratulations on your first show" comment, but nothing. Was my assessment of the show wrong? Was I wack? I had to know. I called Kris and asked him, "How did I do?" He said, "Come to my room." Oh no! That didn't sound good at all. I went to his suite, nervous, and knocked on the door. Kris answered the door with a big smile on his face. What a relief! Kris said, "That was dope! What I want you to do next time is be more vocal on the mic, get involved in the show." He was right. I had my head down the entire time focused on the turntables and show list. Kris then said, "Look, I'm going to make you the permanent deejay for Boogie Down Productions. From now on, you are DJ Kenny Parker. I don't want you carrying bags anymore; that's someone else's job now. Your pay is going to increase, and I'm going to introduce you on my new album as the deejay." Oh, my God! For the umpteenth time in my life, I got blindsided by Kris. We embraced, and he said, "Ok, goodnight... I'm tired."

I went back to my room with a new persona and job title. Once again, Kris blazed a trail and allowed me to slide in behind him. I understood that there would be some resentment from certain people who felt like I didn't earn or deserve such a prestigious position. In fairness, I indeed skipped several steps. I had only been deejaying for two months and still had much to learn. But, what these people didn't take into account was my work ethic. I looked at the passage of time a little differently. In only two months, I improved significantly. I had to practice every single day to reach that skill level. Sure, KRS-One could have chosen almost any deejay in the world to tour with him. Some guys would have left their groups to join BDP. Still, Kris chose me. I realize that there was some nepotism involved, but Kris may have seen something genuine in me. A hunger? A willingness to learn? Who knows? Regardless, I knew two things for sure. I wasn't going to pay these doubters any mind, and I wasn't going to let Kris down either.

The beginning of the decade was the dawn of a new era. Kris and I embarked on a musical journey that would take us around the globe, spanning three decades and well over a thousand shows together. The Parker brothers were once again running around just like we did back as kids in Brooklyn and The Bronx. This time, instead of Prospect Park, the entire world was our playground. KRS-One and Boogie Down Productions would sell millions of records worldwide and set lasting trends that resonate in the Hip-Hop world to this day. Hip-Hop historians mention KRS-One right at the top of every "Greatest MC Of All-Time List." With over 24 published albums to his credit and dozens of guest appearances, many consider KRS-One to have written the most rhymes in Hip-Hop history. Ironically, Kris Parker, the high school dropout who didn't complete the ninth grade, has lectured at over 500 universities in The United States and authored three books.

As for myself, I have deejayed over a thousand KRS-One concerts, including Yankee Stadium, Oakland Stadium, Foxboro Stadium, The Lincoln Memorial, Madison Square Garden, The Barclay Center, MTV, B.E.T., VH1, TNT, The Arsenio Hall Show, and even the PBS Network. I have also become an accomplished club deejay, performing nearly two thousand dates in The United States, Europe, and Asia. I produced (yeah, that's a story for another time) over 30 songs featuring KRS-One and dozens of other songs featuring various artists. I became the first deejay and Hip-

Hop producer ever featured on a reality show (The Real World: Season 1 Episode 2). I produced music for MTV and four national Nike commercials. I've had quite a run.

From time to time, I have reflected on the many hardships I endured growing up in a low-income, dysfunctional family living in New York City. I always felt that every trial and tribulation I overcame made me into the mentally tough person I am today. However, while writing this book, I concluded that it was the exact opposite. I have always been a mentally tough person. That's how I managed to endure all of those obstacles and not lose my mind, faith, and positive outlook on life. My sense of right and wrong never wavered, even as a child, and I never followed the crowd, despite being ostracized for standing my ground. That is something I am proud of accomplishing.

In the first chapter of this book, I asked the age-old question: Is it Destiny, is it Fate, or is it Free Will? Some define Fate as the life you lead if you never put yourself in the path of greatness. That's the direction your life moves in without any effort on your part. Other people make all of the decisions for you. Destiny, on the other hand, is your potential waiting to happen, whatever that may be. Free Will is the ability to choose between different courses of action unrestricted. Do we choose to succeed or fail, or is it our Fate? Of course, I don't know the answer either.

I have encountered thousands of people with various dreams, hopes, and aspirations during my life, but the vast majority of them never come close to reaching their goals. Why? Several factors contribute to success, including, as pointed out in this book, Luck or Divine Intervention or Fate or whatever you choose to call it. However, I find that one component has to be present to achieve any dream. The ability to focus. The power to block out everything else occurring in your environment and direct all of your attention to a single task. I've watched my brother, mentor, role model, and hero Kris Parker chase down an improbable dream, throwing caution to the wind, to reach his one goal. He put himself into a position to either succeed or starve. The ultimate question is, what are you willing to do?

> "You just don't have a story - you're a story in the making, and you never know what the next chapter is going to be. That's what makes it exciting" - Dan Millman

ABOUT THE AUTHOR

Kenny Parker is the longtime DJ and music producer for the iconic Hip-Hop artist KRS-One & Boogie Down Productions. He is a native New Yorker and the younger brother of KRS-One. During his 30-year music industry career, Kenny has performed more than one thousand concerts with KRS-One. His contributions helped KRS-ONE earn the first-ever Source Magazine Award for 'Best Live Hip-Hop Performer' in 1994.

Kenny Parker has appeared in more than 20 music videos and performed over a dozen nationally televised events, ranging from VH1, MTV, BET, and PBS programs to 'Soul Train' and 'The Arsenio Hall Show.' Kenny became the first DJ and producer to appear on a reality show (MTV's 'The Real World' – Season 1 Episode 2), producing two songs for the groundbreaking show. Kenny Parker is credited with more than 50 major label song releases and produced music for four Nike television commercials. The book "SP 1200, The Art & Science" featured Kenny for his pioneering use of the legendary SP 1200 drum machine. Kenny holds a bachelor's degree in psychology. You can find out more about him at DJKENNYPARKER.COM.

www.ingramcontent.com/pod-product-compliance
Lightning Source LLC
Chambersburg PA
CBHW070641120526
44590CB00013BA/807